Sara Tuc

Our House In Arusha

A Memoir

Cover design: Patrick Texier

Our House In Arusha

For my mother, who taught me the magic of stories.

Sokoine Road in downtown Arusha.

Prologue

ON A SOFT NIGHT IN AFRICA when the moon was full, I heard a story that would change my life. In the weeks that followed, like someone pulled by an ancient spell, I said good-bye to my employer and all my friends, ended my eighteen-year marriage, closed the door of my Manhattan apartment, and moved to Tanzania.

The teller of the tale was a quiet Frenchman with a mysterious past. I knew little about him except what he himself had told me. His résumé was bizarre, a long list of odd jobs that included prospecting for gold in Gabon, hunting crocodiles in Zambia, and teaching French to teenage girls in Chile. He said he'd been married three times.

Just before our wedding, a German coffee farmer warned me that I was about to make a big mistake. "The longer you live in Arusha, the poorer you'll be," he said. "Don't give up your life in America. There is nothing for you here."

My new home was a city of mud huts, scrap-metal shanties, and slowly collapsing colonial mansions; it was a world in a time warp, where Masai warriors armed with spears guarded rich people's houses, and women did their laundry in the busy roundabout's new fountain as traffic whirled around them. I still had a set of keys to my old apartment. "You can always change your mind," my ex-husband had said as I left with my luggage.

The farmer, who knew my fiancé better than I did, cautioned me about an expired work permit and several years' worth of unpaid taxes. It seemed the man I was about to marry was in danger of being deported, or possibly jailed. I sensed the farmer was trying to stir up trouble, though I couldn't figure out why. "Don't worry, Peter," I retorted. "I have nothing to lose."

I had left behind a comfortable home, a steady job, a man I loved. But that life was over. The future was in front of me, as plain as an open door. I took a deep breath and walked toward it.

Mount Meru's snowcapped peak as seen from our garden.

Chapter One

The house was a sturdy breezeblock bungalow surrounded by an acre of grass and a tall hedge. A row of
canna lilies lined the gravel drive. More than the
house itself, it was the garden that set us apart. Nobody else on the road had such a lawn as ours, and
certainly no one had canna lilies, all dooryard green-
ery having long since been cleared away by the
neighborhood goats. Who but a muzungu would leave
all that food lying about? What could be the point,
apart from advertising the extraordinary habits of
white people? Aside from its wastefulness, the lawn
was a perfect hiding place for snakes. For this very
reason the yards of our neighbors were swept clean
every morning, polished smooth by the daily application of bundles of twigs. No blade of grass, no leaf lay
between the feet of our neighbors and the good earth
of Africa.

If the lawn served no useful purpose, the same
could not be said of the hedge. The goats of Sekei,
their own dooryards having long since been denuded,
would have liked nothing better than to feast on our
crop of good-for-nothing grass. It was the job of the
hedge to intervene. So while the miserable goats nibbled at the tough vegetation that survived along the

dusty road, our grass thrived. Safe behind the hedge, it grew tall enough to swallow a wandering chicken whole, and still it was allowed to idle, bending and nodding in the highland breeze.

As if to make up for the lawn's shiftlessness, the hedge did double duty. Besides deterring marauders, it shielded us from the curious eyes of our neighbors—at least that was the idea. In reality, it provided the neighbors with cover for their surveillance. We never knew who was lurking behind the hedge, but the low murmur of voices that filtered through its leaves told us we were being spied on.

Above our front door was a hand-painted sign that read TEXIER HOUSEHOLD, EST. 1999. Below the letters were two elephants drawn in profile, their eyes rimmed in black like those of the Egyptian pharaohs. The elephants kept watch over our front yard, which offered all sorts of clues about the kind of people who lived within. The stranger to our house might have noted Patrick's beloved Land Rover pickup parked with the windows down, the seat cushions drenched; Thomas's bicycle resting on its side in the path of my Toyota, his store-bought soccer ball slowly asphyxiating in the shade of a banana tree, an acacia thorn in its side. Even I, unused to household help when I moved to Arusha, soon fell into the habit of leaving a trail of objects for Jenni to pick up.

The road past our house began down by the highway as a smooth stretch of tarmac; the pavement ended exactly where the district commissioner finished his drive to work. Thereafter, the road disintegrated into a mess of gullies and stones, steadily deteriorating as it climbed the hill. The lower road was a river of enterprise: Great slabs of red meat, crawling with flies, hung in the open air; small pyramids of tomatoes rose from blankets spread on the ground; a fraternity of bicycle repairmen set up shop every morning in the shade of a hospitable tree; and the neighborhood knife sharpener carried his whetstone from door to door. Next to the Big Y Club, named for the junction with Putschi's road, was a small shop that sold Sportsman cigarettes one by one; we went there when we were trying to quit. At the ChiChi Beauty Saloon you could have your hair braided or your car battery recharged. Next to the highway was a natural depression into which a stream had been diverted. The water hole may have served livestock in the past, but as Arusha's human population had increased and its herds of cattle had dwindled, another use had been found for the puddle. Every morning a procession of cars lined up on its shore, and a man with nothing more than a rag for a tool could make a few shillings by dipping it in the puddle and wiping the mud from the cars' flanks. The car wash did a brisk business—Arusha had become increasingly dusty and dirty over the years, but its automobiles, with few exceptions, were wonderfully clean.

The upper road ended at a primary school for the children of Sekei and a rest home for old men. The children surged past our front gate twice a day, up the hill in the morning and down in the afternoon, a tide of blue uniforms and striped knee socks and swinging lunch pails. The old men went against the tide—down the hill in the morning to visit the shops on the lower road or catch a bus into town, back up in the afternoon, gingerly making their way over the uneven ground between patches of shade. They traveled in pairs, clasping their comrade's hand for balance and encouragement, stepping to the side of the road as a cloud of red dust rose up from our tires to engulf their flowing white caftans. Rarely did we pick up strangers, but if there was space in our car, the old men got a ride. They sat in the backseat, gazing out the win-

3

dow like sultans, and exited without a word of thanks or good-bye.

The primary school was the only one in the district, and the children who crossed its threshold came from all over Sekei. Unlike our nearest neighbors, the hedge peepers, the children studied us with frank interest, crowding around the front gate on their way to or from the school. Soon after Patrick and Thomas moved in—for they arrived several months ahead of me—Mesuli's handyman nailed a sheet of plywood over the bars, leaving only a small hole to accommodate the working of the latch. After that the crowd dwindled, though I often heard giggles coming from behind the plywood as I sipped my morning coffee on the veranda. Looking up, I would see a small hand snake through the hole, spread its fingers, and wave, as its owner called out the English greeting he'd learned at school: "Good mawning, tee-chah!"

Not everyone was so polite. "Muzungu!" the children shouted as we sailed up and down the road. I never knew for sure whether we were being hailed or accused, unless the point was driven home with a pebble. The doors of the Land Rover were studded with punctuation marks.

The day I moved into the house in Sekei, Mesuli stepped out of the bougainvillea to welcome me; a break in the hedge allowed a flow of traffic between our two houses. Standing on the veranda with a baby in one arm and a toddler by the hand, he listened quietly as I babbled on about how happy I was to be here and how much I liked the house, and how eager I was to get better acquainted with my new surroundings. I announced that I would go exploring on foot. At this last statement, Mesuli's eyebrows shot up. He quickly said he would arrange for a guide. Minutes later, eight-year-old Nelson Mesuli appeared at the door

and off we went. The hill was traversed by a bewildering network of footpaths, and it would have been no
trick at all to wander off permanently. My disappear-
ance would have been the talk of the town and not at
all good for Mesuli's rental business. "My father is the
richest man in Sekei," Nelson informed me as we
scrambled up the steep slope of a ravine. Mesuli had
started out in the district with a small hut for himself
and his goats; now he had two houses and was at
work on a third. Instead of goats, he had tenants. As
time went by, I began to suspect that we were a
greater nuisance than the goats, but if Mesuli thought
so too, he never let on.

The sounds of the house are what I remember
best: the raucous call of the ibis that flew back and
forth between stands of eucalyptus, the metal clang of
pots from Mesuli's kitchen window, the hum of the
electric pump that filled the cistern behind the house.
There were the rhythmic sounds of work being
done—the chop of a hammer, the thud of a hoe. To
my recollection the house was never quiet.

Mornings began with Mesuli's rooster, which
commenced to crow well before dawn. By five o'clock,
when the neighborhood mosque blared its first prere-
corded call to prayer over its tinny loudspeaker, rous-
ing people of all faiths, we were long out of bed.
While devout Muslims all over town were groggily
rolling out their prayer mats and most Christians were
trying to go back to sleep, Patrick had already begun
to embrace the day and was sitting on the living room
couch in a pair of old bathing trunks and rubber flip-
flops and his father's well-worn mustard-yellow cotton
cardigan, happily dunking his bread in instant coffee.
This was an old habit, one he particularly relished
when we were on safari because it disturbed the
wageni, who couldn't help but notice that the bread

was slathered with butter and orange marmalade, a lot of which ended up in the coffee. Which Patrick then drank, of course. As the sky began to lighten, we slid back the bolt and opened the cheap wooden double doors to let in the morning air and sometimes, by accident, a giant banana slug or Mesuli's hen, which liked to roost in an old straw hat that somebody had left on the veranda in a pile of camping gear.

The clank and whine of the metal gate at eleven, the scrape of shoe leather against cement, and a soft "Jambo" from the hallway meant Jenni had arrived. Leaving her shoes on the veranda, she moved through the house on silent feet, speedily accomplishing a long list of domestic chores accompanied only by soothing sounds—the glug of water from the shower tap filling her plastic laundry bucket, the pecking of her knife against the cutting board. The gardener, on the other hand, could do nothing without causing a disturbance. Especially annoying was his method of washing the cars, which involved meticulous polishing of the steering wheel. The siesta hour was filled with inadvertent toots.

❧

On a Saturday morning in March of the year 2000, shortly before the spring rains began, the garden gate clanked and I heard footsteps on the gravel drive. The feet came up to the house and crossed the cement floor of the veranda and stopped. There was a soft tapping at the door.

Jenni had the morning off, and the night watchman had left hours ago, trudging back home in the pale gray dawn to his little hut somewhere off in the shambas. Patrick had taken the Land Rover and driven down the hill to the market in Kijenge to buy bread; Thomas had gone along for the ride. I was in the living room with the curtains drawn, reading a book and enjoying a rare moment of solitude. With a sigh I shut my book and went to the door.

When I opened it, there was Putschi's housegirl with a note from Putschi. The handwriting was elegant and surprisingly feminine, and the note itself was touchingly formal, politely inquiring how we were, hoping we were well, et cetera, before stating that he, Putschi, would like to speak with Patrick at Patrick's earliest convenience, to get his advice on a certain subject. It was signed "R. Trappe," the R standing for Rolf, which was funny because there was only one person in all of Arusha who ever referred to Putschi by his real name and that was Putschi himself.

So I wrote a note in response, saying we would come by shortly, and handed it to the housegirl with a few shillings, and later that day the three of us drove over to Putschi's house.

At the gate we sounded the horn and the housegirl let us in. The several dogs that were lying about the Trappes' patchy yard rose to their feet in unison and came waggling over to greet us. As they milled about, whipping our legs with their tails and wetting us with their noses, the front door opened and little Jessica came prancing down the steps, excited to have visitors. In the doorway stood Putschi's wife, Penny, lovely and shy as a doe. She kissed each of us lightly on both cheeks and ushered us inside, saying, "I'm so glad you've come. It will do Putschi good to have company."

Putschi had been down with malaria for a couple of weeks, and he rose from his place on the living room couch just long enough to greet us. His voice was a scratchy whisper. He had been trying to get his safari business up and running again, now that he had sworn off booze forever and was cold stone sober morning noon and night. But this wasn't what he wanted to talk to Patrick about.

The three Trappes arranged themselves on one of the tiny living room's two sofas, the three Texiers on the other, facing them; on the table between us were a plate of sugar cookies and steaming mugs of tea, a beverage of which the French as a nation have never wholly approved and which Patrick considers almost undrinkable. After a few minutes of small talk, Putschi said, "Somebody I know, a Tanzanian from around here, came to me the other day and asked if I knew anybody who might want to buy liquid uranium. Now if I'm not mistaken, liquid uranium is used in the making of bombs."

"The guy who approached me said he was trying to sell this stuff for some Arabs," Putschi continued. "He told me he had seen it, and he described what it looked like. It was a reddish liquid in two sturdy one-liter metal containers, each with a glass window. I said no, I don't know anybody, and he went away, and that was that. But then it kind of bothered me, you know. I kept thinking about it."

Jessica, whose feet dangled a few inches above the frayed straw mat that served as the Trappes' living room rug, pushed herself forward until her toes touched the floor and, thus poised, fixed Thomas with a hopeful look. "You wanna go out and play?"

"In a minute," Thomas replied, reaching for another sugar cookie. Jessica was only eight while Thomas was almost twelve, and it was pretty clear that "in a minute," meant "never." Jessica plopped herself back on the couch with a sigh.

"One night I was listening to Voice of America on the radio," Putschi continued, "and it was about the embassy bombings in Dar and Nairobi. They said if anybody hears about anything suspicious, anything that might be a connection to the bombings, to call a certain phone number, and then they gave the phone number, but I didn't write it down."

More than a year had passed since the bombings of the American embassies in Nairobi and Dar es Salaam had left hundreds dead and thousands wounded. Although I rarely read the newspapers, there were some things you couldn't escape knowing, even in a backwater like Arusha.

"So here's my question," said Putschi. "Do you think I should report this guy who came to me?"

"Yes, I do," said Patrick. He reached for his cup and brought it halfway to his lips before remembering that it contained the despised tea. Thus trapped, he took a polite sip and returned the cup to the table.

Putschi nodded, slowly, as if he'd been anticipating Patrick's answer. "Well, then, the thing is, who do I report him to?"

"To the American embassy in Dar." I was surprised by the swiftness of Patrick's answer.

"Okay, that's what I thought. But you know, I'm not sure I want to call the American embassy. I was wondering . . . "

"You want me to call?" said Patrick.

"Would you?"

"Sure. I don't mind."

"There's another thing," said Putschi. "Voice of America said something about a reward for information leading to an arrest. I just want to do the right thing, you understand. But if that's how it works out, I'll split it with you."

"What kind of reward?"

"A hundred thousand dollars."

"I'll call them this afternoon," Patrick said, and we rushed home to recharge the phone.

Putschi and his brother, Rick, were among the best hunting guides in all of Africa. The Trappe boys were also known for their impeccable manners, their good character, and the beauty of their women. Putschi, the older of the two, was famous for the promptness with which he paid back loans, right down to the promised day. In a town where friends took the place of commercial lenders, that counted for a lot. Patrick had often loaned Putschi money and even on occasion his hunting rifle, and he was fond of noting that his friend, despite his rough exterior, was "a real gentleman."

If there was anybody in our circle who needed cash more than we did it was the Trappe family. The Trappes' story was a riches-to-rags one; their roots in Tanzania went back several generations, and at one time they'd owned an immense stretch of land. All of it, however, had been appropriated by the Tanzanian government soon after the birth of the republic in 1961 and turned into a national park. Putschi had lost his entire inheritance with the stroke of a bureaucrat's pen. And yet he seemed incapable of holding a grudge.

After thirty-five years in Africa, Patrick, too, had learned that to tote around a bunch of regrets only weighed you down. He had found his way to Tanzania after losing every dollar he had in Sierra Leone. It wasn't the first time he'd been stripped bare in an African country, yet he only ever spoke of Africa with love.

"I came here naked," he often joked, "and I'm still naked!"

We made most of our income during the dry season, and the rest of the year we held our breath, hoping our savings would see us through till the tourists came back. *La vie est un desert,* Patrick loved to say,

10

quoting what he claimed was an old Arab proverb, *et tu est le chameau qui m'aide a le traverser.*

Life is a desert, and you are the camel who helps me cross it.

The reward at stake was a beguiling sum: a nice round figure, generous by any standard, which could be split two ways and still yield enough cash to support a family of three for a couple of years if it was parceled out judiciously. Even—and this was the intriguing part of the calculation—a family who needed to square things with the tax authorities. In fact, the more one studied the situation, the more potential one saw for the kind of boost a brand-new family might do with.

Besides the unpaid taxes, a steady stream of smaller debts clamored for our attention. There was the question, for instance, of how we would pay the next month's rent, and what to do about Thomas's school shoes, which were suddenly too small for Thomas's feet. A note to the headmaster might solve the shoe problem—perhaps Thomas would be allowed to wear his shabby but still serviceable tennies for the few remaining weeks of school. But what to do about the fact that, despite a concerted family effort, Thomas still hadn't learned his times tables? A substantial windfall would enable us to buy the shoes, hire a tutor, and pay the taxes—avoiding expulsion, deportation and possibly jail.

Whether or not we'd be able to stay in Tanzania was one of our bigger worries. We were happy in Arusha, where we had many friends, a good climate, and work we enjoyed. We liked our house and we liked our landlord, Mesuli, who only clucked sympathetically when we needed a few extra days to rustle up the rent. We liked our pretty housegirl, Jenni, who came to work dressed so nicely and went about the house so quietly. We liked our veranda with its view of the garden, where canna lilies bloomed and papayas ripened in the sun. If you stood on one end of the porch and craned your neck you could even see the top of Mount Meru, Kilimanjaro's little sister. On the other hand, Patrick, for one, did not like to think too much about Meru, which last erupted in 1910; that, and the idea that an enormous chunk of it had blown sky high eight thousand years ago, made him nervous.

We were vulnerable, of course, as vulnerable as any newly put-together family in an era that is not kind to families, statistically. In that regard, Arusha was no different from my birthplace of Randolph, Vermont, or Patrick's home town of Paris, France: There was never a day when some family we knew wasn't in the process of breaking up—feuding, dividing, perhaps selling off the furniture and disappearing. To survive as a threesome, we would have to beat the odds.

A Masai elder in the Ngorongoro
Conservation Area, March 1996.

Chapter Two

I went to Africa, the first time, by accident: I had meant to go to Kansas. Africa was no more on my mind than one of Saturn's moons. I had been writing a series of travel articles about North American flora and fauna—alligators in Georgia, armadillos in Texas—and I'd heard about a newly created prairie reserve in the Flint Hills where you could see bison and prairie dogs. That's where I wanted to go. I chose the Kansas prairie because it sounded remote and solitary. Nobody I knew had been there recently, and nobody intended to go.

My proposal, which took the form of a long letter that I worked on for several days, discarding one draft after another, recalled the once-magnificent prairie of which this small patch in Kansas was but a poignant vestige. Prairie grasses, I noted, had once stretched from the Rockies to the Mississippi and from Saskatchewan to Texas, covering some 400,000 square miles, the largest continuous ecosystem in North America. The classic conception of the American prairie is one of sameness, a vast sea of grass stretching into infinity, and yet the prairie ecosystem is one of the most complex in the world. Nearly 80 percent of its plant material is contained underground in a root system so dense and tightly woven that settlers were able to build houses out of bricks cut from prairie sod. Only the Brazilian rain forest supports a greater diversity of species.

Nowadays, my letter continued, most prairie land has been plowed under or overgrazed. The tallgrass prairie—the most fertile part of the ecosystem, where grasses grow up to eight feet high—has been whittled down to one percent of its original acreage. The largest patch remaining is the one in Kansas, a hilly, sixty-mile-wide swath extending from Nebraska to Oklahoma. I wanted to see it in the spring, when the hills are covered with wildflowers.

The prairie preserve struck me as irresistible, particularly since it was due to become the next national park. So I double-checked my facts and figures, spit-shined my lead, and emailed my much-toiled-over proposal to the editor of a magazine received by members of the Auto Club of Southern California—many of whom hadn't noticed the little box on the membership form that you had to check if you wanted to refuse it.

A few weeks later, the editor called: "How would you like to go on a *real* safari?" he said.

My safari was what is known in the travel industry as a "fam" trip—a complimentary trip, sponsored by the hotels I would stay in and the parks I would visit and the tour operators who would take me around. Its purpose was to familiarize me—and the five other writers in my group—with the wonders of Tanzania's national parks. Once fammed, we were

16

supposed to go back to the States and write about our experience, urging others—paying customers—to follow in our tracks.

On day one, we stood on top of the Rift Valley's western escarpment and looked out over Lake Manyara, its shoreline pale petal-pink with flocks of flamingos. Far below us, herds of tiny gazelle, zebras, giraffes, and buffalo grazed on the broad plain, and ant-size elephants feasted on foliage in the forest clearings. On day two, we saw a rare black rhino and her calf, crossing the flat expanse of the Ngorongoro Crater. On day three, a comet streaked across the sky above our tented camp in the Seronera Valley, and the eyes of hyenas glowed in the dark. On day five, a hot-air balloon lifted us up through the morning mist, and we floated over the Moro River, where three lions lay dozing on the bank next to a buffalo kill; in the field where the balloon landed a half-hour later, a sumptuous breakfast awaited. The sky of the Serengeti was as dramatic as the landscape, bursting with stars at night and so big that by day it was a three-ring circus—showers on the right, sunbeams on the left, a rainbow in between. I saw so many animals—lions, cheetahs, bat-eared foxes—that I stopped taking pictures and just looked.

Patrick was still a newcomer to Tanzania, having been there not even a year. His employers, the Moledina brothers, had the largest fleet of any land operator in Tanzania—some 130 cars—and handled the ground operations for a slew of American and European tour companies. Although Patrick's title was general manager, Abbas Moledina did all the managing. The general manager's main role was to brief the clients: meet them for a jet-lagged, bleary-eyed breakfast at their hotel on day one, describe what the next ten days were going to be like, and answer their questions about snakes, ticks, tse-tse flies, Somali bandits, and the myriad other perils, real or imagined, of traveling in a strange land. It was good to have a muzungu to do that, because it gave the clients confidence—one of their own was at the helm. After these briefings, Patrick would return to the office and push papers around, suffocating with boredom, while a Tanzanian driver-guide accompanied the clients on safari. This time, however, Abbas had sent him—the general manager himself—because I was a VIP.

The most important thing Patrick had to do on that safari was to keep Roger happy. Roger, our trip leader, worked for the Stateside tour operator who had engaged Ranger Safaris. It was the Moledina brothers' hope that Roger would return home enthralled with Tanzania and generate a flood of new business for Rangers. Roger was the big fish, and it was Patrick's job to reel him in.

It is hard to imagine two people less compatible than the dueling impresarios of that safari. Patrick owed his success as a safari guide to his talent for improvisation. His style was low-key. He tried not to advertise what he was going to do—no sense in building expectations. Almost inevitably, the truck broke down, or the food ran out, or the road vanished. Once, the tent poles got left behind; another time, we ran out of food and had to buy a goat; the meat was so tough, nobody could eat it. People loved his safaris, from which they returned wholly invigorated, convinced they'd had a brush with mortality and were lucky to be alive.

Roger, on the other hand, advocated a tightly programmed, well-scripted itinerary. Leaving things to chance invited all kinds of chaos and, worse, boredom. "They call me Mr. Africa," he said, possibly referring to the folks in the office, which was at Columbus Circle in midtown Manhattan. In real life, he was Mr. New Jersey—that's where he lived, with his wife in a house in the suburbs. Outfitted, however, in khaki shorts and chukka boots, he resembled a personage, the British explorer, who is in no way dear to the hearts of the French.

To be upstaged by Mr. Africa was not an easy cross to bear after thirty-five years in the bush. Patrick immersed himself in a glacial stillness whenever he and Roger were together, which was as seldom as Patrick could manage. They rode in separate cars and ate at separate tables, but it was impossible for them to avoid each other completely.

When they did come face-to-face, it was often because Roger, in his role as constructive criticizer, felt obliged to comment that the food was monotonous, the iced tea lukewarm, or the roads deplorable. The driver-guides, he complained, were too quiet—they should talk more about the wonders of the Serengeti. Periodically, Roger would scold Adan, to whose car he—and I—had been assigned, for not being more informative. "I shouldn't have to tell them this," he'd say, winding up one of his mini-dissertations. "This is your job." At such moments, Adan smiled and said nothing; once I caught him shaking his head and sort of laughing to himself in despair. Patrick shrugged off the criticism, but inwardly, he was seething. Despite Adan's shyness and an unfortunate tendency toward flatulence, he was one of Ranger's best—hand-picked, along with Felician, to accompany our group.

We writers were not in a mood to be lectured; being on safari was so much fun, it was hard to remember that we were supposed to be working. Besides, the bad roads gave us an excuse not to record much of what was said: It was impossible to take legible notes unless we were at a standstill.

"Stop the car!" Roger yelled one morning. Our little caravan was crossing a flat depression between the Ngorongoro Highlands and Serengeti National Park. We had seen nothing but tufts of scrubby vegetation for miles and miles, and people were starting to doze.

Adan hit the brakes. Roger opened the car door and stepped out. "Come, everyone," he said. We trooped out after him and stood blinking in the sunlight. "This," said Roger, marching up to a young acacia, "is a whistling thorn. Does anyone here know why it's called a whistling thorn?" We shook our heads. "Adan, why have you not told them about the whistling thorn?"

Adan was hanging back, letting Roger have the spotlight. As he shuffled forward, I heard him mutter, "I would, but you never let me speak."

Felician's car pulled up and the other half of our group piled out, yawned, and stretched. "Listen up, everybody!" Roger called.

We gathered in a loose semicircle. "You see this?" said Roger, indicating one of the boluses that studded every branch of the acacia. "This is a gall. In this gall lives a small insect: the cocktail ant." He surveyed his audience. "You might want to write this down." One or two of us dutifully pulled out our pocket notebooks and began half-heartedly working our pens. "As the wind blows through the holes made in the gall by the ant, it makes a high-pitched whistling sound. Hence the tree's name: whistling thorn."

Some of us, distracted by our bladders, had turned our attention to other trees and shrubs; none, however, seemed dense enough to provide good coverage.

Thorn-tree ecology is a story with many twists and turns, in which the tree struggles to maintain just the right balance, employing a multitude of cunning methods to both attract and repel the myriad creatures that nibble its leaves, drink its sap, and spread its pollen. "When a giraffe browses," Roger continued, "hundreds of biting ants rush out in unison to defend their tree. They also deposit an unappetizing fluid on the leaves."

"Tannin," said Adan.

"Not tannin," Roger corrected. "A sticky fluid. White, I believe."

Adan shook his head. "The leaves produce tannin."

"Not the leaves, the ants."

"It is the leaves."

"Okay, but the ants produce . . . something else. Something the giraffes don't like."

"They don't like tannin."

Scowling, Roger wrapped up his lecture, ending with "and that's the story of the ant, the thorn tree, and the giraffe."

He waited while we finished our scribbling before asking if there were any questions. Nobody could think of any. Then, from the back of the class, came an unfamiliar voice.

"Do you know why these gee-raffe head into the wind when they browse these booshes?"

Everyone turned to look at the quiet Frenchman.

"Into the wind?" said Roger.

"When an anee-mal eats the tree, the tree sends tannin from the bark into the leaves. These tannin is a toxin, and it repels the anee-mal, who goes to the next tree. But the wind carries the scent of the tannin to neighboring trees, which respond by releasing their own tannin. And that's why these gee-raffe browse against the wind. You deedn't know that?"

That was round one. Round two took place on the banks of the Grumeti River, again at midday, when everyone was feeling a bit out of sorts. It was hot as blazes, and most of us were having gastrointestinal problems, owing to the overabundance of food and the bumpy roads. A pod of hippos floated in the river, far enough away so that you had to look carefully to make sure they weren't boulders. With my pocket point-and-shooter, I took a snapshot (which did indeed come out, two weeks later, looking like a pile of boulders). Nobody said much.

On our very first game drive, at Lake Manyara, we had been so excited to see anything with four legs and a tail that we had fired away with our cameras even when we were well beyond range, wasting rolls of film. Quickly, however, we had learned to be choosy. Since then, we had seen so many zebra and gazelle that on the excitement meter they were now at about the level of the North American gray squirrel, and since this was possibly our third hippo pool, a group of hippos placidly imitating boulders was only slightly higher. Our tour leaders' efforts to provide us with sufficient amusement had backfired: Our problem was not too little but too much. Too much food, too many beautiful landscapes, too many zebras, wildebeests, gazelle, and now hippos. Our safari was only half over and we were already jaded, only interested in the advanced stuff: mating elephants, a lion kill.

Hippos have some interesting habits. Aggressively territorial, they are responsible for more human deaths than any other animal in Africa. To stake their turf, they bellow and snort and splash the water with their tails while spraying fecal matter. But these hippos were not in the mood for any of that; they were just lolling about, doing next to nothing. After a few polite clicks, the cameras went silent. We began scuffing our toes in the dirt, and squinting at the treetops in case there was something arboreal to point our lenses at.

Anxious to move on, we looked around for our leaders. We found them over by the cars, grunting and gesticulating in a threatening manner—behaving, in fact, rather like a couple of male hippos. They quieted down as we approached, but only a little. The argument had begun with Roger's usual wheedling: the guides should talk about the hippos, the guides in general were inadequate, and this and that. Roger was wide-eyed; Patrick's face was immobile, but his jaw was clenched and the look in his eyes was dangerous.

Quickly sizing up the situation, the women moved in to separate the males. The *Sacramento Bee* reporter led Roger gently away; a corporate speechwriter commandeered Patrick. Round two ended in a standoff.

After that, it was war. At the tented camp, Roger was just warming up for his promised campfire lecture—an account of the time he had spent "living among the Masai"—when Patrick yawned loudly, stood, and announced that he was going to bed. "Don't forget," he added, "we're all getting up before dawn."

This was the cue for the rest of us to jump to our feet and announce that we were tired, too. "I will walk you to your tents," Patrick offered—there were lions and hyenas around—and we walked off in a little procession, leaving Roger with an audience of one, a hotel V.P. who was a newcomer to the group, having flown out from Arusha that afternoon.

We arose before dawn. Everyone was a little grumpy except Roger: This particular game drive had been his idea. The hour was a departure from our usual program of breakfast at seven, checkout at eight, travel to the next park, game drive, lunch. A sluggish start to the day suited most of us pretty well, but it did not suit Roger. "Early morning is the best time to see animals," he had insisted. "Crack of dawn. Everybody knows that."

"You'll see nothing," said Patrick.

"How can you be certain?" Roger challenged.

"Because I know. There is nothing to be seen. Not here. Not in this area."

"If we follow the river, I'm sure we'll see a leopard."

"I'm sure not."

Nevertheless, we rose at five, shivering, and had some tea. Breakfast would come later. Nobody was very animated except Roger.

In the car, however, he turned momentarily peevish. "Where did you all go last night?" he pouted. "I was all set to tell you about my time with the Masai, and you disappeared."

Our two cars prowled along the river's edge. The limbs of the sparsely foliated sausage trees that lined the bank spread out horizontally, and Patrick had instructed us to watch for four dangling legs and a tail. But of the Big Five, the solitary leopard is the most difficult to spot. We looked and looked but saw only fruit dangling from the trees—the long, sausage-shaped pods that give the tree its name. For two hours, we puttered along, stopping now and then so that Roger could photograph a superb starling or a purple-breasted roller. As the minutes ticked by with no sign of a leopard, or any other member of the animal kingdom, he remained obstinately cheerful. "The birdlife in this area is truly amazing," he declared. "Spectacular."

Far, far in the distance a tiny herd of giraffe sailed across the plain. We saw plenty of birds, but we were not a very birdy group, and the early-morning game drive was quietly deemed a failure.

That afternoon, just as we were settling into the lodge at Seronera, Patrick suddenly announced that he was going to see cheetahs. Would anyone like to join him?

Roger, employing Patrick's maneuver of the night before, went off to take a nap: Early afternoon, he asserted, was the worst time of day to look for cheetahs. Several others, fatigued from the early wakeup call, followed his example. The rest of us drove off toward the park's eastern boundary—an area that Patrick had scouted just days before we arrived. Within an hour we had discovered two young male cheetahs. Minutes later, we came upon a mother and three small cubs.

"We haven't seen a leopard," Patrick remarked, as we said our good-byes at Kilimanjaro Airport. More than an observation, it was an apology.

"It's okay," I reassured him.

"It's not okay," he insisted. "You have to come back. I'm doing a recce in the fall."

"What's a reckie?"

A recce, he explained as our queue inched toward the check-in counter, was a scouting expedition—the word is short for reconnaissance. "I'll be going to places I've never been before, to see what's there. No clients, just me and a group of friends. You can come if you want to."

❧

He slipped into my life as quietly as a cat. I barely noticed him. There were so many people in our noisy entourage—tourism officials, hoteliers, publicists, and their assistants—it took me several days to realize he was our guide. His safaris in Sierra Leone, the last place he'd lived, were rough-and-tumble affairs sprin-

kled with mild calamities—flat tires, mechanical fail-
ures, washed-out roads. In Sierra Leone, he was con-
stantly improvising his way out of a jam; if he ran out
of food, the clients ate coconuts and mangoes. With
his fleet of little Suzukis, he would take sunburned
tourists from the beach resorts into the forest: fording
muddy streams, water up to the windshield, eating
local food, kibbitzing with the village chiefs, coaxing
his clients across terrifying hammock bridges, flying
by the seat of his pants. Sometimes—often, in fact—
they even saw wildlife, quite an achievement in the
places he was going, dense with foliage and well acquainted with poachers. He was known all over West
Africa. In East Africa, however, he was an anachro-
nism. "Where are you from?" people would say, startled by his accent.

"I'm French," he'd answer—adding with a wry
smile, "Nobody's perfect."

There would be a moment's pause as the inter-
viewer, confused, tried to formulate the next question.
Sometimes, if Patrick was in a good mood, he'd help
out: "But I've been in Africa thirty-five years."

"Ah! And . . . what brought you here?"

"A plane."

Now there would be a little uncertain laughter,
then another awkward pause. Sometimes the conversation would go no further.

We were halfway up an active volcano when he
said his leg was giving him trouble. He was standing
with his back to me, staring at Oldoinyo Lengai's naked summit.

"What's wrong with your leg?"

He hesitated before answering. "In fact, it's my
knee."

"Okay, what's wrong with your knee?" We had
another guide with us, a Masai herder who said his

name was Robert and then stopped speaking to us, because that was all the English he knew.

"I injured it, years ago."

I waited for him to continue. He fished a cigarette from his pack of Marlboros. "Injured it how?"

"A bullet wound."

The top of Lengai was still six hours away, and it was nearly noon. "All right," I said to him. "Is there anything in your pack we might need?"

From his rucksack, he pulled two cans of sardines, some raisins—our dinner. Then he extracted a small green plastic box.

"What's that?"

"Snakebite kit."

"How does it work?"

Without comment, he opened the box, took out a plastic syringe, and showed me how to use it to extract the venom—the demonstration took all of five seconds. Then he shouldered his pack, wished us luck, and headed back down the mountain. We watched him cross the Rift Valley in the direction of our camp, growing smaller and smaller.

Two days later, he told me about the knee. The setting—a campsite on the shore of a soda lake—was more convenient, the story long and complicated, involving crocodiles, poachers, international smuggling, a drowning, an arrest, a shooting, and a jailbreak. I had to listen carefully, because I wasn't used to his accent. When he stopped talking, I looked at him as if I were seeing him for the first time. "Who are you?" I wanted to say, and in that moment, I resolved to find out.

The campsite was drenched in moonlight. "Maybe we'll see a genet cat," he said. We sat side by side on a bench at the picnic table and poured whiskey, speaking in whispers so as not to wake the others in our party. We giggled a lot, waiting for the cat that never came, and then things started going in a softer direction and he reached out and stroked my hair.

"It's full of dust," I said.

"I don't care."

I leaned against him and let his arms encircle me.

"What's this?" he whispered, feeling the breast pocket of my safari shirt.

"Sunglasses."

He tried the other pocket. "And this?"

"Sunblock. And a pocket notebook."

"You have a lot of stuff."

What am I doing?, I thought. This is crazy.

I stood up and announced that it was really very late and I was going to bed.

"Okay."

"Well, good night then."

"Good night."

I lay in my tent for an hour or so, unable to sleep. Then I got up and sat at the picnic table in the moonlight, listening to him snore. Everything is changing, I thought. Am I ready for this?

He courted me with his stories. In the months that elapsed between visits, that's how he held my attention, with big yellow envelopes that appeared in my mailbox every few weeks. Inside were several pages of his small, delicate script, the sentences ending in exclamation points or trailing off in a series of dots, comic-book style. He had first written about his adventures at the suggestion of a French book editor whom he'd met in Sierra Leone. The tales are full of blows: Fists fly, planes crash, cars and trucks plunge off the road. Then there are the comic turns: In one, he jumps out of a plane and lands in a tree; in another, a drunken cop shoots a chair out from under him. A brand-new bulldozer disappears and is found under a mound of peanuts; a guy with a bag of snakes walks into a bar. The editor had returned the manuscript with apologies, offering to help him find a co-writer. Patrick had stowed it away. It was one of the few items he was allowed to keep when he left the country.

After translating a few chapters into English and mailing them to me in New York, he told me the rest in person, sitting next to me on the living room couch at the house in Njiro and turning the pages of the manuscript. "This part," he'd say, adjusting his reading glasses, "is about the leopard I raised from a cub," or "the old tracker who taught me about the bush," or "the time I was adopted by an elephant herd."

He wondered if I could help him find a publisher. "I know nothing about book publishing," I said. "I know magazines. They're completely different. You need an experienced co-writer, somebody who already has an agent and a publisher and all that."

"I want you."

And so I became his collaborator. My visits became longer and more frequent. It took time to make sense out of a story as chaotic as his, almost every element of which was outside my realm of experience. I had never been charged by an elephant. I had never held a leopard cub. I had never folded a parachute, loaded a rifle, driven across the Sahara, cut my way through the jungle with a machete. His story encompassed parts of the world I barely knew. For thirty years, he had drifted from country to country, through wars and catastrophes, his fortunes rising and falling with those of the continent. But slowly, slowly, his life came together for me. And as it did, my own began to unravel.

¿❦

To leave a cold and dreary North American city in midwinter and, twenty hours later, step off a plane in a tropical place . . . to be greeted there, at the airport, by someone who adores you . . . to feel this adoration coming at you from afar, even before the plane touches down; to search for its source in the crowd of brown and white faces and then, finally, to catch sight of the face from which it radiates and walk into arms that have been waiting for you for many, many days and nights . . . this is how it was when I went back to Tanzania in the year of El Nino.

All over East Africa it had been raining for months, day and night, huge amounts of rain, turning the roads to rivers, washing out bridges, and swamping one safari camp after another. From the plane, the Serengeti was as green as an Irish spring.

The month was January; we were just entering the new year. Ordinarily, the holiday season would have been a busy time for tour operators, but the incessant rain had brought business to a near standstill. Parts of the Serengeti were impassable—every day there was a new report from the guides who stopped by the Mambo Café on their return from the bush: The camp at Maji Moto is shut down, submerged in several feet of water; the bridge at Grumeti Camp is washed out. Every day, more faxes arrived in offices all over town, sent by tour operators in the States and Europe, canceling bookings. The bars and restaurants in Arusha where minivans regularly disgorged tourists at lunchtime were empty except for the regulars—out-of-work safari guides, coffee farmers in town on business, assorted riffraff. They sat under the dripping eaves, waiting for the rain to stop, for their fields to dry out, for the tourists to come back, for the roads to improve. The safari guides whiled away whole days at the Mambo, harassing the Tanzanian wait staff and running up huge tabs. Martina, the Mambo's German owner, a slender and imperious blue-eyed blond who was rarely in a good mood, was threatening to cut off people's credit, complaining that her customers were driving her out of business.

Patrick was no longer working for Rangers. Besides clinching the deal with Roger's company, he'd had a few other successes, the most notable of which was to convince Abbas to spring for a computerized booking system. But innovation made Abbas uncomfortable, and most of Patrick's ideas for improving the business encountered stiff resistance. Soon after our first safari, he'd quit. By the time I came back, he was working for Musa, a plump, round-faced Tanzanian whose small safari business was about to go belly-up. Patrick had been brought in to save it.

Musa, however, did not really want to straighten out his messy affairs. He wanted to conduct them in his own flimflam way. Musa did not deny that he had money problems, but they were not his fault. Some days his insolvency was Patrick's fault for not bringing in more customers, and some days it was the fault of jealous tour operators who were trying to sabotage the business. Chief to blame, however, were Musa's wife and his girlfriend.

"I do everything to make them happy," Musa complained, "but they are never happy."

To appease his girlfriend, he had bought her a car. But when the wife saw the girlfriend driving around town in a brand-new car, she demanded a new car too. So instead of one car, Musa was forced to buy two. This was why he had been unable to pay Patrick's salary for the past eight months.

In the parking lot of Kilimanjaro Airport, Patrick heaved my red duffel onto the backseat of his old Nissan Patrol. In it was a model spaceship for Thomas and some long underwear for Patrick: He had said we would climb Kilimanjaro. Tucked in among my shorts and T-shirts was an electric cattle prod, purchased at Patrick's request; he claimed a small zap was effective against snakebite. When I explained its intended use to the woman at the mail-order house in Oklahoma, she said, "Well, now, that's a new one," and suggested I order the short-handled model. There was a paperback book entitled *How to Write a Winning Book Proposal*—another recent purchase—a tape recorder, a supply of audio-cassettes, and an envelope containing every story Patrick had written down and mailed to me in the past thirteen months. I'd arrived on the first morning in weeks that wasn't drenched with rain, and as we drove toward Arusha, the boughs of the yellow-blossomed trees that sprinkled the green hills dipped and swayed in the breeze. Behind us, Kilimanjaro's glistening snowcap poked above the clouds.

Patrick was bursting with news. "As from now," he said, "I start my own business. Walking safaris. I do the guiding. There are some nice places around, and nobody going there. You think is good idea?"

He could hardly have picked a worse time. All around him, established tour operators—the very companies he was counting on to buy his services—were on the verge of collapse. But the partnership with Musa was clearly finished, and he had no other choice.

"I think it's a wonderful idea," I said.

In the days that followed, I accompanied him as he drove around town, setting up his new business. Together, we put up flyers in all the bars and cafés where the backpackers stopped on their lengthy and improvised treks, and we hand-delivered business proposals to the local tour operators, trying to persuade them to offer his walking safaris to their clients.

If Patrick had wanted to test my ability to live in such a place as Arusha, those thirty days would have sufficed. On my first two visits, I had barely glimpsed the town, but during the soggy month of January '98, I got to know it quite well. The city was sprawling, crowded and chaotic, the hills and roadsides cluttered with shanties, the downtown streets overwhelmed with an array of traffic that spanned the entire evolutionary spectrum of land transportation from ancient times to the present: Pedestrians, most of them heavily laden, picked their way along the grungy footpaths that paralleled the roadways; donkeys and human-powered wheelbarrows and carts hugged the edges of the road; so did the bicycles that served as pushcarts, loaded with everything from loaves of bread to two-by-fours, the cyclists walking alongside them. Bicycles with riders, some carrying passengers front and back, zigzagged through the vehicular snarl, bells ting-a-linging. Motorized traffic came in all shapes and sizes: Peugot taxicabs, Land Rovers, cargo lorries. Lethal daladalas—public buses—ever overcrowded, swerved to the side of the road like birds of prey snatching a meal, competing for the chance to pick up even more passengers. The madness was compounded by the potholes, which caused the traffic to veer this way and that along an unpredictable course, so that simply driving down the street was like playing a game of chicken.

Most of the newcomers—people from the countryside who'd arrived with virtually nothing, hoping to partake of the city's relative prosperity—lived on a few shillings a month in squalid and dangerous conditions. Downtown, street urchins and grandmothers begged for change, and gangs of boys lurked in the shadows, surveying the parked cars and waiting for the opportunity to steal anything that wasn't locked up or bolted down.

"What's with the red X's?" I asked as we drove through town on an endless series of errands. The facades of the cheap little houses and shops that lined most of the major roads had been spray-painted with the angry-looking symbols.

"They're marked for demolition," Patrick said. "They were built without a permit, in the highway right-of-way. Someday they'll be torn down—maybe. Nobody's in a hurry."

Some of these doomed structures had taken years to build, he added, because their bricks were purchased a few at a time, as the owner saved up. That explained the many houses I'd seen in various stages of arrested development, each consisting of three or four walls that had not yet reached shoulder height. Many had been like that for months.

Commercial buildings had sprung up with greater speed, chief among them the Chinese-built Arusha International Conference Center, a bewildering labyrinth of office warrens, catwalks, dark and spooky unmarked passageways, and rattletrap elevators. The United Nations tribunal on war crimes in Rwanda was going on there at a very slow pace—it promised to juice up the town's economy for years, generating business for local merchants, doubling and tripling housing prices, and providing jobs—at much higher wages than local citizens wanted to pay—for Tanzanian chauffeurs, housemaids, and clerical workers.

The Arusha of yesterday existed everywhere in small patches. It could be seen, for example, along the stretches of riverbank reserved, by common consent, for doing the laundry, where on sunny days groups of women stood ankle deep in the stream, bending from the hips as they scrubbed, bright-colored garments laid out behind them on the white rocks to dry. And at the roundabout at the intersection of Njiro and Old Moshi roads, a grassy circle where somebody's white cow regularly grazed, placidly munching as the traffic whirled around it. The city's cows were no longer herded through the streets, however, and most no longer went to pasture; they stayed in the front yard, and the women and children walked to the nearest un-occupied grassy plot, perhaps miles away, and carried great bundles of freshly cut grass home to the cow on their heads. The scent, too, of the old town mingled with that of the new; the combined aroma was a mix of wet or dry earth, thick vegetation, charcoal cooking fires, diesel fumes, and smoldering piles of trash. White folks mostly disparaged the changes. True, you could now buy butter in town—and yogurt, and current best-sellers, and Gameboys—but you could no longer find a parking space, and you would be crazy to leave your house unlocked, as people once did without hesitation. But I liked Arusha. "If I were a painter, I would paint this place," I said to a visitor from England, an investor in a tour company that was flying hot-air balloons over the Serengeti. We were having drinks in the garden of the Novotel, an oasis of calm in the roiling city. "To be sure," the man replied, winking at the person next to him, "Arusha could use some painting. But I say bull-doze the place and start over."

The office of Leopard Tours was located on the second floor of the Novotel. We stopped by every day or two. Usually I waited in the hallway while Patrick and the Indian secretary had their small chat. The con-versation went something like this:

"Good morning, sir!" the secretary would sing out. She had begun to greet Patrick like an old friend.

"Good morning," I'd hear Patrick say, his voice drifting out into the hallway through the open door. "Is he in?"

"No, not today. I'm afraid he is still in Dar."

"Still? He was due back yesterday."

"Yes, but he has been delayed. You know the road is veddy bed."

"Yes, I know. All the roads are bad. So much rain. When do you expect him?"

"Maybe tomorrow. Maybe the day ef-tuh. It is hud to say."

"Okay, I try back tomorrow. Thank you very much."

And we'd leave. I never had to stand in the hallway very long.

The purpose of these visits was to ask a favor. As soon as Patrick formally quit his job with Musa, his work permit, a document on file in some mausoleum in Dar es Salaam, would become invalid and he would have three months to find another job or leave the country. As an independent businessman, he would have to invest an impossible sum to obtain a license to work in Tanzania. So he needed a sponsor, the owner of a legitimate company who would list him as an employee but basically leave him alone. He thought the Tanzanian owner of Leopard Tours, for whom he had done a little guiding before going to work for Abbas, would help him out. So every day or two we stopped by, to find Mr. Leopard Tours not in.

"Maybe you should try calling first," I suggested one day. Mr. Leopard Tours, we had just learned, had returned from Dar with a bad case of malaria and was home in bed. "It would save a lot of running around."

"I prefer this way," Patrick said. "Besides, I have no phone."

He used to have one. It came with the house. At first, he considered himself fortunate: It could take up to three years to get a landline installed. The house, which belonged to Musa—it had come with the job—not only had a line, but there was even a phone attached. Patrick picked up the receiver to see if it worked. Miraculously, it did. But he had nobody to call, so he replaced the receiver in its cradle. Three days later, he picked it up again, and this time the line was dead.

He drove to the phone company's office downtown. A clerk rummaged around in some files and pulled out a piece of paper. "You have an outstanding bill," she said. "Eight hundred forty-six dollars."

"How can that be? I've just moved in." The woman showed him the paper. Many of the calls were to Mumbai.

"This is not mine," Patrick said. "I know nobody in Mumbai."

"Perhaps it was the previous tenant who made the calls," said the woman. "Nevertheless."

"Nevertheless what? You want me to pay somebody else's phone bill?"

The woman shrugged. She didn't care whether he paid the bill or not, but rules were rules. "If you want the phone turned back on, yes, suh, you must pay."

He went without the phone.

Thus we spent two full afternoons chasing down a set of used tires that a French tour operator named Thierry was rumored to be selling. "He's not here," said the askari who opened the gate at Thierry's compound far out on the town's western edge. "Maybe he's at his home." We drove back the way we came, and roamed around some unmarked streets until we found Thierry's house. "Mr. Thierry is not here," said the housekeeper. "Have you tried his office?"

As the weeks went by and Mr. Leopard Tours continued to be home in bed with malaria, the secretary tried to be reassuring. "Have faith in Gud," she said. "It will all work out." Meanwhile, Musa wasn't aware that Patrick no longer worked for him. Patrick didn't want to tell him until the matter of the work permit was resolved. For all Musa knew, Patrick was on strike until he received his back pay. The two had taken to hiding from each other, which was tricky, since their houses were only a few feet apart. To avoid an embarrassing encounter, we stayed indoors when Musa's car was in the driveway, and dashed to the Nissan whenever we went out, revving the engine to warn Musa to stay indoors until the coast was clear.

In the end, Patrick went to Musa's office, and the two men came to an agreement.

"Well, Musa," said Patrick, "I understand you have no money. You can't squeeze water from a stone that is dry. But I need to pay Thomas's school fees. So here is what I propose. Let me stay in the house till the end of the school year. I will lead my walking safaris and make what little money I can."

Musa sighed. "Mr. Patrick, what you say is true. There is no money to pay you, but the boy must not suffer. Stay in the house. Karibuni," he added: You are welcome.

"This is the fault of Rangers," Musa complained, as he stood to signal that our business was finished. The explanation was for my benefit; he didn't want to leave me with a bad impression. "They are angry that their general manager, a muzungu, comes to work for me, a Tanzanian."

A few weeks later, when Patrick began to make a little money from his walking safaris, he moved to the house in Sekei, taking Musa's furniture with him. Without Musa's permission. This inspired Musa to look for opportunities to harass Patrick, the absence of a work permit being a vulnerable point. And so the contest between them continued.

On the Friday before I left town, Sue Forrester leaned across the big slab table at Masai Camp and said to me, "Leaving so soon?" She seemed disappointed. "The kids at school are all talking about you, you know."

"They are? What are they saying?"

"They're saying it's about time Tom's dad had a proper girlfriend."

I smiled, embarrassed, resisting the urge to hide the gold band on my ring finger, which Sue had undoubtedly already noticed—she was too clever to let an important detail like that go by.

"I have a job to get back to," I mumbled.

૨**

Despite the rain and the grousing and the many things that didn't work—the phones, the cars, the electricity, the roads—in those thirty days I thought I glimpsed a better life. The house with few furnishings, the hours spent on futile errands—looking for people who couldn't be found, mending things only to have them break again—the barrenness of the little shops downtown, the brownouts and blackouts, and the common wisdom that said things would only get worse—none of it particularly bothered me. This is a place, I thought, where life could be different, slower, more measured. A place where you could drive through town and see people talking with their neighbors, doing laundry together in the sun, spending half a day on a task as simple as fetching grass for the cow. A place where a family might sit together in the evening and talk or play games or read books out loud because there was no TV. The house in Njiro, though grand in comparison with its neighbors, struck me as admirably simple. Apart from a few sticks of the standard pine furniture made in town, there were some straw mats laid down on the linoleum floors, and the necessary kitchen- and tableware, and little else. The background noise I recognized from the audiotapes that Patrick had been sending me: the neighbor's cow, the whine of the metal gate as it swung on its hinges. Then there were the sounds of Jenni's quiet presence—the chuff of her footsteps crossing the cement floor of the veranda as she scraped the mud from her shoes before removing them to enter the house, the clatter of dishes and the burble of laundry in the sink, the exchange of greetings between her and the maid next door. Above all, there was the sound of the rain, pattering on the leaves of the banana trees in the garden and drumming on the tin roof, making such a racket at times that Patrick and I, sitting together in the living room, had to shout at each other to be heard.

In the evenings, we fixed our own dinner and stacked the plates in the sink for Jenni to wash the next day. Then Thomas and I sat on the floor and played card games or jacks while Patrick opened up his early-model laptop and, with his back to the room, worked on his flyers. Or the three of us played guessing games until seven-thirty, when Patrick said, "*Au lit, mon grand,*" and Thomas reluctantly headed down the hallway.

Once Thomas was tucked in, we'd pour ourselves a nightcap and talk, often by candlelight, the electricity too feeble most evenings to power anything but the laptop. This was when we worked on our "winning book proposal." I asked the questions, Patrick supplied the answers, and I wrote them down. We began at the beginning, with his first trip to Africa, and kept right on going all the way to Tanzania.

Old Moshi Road, in front of the Mambo Café.

Chapter Three

Behind the Mambo Café, a converted mansion in the old part of town, was a garden shed equipped with a phone line. This was our link to the outside world before cell phones came to Arusha. During my El Nino visit, I stopped by Multilink Services, as the shed was called, to find the desk shoved aside and the wall opened up with its guts spilling out: a tangle of multicolored wires trailed across the floor. Outside, standing in a newly dug hole, was the telephone fundi, his feet in several inches of water. I found Melissa, Multilink's owner, hunched over a cup of tea on the Mambo's front porch, head in her hands. "The fax line is lost," she said. The telephone fundi never found it, and Multilink folded, a victim of new technology.

By the spring of 2000, Arusha had not one, not two, but three mobile phone companies, along with a growing number of cyber cafés. If, when you drove by the Forresters' house, you happened to see Sue Forrester standing on the roof of the Land Rover in her flipflops and flowered skirt, turning in circles, you knew she was on the phone, searching in vain for a better signal. Some folks subscribed to all three services in the hope that when it was time to make a call at least one of them would be working.

The town was no longer a peaceful backwater; every day it became more ramshackle and more cosmopolitan. The once-forlorn shops were filled with foreign goods; at the market in Kijenge, you could buy olive oil and even Camembert. The olive oil cost more than a pair of shoes and the Camembert, which was made in Kenya, didn't really taste like Camembert, but it was better than no cheese, and certainly better than the stuff they produced in the dairy at the Greek school, which lacked taste and had goat hairs in it.

The Mambo regulars were having to compete with an upscale crowd of U.N. lawyers and high-end safari clients. Martina had jacked up the prices, added a brick terrace with canopy, and then, tired of our grumbling, had disappeared to her flower farm in Usa River, leaving the restaurant in the care of Emilio, robust, genial, and Italian.

The roundabout where the white cow grazed had developed into a proper landmark: Many months of slow construction had finally yielded an ornamental fountain with a circular pool. Then, overnight, a towering monument was added: a giant inflatable replica of a bottle of Kilimanjaro beer, the local brew, its neck pointing skyward like a steeple. The fountain had been appropriated by the women of Kijenge, who gathered there on laundry day, saving themselves the trip to the river with their heavy loads. The cow had been displaced, though some days it turned up to graze in a small plot on the other side of the highway, lifting its head now and then to eye the women clustered around what might have been, in a better world, its new watering trough.

Despite the changes, I continued to think of Arusha as a quaint and remote highland village. It was tempting to believe that nothing had changed, since the town had its own quirky way of counteracting every advancement. Thus, instead of one crummy phone service we now had three, as well as a steady stream of viruses courtesy of the cyber cafés. Even the ornamental fountain came with a hitch, for soon after the women's takeover, the town fathers, in apparent opposition, turned off the water.

The town was flooded with refugees in search of high ground, and we needed to believe that Arusha would take care of us. In the past ten years, the town had doubled in size, taking in 100,000 newcomers. The very rich and the very poor lived side by side, and underneath its humdrum surface, the town simmered with tension. But the bombings of American targets, even those in Dar and Nairobi, belonged to another world. It was hard to think of anything in our town that was both (a) American and (b) worth blowing up. The closest thing to a cherished American icon I could think of was Meat King's annual shipment of Thanksgiving turkeys. The arrival of the turkeys each November was announced with a good deal of fanfare, causing American ex-pats from across a wide area to swarm the German-owned shop (one of the few places in town where you could buy meat without fear of being poisoned). But while the turkeys were a clear instance of foreign pandering to American interests, they were unlikely to put Meat King on anybody's hit list.

West of the beer-bottle roundabout was a campground for budget travelers. How Masai Camp became the Friday-night watering hole of Arusha's muzungu crowd nobody knew; the process was as mysterious and intuitive as the movements of any herd. The big slab table nearest the bar was where the old guard gathered. It was no secret what the town's white elite, many of them the descendants of European settlers, thought of the new regime: Independence was the worst thing that had ever happened to Africa. The Africans weren't ready for it, they hadn't the education or the brains, they weren't even smart enough to know how dumb they were, how much they needed the whites. Tanzania had looked like the perfect bolt hole — a country so primitive it hadn't had a chance to go bad. But it turned out you could get nothing done here. The Tanzanian workers were lazier and more ignorant than the watu back home, the Wahindi more treacherous, the bureaucrats equally as greedy and corrupt. If, by working like a donkey, you did manage to make a little profit, the government sucked you dry. These opinions were expressed freely in front of Tanzanian waiters, chauffeurs, and household servants.

"The big mistake was to let the Asians stay," a third-generation Kenyan informed me one Friday night, leaning across the big table to look me straight in the eye. "They were brought here to build the railroad, you know, in Kenya, and after, the provincial government allowed them to stay on. My grandfather was one of four who advised against it. Lord Delamere was another. My grandfather was deported for his views. Lord Delamere wasn't, however, because he was a lord. Anyway, the first thing the Asian shopkeepers did was to teach their African employees how to skim twenty cc's off each bottle of cooking oil and set it aside for their own consumption. No, it was a great mistake to let the Asians stay and set up their shops."

As the only American in the group, I was used to such lectures, many of which were for my edification. I ignored them, not realizing that they worked on you in a subtle way.

The morning we sat in Putschi and Penny's living room, two families drinking tea and eating sugar cookies and talking about bombs, my confidence in Arusha yielded an inch to the rising tide of suspicion. Maybe there was no backyard bomb factory. Maybe the stuff Putschi had seen was bogus, the broker just another scammer trying to pay the rent. On the other hand, we were surrounded by entrepreneurs who had adapted to the changing times, turning bicycles into taxis and puddles into car washes, selling electricity through the back door of hair salons. Here was a cottage industry for the new millennium.

The first time Patrick dialed the U.S. embassy's main number in Dar es Salaam, he got the Mobitel recording that informs you your account is depleted, so we drove to the clock-tower roundabout. The clock tower was a particularly busy intersection, whirling with traffic. Masai women hawked their wares on its fringes, scruffy beggars young and old sidled up to the parked cars and pleaded for "mah-nee," boys lurked in the shade, waiting for the opportunity to burglarize somebody's car or grab somebody's camera; tourists wandered in and out of the souvenir shops and the currency exchange and the post office and the cyber cafés, and locals ran the gauntlet in pursuit of sundries like Parmalait and Weetabix at the corner grocery, or prescription items at the Indian pharmacy. Two big overland trucks carrying college kids on spring break from the U.K. were parked in front of Max's Patisserie and Cyber Cafe, and inside, a dozen sunburned travelers, their dirty hair braided and dreadlocked and bandannaed, were checking their email and splurging on lattes. We bought a phone card and a loaf of bread, then got back in the truck and drove to a quiet side street to make our call.

It took Patrick a few more tries on the mobile to reach the embassy in Dar. Just as he made a connection, a Masai girl with a big papaya appeared out of nowhere, planted herself next to my partially lowered window with a "Jambo, mama," and held out the fruit invitingly.

"I'd like to speak to the chief of security," Patrick said. He waited while the switchboard operator put him through.

"Fruti," said the girl. "I give you good price."

"No, thank you." The girl didn't move.

The chief was not in, so Patrick explained the situation to a deputy. "I'm calling from Arusha. I heard that somebody here is trying to sell liquid uranium."

A movement in the side-view mirror caught my eye: Another girl was approaching; this one had a basket of mangoes on her head. I rolled up my window.

"Yes, Arusha," Patrick shouted into the phone. He began spelling his name for the deputy. The girl with the mangoes began tapping on the window.

The deputy promised to give the chief the message.

"Thank you very much," said Patrick, and he hung up. The girls circled around to his side of the car.

"You didn't leave your phone number," I said.

"Oh shit."

So Patrick called the embassy again, spoke to the deputy, and this time left his number. Then he started the engine, and by the time we pulled away, the girls had given up and wandered off.

The chief of security didn't call back and neither did his deputy, and after a few days we tried again. This time, I made the call. "I'm an American citizen living in Arusha," I said to the man on phone duty. "My husband spoke to somebody at the embassy a few days ago—he's the one who called about the liquid uranium."

"The what?"

"Lick, wid, yoo, rain, ee, um." I was only trying to make the words intelligible over the bad connection, but I must have sounded condescending because Patrick shot me a look. It wouldn't help our cause to annoy the embassy's front line. I took a deep breath and went through Putschi's story again. The chief, however, was still not in.

For Thomas's twelfth birthday, at the end of

March, we took him to dinner at Mama's Pizza. It was also his friend Andy's birthday, so the Forresters came too. Right away, it was obvious that the boys had chosen the same gift for each other, for there is very little you can do with a sheet of giftwrap to disguise a soccer ball. There were two models available in town, one expensive, one not; when the wrappings came off and two top-of-the-line balls emerged, everybody applauded in relief. Andy announced that the new ball exactly matched the one he already had at home. "You can never have too many soccer balls," Sue pointed out hastily, "what with the thorns and all."

Thomas was still wearing his tennis shoes to school every day—either the headmaster hadn't noticed our persistent flaunting of the dress code or he had decided it didn't merit expulsion. Hopeful that Thomas would finish out the year without getting busted, we gave Mesuli the shoe money as a down payment on the April rent. Then I emailed a bunch of friends in New York, one of whom emailed me back with an offer. If I wanted, he said, I could come help him edit a vast collection of recipes that Martha Stewart was publishing on her Web site. So just before Thomas's Easter break, I flew to New York. Patrick came with me. Thomas went with his friend Simon's family to the coast.

"Daddy will be back in two weeks," I said the night before we all left. "I'll come later."

"How much later?"

"A few weeks later."

"How many weeks?"

I would be gone eight weeks, but that sounded excessive even to me, so I said, "Oh, three or four."

"I wish I had a real mother," Thomas said. "One who would stay home with me."

I cringed. I had been going back and forth between New York and Arusha for too long, and I had intended to settle down after the wedding. I didn't want to go to New York and be an elf in Martha's workshop, but somebody had to make some money around here. I laughed at the expression on Thomas's face—he was a first-class pouter—and gave him a hug. "I'll be back before you know it," I promised.

❧

In New York, the trees on my old block were just starting to put forth leaves. The apartment in Washington Heights was unoccupied—my ex-husband was working out of town—and I let myself in with the set of keys I had kept for such occasions. It felt strange to be there with my new husband.

My third-floor neighbors watched our comings and goings with curiosity: Who is that man, and where is her husband? Though the neighbors and I had shared the same hallway for years, we were only casually acquainted; they had no way of knowing that the couple who lived in 3B were no longer married.

"Hello, dear," said Mrs. Bankoff, the landlady, greeting me as I got on the elevator with husband number two. She was a kindly octogenarian who looked after her tenants as if they were an extended family and set out bowls in the courtyard twice a day for the neighborhood's stray cats. "I haven't seen you for a while."

The door slid shut and the motor thrummed, sending the elevator upward; the three of us stood toe to toe in the cramped space.

"Yes," I said, "I've been away. In Africa. You know I'm in the travel business now. Safaris. This is Mr. Texier, my partner. He's the guide; I, um, pour the tea."

To Mr. Texier I said, "This is Mrs. Bankoff; you're

standing in her elevator. Her father built this place."

"You picked a nice time of year to visit New York," said Mrs. Bankoff, smiling at Mr. Texier, as the elevator jolted to a stop on the third floor. The automatic door slid open.

"Have a nice day, Mrs. Bankoff," I said.

"You too, dear."

And Mr. Texier and I exited.

"Sorry," I said, unlocking the door to 3B.

"No problem," said Mr. Texier.

We spent the next few days strolling around the city, enjoying a fortunate stretch of warm and sunny spring weather, and watching TV in the evenings. That was how we discovered that the director of the FBI was in Tanzania. The evening news carried the story; a clip showed the director standing in front of a building in Dar that might have been the embassy, though I didn't notice; I was too busy trying to find the cordless phone. As the director yacked about how "we" were going to ferret out the terrorists responsible for the embassy bombings and prevent such atrocities from happening again, I called information and asked for the FBI's New York headquarters, located downtown near the World Trade Center. An Agent Carter picked up the phone.

"I just saw your director on TV," I told him. "He was in Tanzania talking about terrorism. I might know something about that." And I told him my story.

Barely a month had passed since our conversation in Putschi and Penny's living room. Agent Carter listened carefully, asking lots of questions. Then he repeated what I'd said, reading from his notes. His accuracy and thoroughness were impressive. He took Putschi's phone number. "My husband will be back in Arusha on Tuesday," I said. "Here's his cell phone number."

Now, I thought, we'll see some action.

After Patrick left for home, his suitcase bulging with brand-name items ordered by friends, the city felt desolate. Martha's workshop was an untidy warren overflowing with editorial clutter. I was part of the overflow, squeezed into a dark hallway outside the men's room next to a freelance copy editor named Webster. I shuttled back and forth between the office and the apartment, skulking in and out of elevators and subway cars, avoiding Martha and Mrs. Bankoff and feeling like an intruder in places I used to call home. Months earlier, my friends had given me a big send-off, wishing me happiness with a finality that suggested they might never see me again—and now I was back already, acting as if I wanted to reclaim my former life though such a claim was clearly no longer appropriate. In the ghostly silence of 3B, I wandered from room to room, studying the artifacts like a visitor in a museum. Every object told a story about my ex-husband and me.

As the wife of an actor, I had lived a nomadic life, moving fifteen times in as many years. My husband and I had a system: He went ahead with the pots and pans, I covered the rear. I arrived to find the dishes stacked, the shoes in rows, a loaf of bread rising in the oven. We were a good team, he and I.

I made the coffee, and pulled back the curtains so he could see the sky while he drank his morning cup in bed. He balanced the checkbook, changed the oil, and danced like Fred Astaire. He was the best roommate I ever had. When I was working days and he was working nights, he wrote me notes that I saved in a drawer: "Sweet one, here's your dinner. I love you very, very, very much. Microwave on 7 for 10 minutes." We had pet names for each other, we had silly sayings with secret meanings, we had a repertoire of songs for which we had worked out the harmonies.

He made me laugh.

Our battles were epic—doors slammed, walls trembled, rockets flared; I remember a tuna salad flying through the air. We argued about everything and nothing: whether actors should go to college, whether vitamin C prevented colds. Starting in New York and working our way west, we set off fireworks all across America. At length, we came to California: land's end.

I was sitting under a wisteria-draped pergola wrestling with the Sunday *New York Times* crossword puzzle one morning in June when my husband appeared in the kitchen doorway in bathrobe and slippers. The screen door opened, and he descended the steps to the patio. His bare legs looked pale and vulnerable next to the dark blue terrycloth of his robe. A metal chair screeched against the concrete as he pulled it back from the table and set it on a patch of lawn. "I need to talk to you," he said. Then he pulled another chair over and set it down facing the first one. It was the setup for a serious conversation.

We took our places. Our marriage was ten years old and had withstood all kinds of tests, most of the major deal breakers, in fact, with the notable exception of money, about which we never argued. So I figured I was well prepared for whatever might come next. My husband leaned forward, stooped under the weight of what he had to say. Over his shoulder, the one scrawny tree that occupied our backyard reached its bare branches to the sky like a suppliant; the thing had been dead for years and our landlady, who lived next door, wouldn't cut it down. She refused to admit it was dead. Every little while she came over with a pair of loppers and cut it back a little further, explaining that she was trying to "shock it" back to life. The tree made me both sad and irritated. I couldn't look at it without wanting to turn it into mulch.

My husband began. "I've been going to a twelve-step group," he said. "For sex addicts."

I have to admit, that took me by surprise.

"But," he hastened to add, "I don't really think I'm an addict."

I waited.

"What I think I am," he said, "is gay."

I took a deep breath. We had tackled this thorny subject before, many times, and emerged from the thicket bleeding, many times. My husband stared miserably at the drought-resistant grass, and my heart ached for him, and for us. He had tried to be faithful, he said, but he had failed. He needed to forgive himself and to accept that his sexual feelings were a natural part of him, and not something he could change. He said he loved me, and that he didn't want to lose me, but that he would understand if I did not want to be married to him anymore.

By now, we were both staring at the grassy lawn, as if we might find some ancient wisdom written there. I knew he loved me. That was the problem—we loved each other. We had tried therapy, drugs, and religion; nothing resolved our dilemma.

So there on our Los Angeles hilltop, we called a truce. We were what we were. We couldn't change, so we would stop trying. My husband would keep his secret life hidden, from the world and from me. That was the deal, and he honored it scrupulously. Our marriage lasted eight more years.

After we moved to Washington Heights, completing our circular odyssey, there were days when my husband couldn't get out of bed. Days when he could barely speak. Days when he said the pain was physical, a sensation in his chest that was like being stabbed with

a knife. There were days—I found this out only later—
when he thought about threatening to jump off the
George Washington Bridge. Not jumping—threatening
to jump. Then maybe someone would realize how bad
it was and get him some help. I figured his black mood
would pass. It honestly never occurred to me that I
could be part of his problem.

The day I made my own confession, the Hudson
River looked cold through the bedroom window, the
sky colorless, the rock escarpment on the opposite
shore dark and foreboding, like the walls of a medie-
val castle. As I unpacked my red duffel, my husband
sat on the bed, asking questions. I had just returned
from my third trip to Tanzania, and I knew I had
some explaining to do.

"How was Kilimanjaro?"

"We didn't climb it."

"You didn't? How come?"

"It was too rainy. Everything was flooded. We
spent a lot of time in Arusha."

The pale afternoon light of the late-January sun
had begun to fade, and we stretched out on the bed
together, my head on his shoulder. He was the first to
speak.

"Did you fall in love in Tanzania?"

I had been preparing myself for this conversation
for weeks. I didn't want to have it, and I hadn't expected him to take the lead. But he was perceptive;
sometimes he knew what I was thinking even before I
did. Still, I hesitated.

"I fell in love with a ten-year-old boy."

"That's nice. And his father?"

My heart was pounding.

"Are you in love with him, too?"

"I don't know. I could be."

"Ah. I see." His arm stayed where it was, encir-

55

cling my shoulders. "This is big."

We lay still for a minute, then he got up and began pacing. I sat on the bed, waiting for him to explode. But he only stood with his back to the window and exhaled, as if he'd been holding his breath. "This is big," he repeated softly.

He said he was surprised, but in his heart, he must have known. I was grateful for his intuition, and relieved that he had chosen to make this easy for me, and not to react in a way that would have caused me to feel guilty. More guilty than I already did. I asked him if he thought I'd made a mistake.

He sighed, sad but sure of his answer. "No," he said. "I think this is happening because it's right."

For the next eighteen months, I went back and forth between two continents and two lives. In New York, I was one person, in Tanzania another. Something had to happen.

Eight years after my husband's Sunday-morning confession, almost to the day, I slipped off my wedding band. My husband needed his freedom—that's what I told myself. He couldn't choose it because he didn't want to hurt me, so I chose it for him. For us.

Fifty dollars and a paralegal took care of the official business. "It's a busy year for divorces," said the young man who handled our case; he told us we could expect results in five months.

We filed for divorce in May; in July, we celebrated our eighteen-year wedding anniversary at a favorite neighborhood restaurant. "I think we should always celebrate our anniversary, don't you?" I said. Looking at my husband sitting across from me, I thought with surprise, "We're middle-aged. How did this happen? We were children when we met."

The document stating that our divorce was final arrived in the mail in August; my husband opened it, and showed it to me when I got home from work. "You should keep the original," he said. "You will need it to get remarried."

I took only one suitcase with me when I moved to Tanzania. When I shut the door of the apartment in Washington Heights everything was undisturbed, just as if I still lived there. My books were still on the shelves, my father's oil paintings still on the walls. The family heirlooms I treasured—the grandfather clock, my grandmother's quilts—were all in place, and so was every souvenir my husband and I had collected over the years.

As we left for the airport together, he tried to reassure me. "This is still your home," he said. "You can always come back, you know."

"I know," I said tearfully. We both knew that when I came back it would be to visit.

At the airport, my husband—for I still thought of him as my husband, and I couldn't help it—came inside and we had lunch at a long empty bar topped with fake black marble and he took a picture of me as I looked on our last day together. When we said good-bye, my heart was pounding, but I didn't cry. I couldn't latch on to the moment; it was too big, and my emotions were a jumble. I had wanted him to be relieved by my decision, and I knew he was. I just hoped that neither of us would regret it down the road.

Five months into my second marriage, I still grieved. I also had spells of doubt: Had I acted selfishly? Antidepressants and a therapist named Eli had saved my husband's life after my own medicine had nearly killed him, and yet I worried that without me he would perish. Alone in the apartment we'd shared, surrounded by mementoes of our life together, I picked up the phone. "How's the play going?" I asked.

There were problems with the set—he mentioned

something about exploding lights that sent showers of broken glass down onto the stage. The night before, they'd had to stop the show and get out the brooms. Other than that, he was fine.

"I miss you," he said.

"I miss you, too."

❧

Just before I left New York, an agent Summerhill called me to follow up on Putschi's lead. I repeated my story.

"My husband is there now," I said. "In Arusha. He's the one you should call."

Almost two months had passed since Putschi's housegirl had come knocking. I gave Agent Summerhill Patrick's and Putschi's cell phone numbers, and the number of the Mambo Café. "He's there a lot," I said. "You can leave a message with Emilio, the owner."

Patrick was so well known in Arusha that anybody, even the FBI, could have found him without half-trying if they wanted to. Putschi was even easier to locate, especially these days, because he rarely left the house. Agent Summerhill dutifully took down the numbers, repeating them back to me. But somehow I knew that no FBI agent was going to be dispatched to either doorstep. Too much time had gone by, and too many phone calls had been made. I hung up the phone and forgot about Agent Summerhill for a long, long time, remembering him again on a radiant September morning as I stood in lower Manhattan, looking at a smudge in the sky where the World Trade Center had been.

Our wedding at the Boma, November 1999.

Chapter Four

The old German fortress where I became a bride for the second time harkened back to Arusha's days as a garrison town. I knew nothing of its origins at the time of our wedding, and sensed nothing special about its shabby gloom. Much later, I learned that its construction was a humiliating task carried out by once-proud warriors, who were forced to use their spears as pickaxes and their shields as pallets for carrying stone. The brutality of those days had not been forgotten, but few newcomers bothered to acquaint themselves with the town's history. One hundred years after its ignominious beginnings, I knew the Boma only as a place to get married.

In the pictures of our wedding Thomas is radiant, his face joyful. He has spiked up his hair with gel, bought by me in a moment of indulgence at the market in Kijenge, and his blue-and-white-striped shirt matches his papa's. He pouted when I insisted he wear his navy blue school trousers, but they were the only nice ones he had—fortunately, we were able to find a reasonably clean pair among his messy belongings. I'm not sure which delighted him more—that we were finally getting married and he would have a proper mother, or that we had chosen a Tuesday for the event, which meant skipping school.

The groom shows signs of wear and tear, normal for a man of fifty-five, the hair shaved close to disguise the fact that it is thinning, an empty space where a couple of right-side molars used to be. The replacement teeth were residing, when the pictures were taken, in a blue plastic bag that hung from a wooden peg in the bathroom of the house in Arusha. Patrick had given up wearing them after they fell in the soup at the home of the French ambassador to Ivory Coast in 1984. Amazing that he was still carrying them around with him, after all the possessions he'd parted with over the years. They were expensive, though, and you don't just throw out a set of good teeth. His wedding attire had come from the back of his closet, stored there in case a fancy occasion ever arose. He even had a tie—it was tricolored, like the French flag, and had teddy bears in sailor suits marching up and down it. The rest of his costume consisted of a blue-and-white shirt (nicely pressed by Jenni), a pair of black leather boots that Thomas had spit-shined, and a pair of blinding white trousers several sizes too small. He looked like a bandleader. That the pants were dangerously tight fazed him not at all. Stepping into them for the first time in fifteen years, he simply took a deep breath and zipped up. His dust-colored canvas-and-leather safari vest—a last-minute decision—covered the bulges: Voila.

We were married in November, a good month for a wedding in Tanzania. In November the rains come and the jacarandas turn blue, pushing out blossoms no bigger than your thumb; their masses of petals float above the rooftops of Arusha like puffs of blue mist. Rain on a wedding day is a sign of luck—rain makes a knot grow tighter, they say—and so is a jacaranda blossom that lands on the windshield of your car. You can be fairly sure that one or the other, raindrops or blue petals, will fall out of the sky to bless a November wedding.

The day of our wedding, we had a steady downpour until noon. Our reception was to be under a roof, so there was nothing for the rain to spoil except Thomas's crepe-paper flowers, which he had been working on for the better part of the morning. The flowers were to go on the Land Rover pickup, but they were piling up on the coffee table as Thomas labored over them, and the Land Rover was dripping next to the front porch.

Then, with less than two hours to go before our two-o'clock appointment, the rain stopped, the sun came out, and toads hopped across the lawn, lured from their hiding places among the canna lilies by swarms of newly hatched termites.

Jenni emerged from the kitchen, where she had been preparing lunch, and padded barefoot down the corridor with her blue plastic wash bucket; I heard the staccato gloog-gloog of water as she filled it from the shower tap. A moment later she appeared in the living room doorway and, leaning to starboard to balance the heavy bucket, walked past us and out the front door. As if on cue, Thomas gathered up his decorations and a roll of cellotape, and while Jenni scrubbed the Land Rover with her floor rag, he festooned the grille and roll bars with flowers and streamers.

I laid a bath towel on the dining table and began ironing my dress, a simple ankle-length sheath made by a Tanzanian dressmaker whose tiny stall, located in the warren of shops that surround the central market, did a brisk business. The silky blue fabric was the same color as the blossoms of the jacaranda trees that were now in full bloom all over town. It brought out the blue of my eyes and went well, I thought, with my hair, which could no longer be called anything but gray.

My move from New York City to Tanzania had been hard on my hairdresser. The transition was spread over three years. When it began, my hair was the color of rust. Every few weeks I'd go around the corner to the Cuban hair salon and Juanita would touch up my roots. "Is it dangerous?" she asked, when I told her I was going on safari in the Serengeti. "Not a bit," I said, but Juanita frowned in doubt as she dragged her *peine grande* through my hair. "Me, I prefer go to Lourdes," she said. "To see the Virgin."

Back for a touchup a month later, I showed her my pictures of lions, zebras, and gazelles. "Dios mio," she murmured, studying a wildebeest. "Thassa ugly cow." She sounded gravely perplexed, as if God couldn't possibly have intended one of his creatures to come out looking like that. Her reaction was similar when I told her I wanted to go from rust to medium brown. Alarm gave way to confusion and finally pity, but all she said was "Brown no match your skin."

I knew she worried about me—I, who didn't go to church and had no children and often traveled to distant countries without my husband. Our neighborhood in Washington Heights was well known to be full of brujas; perhaps I was under a spell.

But my mind was made up, and in the span of a few months I went from medium brown to fawn to tawny gold on my way to natural, that is to say, gray. A lustrous silvery gray, but gray nonetheless. Juanita fought me every step of the way. "But you are so young and beautiful!" she lamented. "What will your husband think?" It was not easy to stand firm.

Every time I got off the plane at Kilimanjaro Airport, my hair was both lighter and shorter. It took a full year for the roots to grow out enough so that

Juanita could snip off the last of the color. Together we studied my new reflection in the mirror. "In fact, I like it," she announced, gracious even in defeat. And with the blessing of my colorist I moved to Arusha and began a new life.

By 1999, Arusha was a fast-growing city, a mix of shanties and grand stucco mansions. If you were of the class that had money, you were supposed to flaunt it. Thus it was customary for people with less than a tenth of our income to rent for their wedding day a shiny white limo decorated with real pink roses, not crepe paper. Certainly a Land Rover pickup was not considered a proper wedding chariot, even by people too poor to actually own any sort of vehicle other than maybe, if they were lucky, a second-hand Chinese bicycle.

The bride, if at all possible, was supposed to arrive at the flower-filled church in a gown of white satin and lace, the groom in a tuxedo. Anyone of our means should have hired a band for the reception and prepared heaps of food. But we were happy with our plans. We didn't want to burden ourselves with a bunch of arrangements that might come undone at the last minute, as weddings have a way of doing.

Setting the date had proved difficult. We had made half a dozen trips to the Boma, back in October, in search of the civil servant in charge of marriages. Always his secretary met us with the same apologetic face, those sorrowful eyes, the wan smile, and said (softly, the way the Tanzanians do, so you have to lean in to hear them, as if life is just too futile to even bother to raise one's voice enough to be heard anymore): "Mr. Makombe is not in. You must come back lay-tah." When will he be back, we inquired, unable to stop ourselves from asking the meaningless question. The secretary's eyes wandered over the room's grimy walls, searching in vain for the answer. "Mebbe at fah," she said—or three, or eleven, making up an answer so that we would go away and leave her in peace. Okay, we would say, see you then. Doggedly, we would return at four, to find Mr. Makombe not in.

We were beginning to wonder if the wedding boss even existed when we got lucky, arriving one day just as he was leaving. He and Patrick hurriedly compared appointment books and came up with a date: November 16, a Tuesday, at two o'clock. We paid in advance, twenty thousand shillings, which was probably the muzungu price since twenty thousand was a month's salary for most people. Still, when you considered that a can of tuna at the grocery store in Kijenge cost three thousand shillings, the fee was a bargain.

After we set the date, Patrick called his mother in France with the news. They talked for a few minutes, then I heard Patrick's footsteps coming down the hallway. I was at my desk near the bedroom window composing emails to friends in the States and copying them onto a floppy to take to Max's Patisserie and Cyber Café, where Max's Internet connection would launch them into cyberspace. Patrick was holding the cell phone in his outstretched hand. "She wants to talk to you," he said.

I took the phone cautiously: "Hello?" I had never spoken to his mother before. From far away came an unfamiliar voice, high and feminine and throaty, with a strong French accent. "Hello? Sah-rah? I weesh you much happiness. It weel be good for Thomas to have a muzzer. Sah-rah, I keese you. Bye-bye."

Patrick told her we would come to France in April—she could have a look at her new daughter-in-law then. Neither of us expected his mother, who was seventy-five, to jump on a plane and fly down for the wedding, particularly since it was just the latest in a series: Patrick had already been married two times, or three, depending on how you counted.

Patrick paid for two gold wedding bands from the Lebanese jeweler who had the shop near Meat King, and Jenni led me in and out of tailors' shops until she found a dressmaker who quoted what she considered a fair price: eight dollars. The fabric itself cost about six, so the whole dress set me back less than a set of WalMart pillowcases. Jenni explained to the dress-maker what I wanted, then instructed me to draw a picture in the dressmaker's sketchbook. A few days later I returned and tried on the dress as, standing be-tween me and the busy sidewalk, Jenni and the dressmaker's apprentice held up a thin wool blanket to obstruct the view from the street of me in my un-derwear.

In mid-October, I received an email from Eric, the editor who had sent me to Tanzania three years ear-lier. He had quit his job with the travel magazine, and he and his wife were on a world backpacking tour; they would be arriving in Dar es Salaam in Novem-ber. "Come to Arusha," I emailed back. "We're getting married on the sixteenth. You and Bev can be our witnesses."

The first of our wedding-day snafus was the dis-appearance of the groom. At ten o'clock in the morn-ing, Patrick and Eric drove the Toyota Tercel—my car—into town "to help Karl make the punch." Karl, a skinny South African with the face of a fox, long wispy blond hair, and a neatly trimmed mustache, was a bartender at the Discovery Club, a job he shared with his much sturdier-looking wife, Gail. That's where our reception was to be, starting at four o'clock. Killer punch and what the British ex-pats call bitings—pretzel mix and stuff, nothing fancy.

The punch was Patrick's own recipe, a sangria-like concoction that recalled for him past birthdays, weddings, national holidays, and Saturday nights in various former stomping grounds: Ivory Coast, Nigeria, Sierra Leone, Gabon, Cameroon. . . . He seemed anxious that Karl—who was a professional hunter before he became a professional bartender—get it right; indeed, it had been the subject of more discussion than any other aspect of our wedding, he and Karl having sat down together at a booth in Discovery one slow afternoon, Karl with a notebook and pen, to itemize the list of ingredients and their proportions. It gave Patrick and Eric a good excuse that morning to leave the house, allowing the women some privacy for their own wedding preparations. Three hours later, with time growing perilously short, the punch makers were still making punch. Jenni and Bev, the best man's wife, were in the kitchen, throwing together some lunch that we no longer had time to eat. Only the Land Rover was showered and scrubbed and dressed in its wedding attire, ready for the ride down the hill to the Boma.

"Look, Sara!" called Thomas through the open window. He was standing in the truck bed, turning this way and that to admire his handiwork. I stood the mulish iron on its end—the obstinate thing was spitting and spewing and making a mess of my dress—and stepped onto the veranda to admire the pickup, all decked out and clean for the first time in weeks—it really had been improperly muddy for a bridal conveyance. "It's beautiful," I told Thomas, silently noting his grubby fingernails and wild hair, stiff with dust. "Now what are we going to do about you?"

As he trudged off to the shower, I picked up the iron again. From the kitchen, I could hear the rattle of plates and the chopping of vegetables. The iron hissed and spit, and a dark splotch appeared on the bodice of the blue dress. Stupid thing, I muttered, cursing the cheap appliance. I blotted the wet spot with a clean dish towel from the kitchen drawer, but whatever fabric the dress was made of — in my anxiety, it struck me as something one might line a coat with — did not like steam, and the water mark left by the iron refused to go away.

"Jenni!" I yelled toward the kitchen.

It was Jenni who kept our household running smoothly, calling "Wait, sir!" each and every time Patrick walked out of the house without his cell phone, picking Thomas's fish hooks up off his bedroom floor before anybody could step on them, and restoring order to the chaos of our kitchen on a daily basis. She was unflustered even by the waywardness of our electrical power, managing to get the electric pump going often enough to keep the water tank filled, ironing every shirt, pillowcase, and undergarment in the house, rescuing forgotten items from the fridge and turning them into soup. Her only fault was that she was too good for us, more capable than the job required, and though we paid her well by Arusha's meager standards, we knew that we were in her debt.

One day when Patrick was on safari, I screwed in a light bulb in the bathroom and the thing exploded — I'm lucky I wasn't blinded — and the lights in half the house went out. Mesuli, our landlord, lived just next door and spoke good English, but he was a cook by profession and knew nothing about fixing anything. "I am going to call the fundi," he would say, shaking his head and sighing whenever there was a problem with the electricity or the plumbing. Then he would summon his mechanic.

My Swahili was terrible, but I did know the words for "no electricity" because it happened all the time. So when the light bulb exploded I swept up the shards and splinters of glass, then went over to Mesuli's, stepping through the break in the hedge between our two houses. The first person I saw was the askari—at least I took him for a watchman, though there were often so many people at Mesuli's house that it was hard to know who was who. The askari and I exchanged the usual pleasantries—"Habari ya kazi?" (How's work?) and "Habari nyumbani?" (How's the family?), and then I said, "Hamna umeme"—the power's out—and the askari summoned Mesuli. Mesuli led the way back through the hedge, set a chair under the fuse box in the hallway outside the kitchen, and climbed up to have a look. He climbed down. "I am going to call the fundi," he said. It was Saturday evening, and the fundi was unavailable until Monday morning, so after Mesuli left I went to the kitchen and began chopping vegetables by candlelight.

Monday morning, no fundi. When the metal gate at the end of the drive finally clanked open it was to admit Jenni, coming as usual to clean the house and prepare lunch. It was her day to iron, too, so when I explained that she couldn't because hamna umeme she too set a wooden chair under the fuse box and climbed up on it. This made me very nervous. "Jenni, be careful," I pleaded, thinking of the exploding light bulb, but she only laughed quietly, the way she does. She moved things around a bit in the fuse box, and we had light.

I went next door. "Never mind the fundi," I said to Mesuli. "Jenni fixed it. She's very clever, you know," I added, suggesting a certain difference between him and her, because of course he himself had stood on the exact same chair and looked into the exact same fuse box and accomplished zilch. Mesuli laughed. He knew I was teasing, and besides, he had a comeback. "I know," he said. "My wife trained her." It was true:

Mama Mesuli worked at the Novotel, where she taught people how to cook muzungu food—European cuisine. Jenni was one of her star pupils.

But even Jenni couldn't remove the stubborn water spot from the front of my blue dress, and at one o'clock, with no groom in sight, it seemed inevitable that we would arrive late at the Boma and maybe even show up at our reception unmarried. Amazing, I thought, as Jenni handed me the dress, how even the simplest wedding could go awry at the last minute.

At five past one, as I was entertaining the possibility that Patrick had changed his mind—deciding perhaps that he'd been married enough already—he and Eric returned, only slightly tipsy from sampling the punch, nothing some lunch wouldn't cure. We ate hurriedly, and changed into our wedding clothes.

"Take my camera," I said to Thomas, just before we left the house, strapping the case to his belt. "Make sure you get lots of pictures." Patrick and I posed in the garden for the first round, surrounded by canna lilies and banana trees and flying termites, their wings glinting in the sun.

Juanita's salon was the kind of place where women traded confidences; even if you didn't mean to, the señoras would coax them out of you, seducing you with their accomplished fingers and murmuring voices. Especially Juanita, who sang Spanish melodies in a soft soprano as she parted and snipped, parted and snipped. When she learned that my husband and I had no children, that we had tried for many years without success, she took an interest. The next time she went to Lourdes, she said, she would speak to the Virgin on my behalf. She had prayed for this very thing when she and her husband were trying to conceive, and now she had a teenage daughter. I wasn't sure I wanted children anymore, but I didn't say so. Juanita could pray all she wanted, but for me to conceive would take something on the order of an Old Testament miracle, for my marriage had grown quite chaste.

The day I met Thomas, I got off the plane in Nairobi and began searching the crowd for his father's face. Patrick saw me first, and waved; Thomas was the small boy by his side. Along the highway between Nairobi and Arusha, we saw giraffes and gerenuk. Thomas had a little pair of binoculars that Patrick had given him for the journey; he offered them to me so that I could have a look. A young goatherd raced across the scrubby plain, waving at our speeding car. "Which do you think is better?" I said. "Going to school with your friends, or spending the day alone in a field, tending goats?" Thomas studied me solemnly. "Tending goats," he said.

He was as cute as a nine-year-old boy can be, with long skinny legs, unruly honey-colored hair, big brown eyes with thick lashes, a button nose, cherubic lips, and a mouthful of crooked teeth. His skin was smooth and tawny, his face round, and his fingers and toes long and elegant, except for the nails, which were long, yes, but elegant, no. He loved snakes and fish and trucks and planes, and despised homework and asparagus and toothbrushes and early bedtimes.

I was just another tourist. Tourists went away, promising to return; nobody ever saw them again. The person who asked him about tending goats went away and never came back. He forgot all about her. The next time we met, I was a stranger.

He was still sizing me up when evening came and his father drove to Kilimanjaro Airport to drop off some clients, leaving Thomas and me at the house in Njiro. Patrick promised to be home by ten. Ten o'clock came and went. Then ten-thirty. Then eleven.

"Aren't you tired?" I asked. We were drawing pictures at the pine-slab table. Thomas was drawing me drawing him, and I was drawing him drawing me.

He shook his head. "I want to wait for my dad." Every little while, his pencil stopped moving. "What time is it?" he'd ask again. "What's taking him so long?"

It was almost midnight when we heard the Nissan's engine. Thomas ran to the door and threw it open, then stood on the veranda in his bare feet as Patrick emerged from the car. "Papa, you're late!" he scolded.

At a coffee plantation in Karatu, we walked together through a field. "I don't have a mother," he said suddenly. "She left, and I don't know where she is."

"I know." I was on his right, and his face was turned in my direction. I could feel him looking at me, waiting for me to continue. But I had another life in America, and I couldn't be the mother he needed, not then. We walked on through the field in silence.

The day I married his father, Thomas placed full confidence in me, assuming without hesitation that it would be better having me for a mother than having no mother at all, even though I had come to him wholly inexperienced and untrained. He was astonishingly trusting, given his former experience with mothers. I was the latest in a disappointing string whose only jewel was Sento; that she was only a nanny and not a real mother was of no significance to Thomas until the day he left Sierra Leone without her. His original mother, somebody by the name of Anne, had disappeared from Sierra Leone nine years earlier, and nobody seemed to have the faintest idea where she might be. His father was unable to explain how his mother had become so completely lost in the age of the telephone and the postage stamp. His next mother was an Argentine painter who fed him eggs after he explained he was allergic and nearly killed him. After that he spent a year boarding in the French country-side, an arrangement that included a temporary mother. *That* mother had been so thoroughly unpleasant that he had erased her name from his memory.

"I hate the Dursleys," he said to me one evening as we slumped together on the living-room couch, reading *Harry Potter and the Sorcerer's Stone* by candlelight. Thomas loved Harry, an orphaned wizard boy who had been raised by evil relatives. "They remind me of that family I lived with in France."

His head was on a pillow and the pillow was in my lap; I put the book aside and stroked his hair. The only part of his past that Thomas ever talked about was Sierra Leone, where he had been happy. I tried to find out more about the Dursleys of France, starting with an easy question. "What were their names?"

"I don't remember."

I tried again. "Did they have children?"

"A girl."

"How old?"

"I don't know. Let's finger-wrestle." He sat up and grabbed my hand.

I could get nothing more out of him. The Dursleys of France were back in the dungeon, the door heavily bolted. It was as if he would just as soon forget that family had ever existed.

I was bound to disappoint him, and so I did, soon after the wedding, when I began disappearing for days, weeks, and months at a time. His stoic forbearance inevitably recalled for me the morning of November 16, when I held up my ruined wedding dress, inviting him to commiserate with me over the dark splotch front and center.

"It doesn't matter, Sara," he said. "You can hardly see it." Then he threw his arms around me in a rush of spontaneous joy. "I'm so happy!" he said, brown eyes shining.

❧

At the Boma, the secretary looked from Patrick to the rest of us, clustered in the doorway in our dressy clothes—and frowned. "I'm sorry, suh," she said finally. "Mr. Makombe is not in."

Despite the wedding chief's habitual elusiveness, it had never occurred to us that he might not bother to keep an actual appointment for an actual wedding. Silly us. We were more embarrassed than angry, and momentarily uncertain: Now what do we do? The secretary, wearily apologetic, suggested that we reschedule, but that was out of the question. What about the reception, our guests, the punch? What about the crepe paper flowers? And if there's one thing a wedding reception absolutely must have, it's a bona fide bride and groom.

"Wait outside," Patrick instructed the rest of the wedding party. He looked rattled. Everybody hustled out onto the second-floor veranda, leaving him to powwow with the secretary. We stood around, gazing down at the dusty courtyard. After a moment, Patrick appeared in the doorway of the absent Mr. Makombe's office and called to Eric. The two of them disappeared inside.

"Smile, Sara," said Thomas.

I turned to face the camera lens. "Well," I said brightly, "here we are." A bead of sweat trickled down my back.

Our wedding was going no more smoothly than the engagement, and as the minutes ticked by, I began to feel sorry for the groom. Five years separated Patrick from his most recent marriage, which had ended in a clean break. When he and wife number three tired of each other after a few months as husband and wife, they went to the nearest courthouse, where, for a fee, a clerk opened a ledger and drew a line through their names. They could have saved themselves the ten dollars if they'd been less hasty, for shortly thereafter, the courthouse, and all its records, burned to the ground. The exed wife went back to Argentina and had been unheard-from since.

My situation was different. Only yesterday, it seemed, I had been married to a man I still loved, and though I had done my best to segue from one marriage to the next, the transition had been rough, and my installation at the house in Sekei had precipitated a long spell of dithering. We had already gone around town, Patrick in the lead, saying that we were getting married. We'd told Thomas, and our mothers. All of our friends in Arusha were ready and waiting for what they reasonably expected to be the social event of the year. The last big wedding was so long ago that the marriage itself was almost over, the bridal couple looking grim and publicly talking about divorce. "We need to set a date," Patrick reminded me. He knew that he risked a flood of tears. In our not-yet-official family, I was the worrier and the weeper. While my marriage was collapsing and I was slipping away from New York to spend weeks in Arusha, I once overheard Patrick assure Thomas that it was normal for women to cry a lot, even on a daily basis.

"Not yet," I said. "I'm not ready." I knew how much he wanted this marriage, and I was sorry to put him off. But I had given up everything — my husband, my home, my friends, my carefully constructed life — to come live with him and Thomas, and for now that would have to be enough. After a few tries, he gave up. "Tell me if you change your mind," he said. "I won't ask again." Then he went off to Lake Tanganyika with clients, and while he was gone I gathered my courage. Two weeks after his departure, the Land Rover drove through the gate and a stranger tumbled out of the driver's seat and landed in the bougainvillea. "It's Daddy!" Thomas yelled, recognizing his father under a thick layer of reddish-brown road dust. Patrick limped toward us, his foot numb from pressing the accelerator for twenty-three hours without a break. "I couldn't wait to see you," he said. That night, I told him I'd reached a decision, and the next morning he drove straight to the Boma and met with the wedding chief before I could change my mind again.

When the men emerged from Mr. Makombe's inner sanctum, they were accompanied by a smiling young Tanzanian who extended his hand in greeting.

"Good afternoon, madam," said Mr. Happy God Matoi. He apologized for keeping me waiting, explaining that his boss had been delayed by "urgent matters" or some such baloney.

"But do not wuddy," he assured me, his voice calm and soothing. "I will puf-fahm the merry-edge. Come this way, please." And we followed Mr. Happy God Matoi into a dingy little office with turquoise blue walls.

"What took so long?" I whispered to Patrick.

He rubbed his fingers and thumb together, the sign for money. They had been haggling over Mr. Ma-

77

toi's fee. In the end, Patrick, or perhaps Eric, gave him twenty thousand shillings, the same amount we had paid his boss.

The room was your basic Tanzanian office—so cramped that you could barely move around in it, yet all it contained were a couple of cheap wooden desks shoved up against each other, face to face, a few chairs, and some forgotten piles of paper collecting dust, large quantities of which had drifted through the open windows.

The seven of us squeezed in: Mr. Happy God Matoi sat at one desk, Patrick and I at the other, facing him; Bev, Eric, and Thomas occupied a row of chairs next to the door; a friend with a video camera jammed himself into a corner.

Mr. Happy God Matoi slowly swept the room with his serene smile, as if to remind one and all of the solemn pleasure of the occasion and set the tone before beginning the proceedings. His gaze came to rest on Patrick.

"You are Christian?"

"Yes," Patrick responded.

From a desk drawer, Mr. Matoi extracted a leather-bound copy of the Holy Bible and placed it in front of us. A puff of dust rose up around it.

The secretary came in and handed each of us, bride and groom, a sheet of paper on which were printed our vows, a short paragraph typed perhaps back in 1960-something on a 1930-something Underwood, then copied over and over through the years until it had reached its present iteration, which was barely legible. I read through it hurriedly, to find out what sort of marital contract I was about to commit to, and found nothing objectionable. Patrick skipped this step; his eyes were a bit glazed, and I sensed that he was still recovering from the awkward beginning.

He glanced down at the sheet of paper, which I knew he couldn't make out without his reading glasses. The glasses stayed in his pocket.

Then Mr. Matoi made a little speech: "Marriage in Tanzania is between a man and a woman," he explained, "not a man and a man, or a woman and a woman. In some countries, that's okay, but not here." He paused, seeming to wait for some sort of response. We nodded gravely.

"Another thing: Marriage in Tanzania is meant to be for life. Sometimes things don't work out, and then, if necessary, the marriage may be tuh-minated, and you have dee-vuss. But for that, you don't come here, not to this office. That's another office." He waved his hand toward the clattering street.

I glanced toward the open window and fiddled with the length of chiffon that I'd flung over my shoulders in an effort to look bridal. I needed to believe we would be okay—all of us, that is. My first husband, my second husband, Thomas, and me. Trust in God, the Tanzanians advised us, a hundred times a day. Even a pagan like me could intuit the wisdom that had turned me around when I was headed toward Kansas; sprung the general manager of Ranger Safaris from his office prison just as I was passing through; answered my hairdresser's prayers and given Thomas a mother; and produced Mr. Happy God Matoi and his dusty Bible. Surely the organizer of this elaborate scheme had plans for my ex-husband, too.

"Here," Mr. Matoi was saying, "we concern ourselves only with marriage, and we tell the people that marriage is supposed to last forever." We nodded again: That was our plan, too.

Mr. Matoi moved on to a few final practical matters: "Will this marriage be polygamous, monogamous, or potentially polygamous?" he inquired. Everybody looked at Patrick.

"Well," said Patrick, clowning. "Hmm…"

"He wants it to be monogamous," I said.

"This is what I was going to say," said Patrick.

Mr. Matoi laughed politely and ticked a box on the sheet of paper in front of him.

With that, Mr. Happy God Matoi instructed us to recite our vows, Bible in hand. Patrick finally put on his reading glasses. Vows said, Thomas came forward with the rings, which he had somehow managed not to lose even though we gave them to him back at the house more than sixty minutes and three miles ago. All the necessary parties signed the necessary papers, in indelible ink, a moment that was recorded by all three cameras, and we were officially married.

The rest of the day went smoothly. Eric, a little weewah from sampling the punch, threw up on the way to Mezza Luna, where we passed a quiet hour in the garden before moving on to the Discovery Club, and after that he was fine. Loads of people showed up for the reception, including some we barely knew. There were Kenyans, Zimbabweans, Senegalese, and South Africans. There were Germans, Swiss, Finns, Scotts, Brits, French, Indians. There were even a few Tanzanians, including Jenni and Moses, her fiancé.

The upstairs veranda overflowed with people, all speaking English in a variety of accents; their voices drifted out over the street, lifted by a cool night breeze. There was an ample supply of punch, and Karl and Gail had remembered the things we'd forgotten about, such as flowers and champagne. They'd bought several bushels of roses from one of the many flower farms on the edge of town, and several bottles of South African sparkling wine.

"You must save the cork," Karl instructed, "for luck." He took out his pocketknife and nicked the top of the cork, then embedded a Tanzanian shilling in it, which is what you're supposed to do. "Don't let the coin fall out," he warned.

Before going to bed, Patrick took the champagne cork out of his vest pocket and set it carefully on the bookshelves in the living room, where we kept our personal treasures. The shilling was still embedded: He had wrapped it in a bit of cellotape, just to be safe.

 है▲

In the weeks that followed the wedding, word got around the little town of Randolph, Vermont (population 5,000), that one of its progeny had (a) divorced and (b) remarried, and (c) was now the wife of somebody named Patrick, who might or might not be a tribal chief. "Dear Sara," my mother wrote. "Here's what happened to Ellie's plan to share the news of your wedding with her church." Ellie and Fred Streeter shared a fence line with my mother and had known me for forty years. "I wrote out a little announcement which Ellie said would be read in church. She handed it to Tim, the pastor, to read at the proper time. When it came to that time in the service, he read other news, but not what Ellie had given him. I guess she spoke up from the congregation, asking him if he didn't have something else he was planning to read. It turned out that he had lost it! He called on Ruth"— my aunt, another Episcopalian; my mother went to the Congregational church—"to help him out. She knew about Ellie's request, but was not prepared to make an announcement herself. However, she said something like this: 'My niece, Sara Tucker, was married last week in Africa. She did not marry a tribal chief.' I don't know what else she said, but apparently

one of the members of the congregation misunder-
stood her, and after the service came up to Ruth and
said, 'Sara married a tribal chief?' "

Many of the people hearing this news had quite a
lot of catching up to do, and I wondered whether an
article I had written for the *Randolph Herald* some
months earlier might have added to the confusion. The
article was about Tanzania—a country, I explained,
that I visited often; it was accompanied by a snapshot
of me standing shoulder to shoulder with a diminutive
Masai chief in traditional dress, the two of us looking
very chummy. Was this perhaps the image that flashed
into people's minds when they thought of my new husband?

Arusha having no door-to-door postal delivery and
very few post office boxes for rent, Patrick and I had
arranged to have our mail sent to the Mambo Café.
Almost every week the Mambo received another card
from America congratulating us on our nuptials.
Cards from my aunt Lois and my aunt Ruth, cards
from the Lunch Bunch—friends of my mother's who
got together at a restaurant once a month and had
known me since birth—cards from other relatives and
friends, many of them plucked from the section of the
card rack labeled "Humor."

After the wedding, I collapsed. Just like that. One
minute I felt fine, and an hour later I was lying in bed
with a fever, drenched in sweat, every muscle aching,
and a pain in my belly like somebody had kicked me
with an iron boot.

"It's malaria," said Patrick, and he brought me a
glass of filtered water and some pills from the medicine drawer in the kitchen. "You'll start to feel better
in two, three days. Four at the most."

For the next two weeks I lay in a stupor. I couldn't

eat, I couldn't think, not about anything except the pain. Sometimes I dozed. Mostly, I just waited for the minutes, hours, and days to pass, languishing under the mosquito net canopy, inert, moaning now and then just to make sure I wasn't dead yet. "It's not malaria," said the doctor whom Patrick finally took me to, but that was the extent of his diagnosis. If he recognized the symptoms of what I later concluded was a common illness, he said nothing. In layman's terms, too much had happened in too short a time, and I had to lie down. After a while, I felt better. I got up again, and life went on.

The road to our house in Sekei.

Chapter Five

Of all the houses on our road, only Mesuli's and ours advertised themselves as worth burglarizing, and ours was the better target of the two. It was public knowledge that Mesuli had a TV and we didn't, but we had one more car than he did and a couple of laptop computers. Our house had strategic advantages as well, from a burglar's point of view, such as the fact that we were often not at home whereas Mesuli's house was almost never empty. And yet we had never taken more than minimal precautions against intruders. We had locks on the doors, of course, and metal grates on all the windows, and when we left the house we always put the key in a hiding place. But the hiding place was—guess where? Under the doormat. And the night of our wedding, when we arrived home late to discover the key was not under the mat, just one swift *blam* of Patrick's red-stockinged foot was enough to make the door fly open. After that, we ratcheted up our security measures: Mesuli's fundi put a strong bolt on the front and back doors, and we moved the key's hiding place. To the plant pot. The one at the top of the front steps.

Our wall safe was an unframed canvas, a good-bye present from wife number three, the Argentine, who had executed the painting herself. It was large, colorful, and eye-catching in its depiction of a matador and bull. Behind it were a few bills tucked so precariously that an accidental bump was guaranteed to dislodge them. Just in case the would-be thief should miss this opportunity, the helpful matador dangled his red cape invitingly, as if calling out, "Over here! Over here!"

The man assigned to guard our property was an old guy who drank. His main job was to open the gate when we came home late at night so we didn't have to get out of the car and open it ourselves. Nine times out of ten, it took several blasts of the horn to summon the askari, because he was sound sleep.

We knew nothing about him. We didn't even know his name. When Patrick ran out of cigarettes or beer in the evening and needed somebody to walk down the hill to the Big Y Club, he stood on the edge of the veranda and called into the darkness, "Askari!" and the askari came. He had managed to keep his job even though he was half-hearted in his duties. Who could blame him? It was a shitty job, sitting up all night, alone, in all kinds of weather, with nothing to do, just waiting to be attacked.

Traditional wisdom held that it was a poor idea to arm your askari, never mind that Arusha's burglars were modernizing like everyone else; their gear now included automatic weapons. Most askaris, on the other hand, were equipped with a flashlight, a whistle, and a blanket. Our askari had only the blanket, which was supposed to protect him from mosquitoes.

"If thieves come," I once said to Patrick, "armed with guns and stuff, what is the askari supposed to do?"

"Yell," he said. "Call for help. The thieves will run away."

The day after Patrick returned from New York with his suitcase full of shopping items, he sent me an email: The house had been broken into while we were gone, and a few things had been stolen—his ancient laptop, his shortwave radio, some clothing. The hunting rifle had not been taken—Patrick had had the forethought to leave it with a friend while we were away—and the thieves had not found the cash, because there was no cash to find. In a postscript, he mentioned that he still hadn't heard from the FBI.

The break-in had occurred on the askari's watch. The askari knew nothing about it—he was very sorry but he must have been asleep.

To my surprise, I learned that this was not the first time the askari had slept through a burglary. In his email, Patrick alluded to an earlier break-in; it had occurred before I moved to Arusha and he hadn't thought to mention it before. I knew he had a soft spot for the old guy, whose peaceful snoring was so integral to our nocturnal soundtrack, but he had Thomas and me to think about. The old askari had already received a warning and a fine. This time, Patrick fired him.

A messenger delivered the askari's subsequent protest letter, hand-written in shaky block letters and passable English. The grievances it itemized could be fully rectified by the payment of a sum equal to less than one hundred dollars. Patrick sent the messenger away empty-handed. Sometime later, the askari himself appeared at the house. He stood on the lawn, drunk and accusing, making such a ruckus that Mesuli came running. Immediately, the old man switched to a tearful whine, and Mesuli led him away.

The new askari was someone Mesuli knew; he came highly recommended. "He doesn't drink," said Mesuli, "he doesn't sleep; and he won't cheat you."

The man lived in the neighborhood and was somehow related, like so many of our neighbors, to Mesuli.

To protect himself in the line of duty, the new askari equipped himself with a homemade bow, which he stored in the damp little shed under the cistern. "Don't you touch that," I warned Thomas. "That is not a toy, and it doesn't belong to you." This was after I found him shooting arrows at the wooden fence in the backyard.

Just as Mesuli had promised, the new askari was a reliable employee. He came to work on time, and when we drove up the hill toward home after dark he would hear the car engine from afar; by the time we reached the gate it was open. When we forgot to take the keys out of the ignition, he brought them to us, calling softly at the front door: Hodi! He rolled up the car windows when we carelessly left them down.

The new askari followed a steady routine. Six nights a week, we heard the clank of the gate at seven-thirty, an hour after sundown, then the crunch of the gravel as he walked up the drive. His footsteps paused when he reached the kitchen window, under which was the switch for the electric water pump. We heard the hum as the pump went on, and an hour or two later, the trickle of water as it overflowed the tank, then a quick series of steps as the askari ran to turn the pump off. Sometimes in the night, I heard him cough, or I heard his footsteps circling the house. Then, at first light, the clank of the garden gate again as he left.

We hardly ever saw him. Mostly he sat in the darkness at the end of the driveway near the cistern, just beyond the patch of light from the kitchen window. Sometimes I would catch a quick glimpse of his face in the glare of the headlights, partly concealed by the gray wool blanket that he draped over his head on cold nights.

One Sunday morning we passed a small group of men on the road; they were carrying Bibles, on their way to or from church. One of the men smiled and lifted a hand in greeting. He had a gentle, sad-eyed face, and looked very frail in the light of day. "That's our askari," Thomas said.

❧

Just before our first anniversary, Patrick landed a job. It came with a good salary, housing, a company car, meals, and other perks. This was not just any job but the job of his dreams. He had been hankering after his own patch of jungle ever since he was a kid. The patch he got was a big national park in Togo, for which the Togolese needed a director with experience in antipoaching.

The job was good news indeed. Not only did it solve our money problems but it also made sense, at long last, of Patrick's higgledy-piggledy résumé by combining his many talents in service to a noble cause. He had done antipoaching, yes, in Ivory Coast. He had even done a little poaching. And he had other important qualifications. For one, he was capable of speaking for whole paragraphs without uttering a single cuss word, and thus fit to be a dignitary. The chief of a national anything should be a man of decorum, even and perhaps especially when the nation is a small and rather shabby one. Plus, he was well-educated, having failed to achieve his engineering degree by only the tiniest of margins—not getting his degree being the only foolproof way he could think of to avoid becoming an engineer, which was his father's idea and not his own. Never mind that: He can repair his own car. He speaks perfect French. He speaks several other major languages as well—or almost as well—and several others well enough; plus, he can say hello and/or thank you in Krio, Ebu, Mandarin, Arabic, Russian, and Greek; he has memorized the capital cities of every country in Europe, Asia, and the Americas, and has seen many of them with his own two eyes. One of his most cherished souvenirs, in fact, was his Chinese driving license, issued in 1992, the year he drove a supply truck in the Paris-Beijing rally. In these modern times, the person in charge of protecting a country's resources, even a bit of turf in a small African nation, should have a global perspective.

There was only one problem. "What about Thomas and me?" I asked when Patrick said he was going to start the job on a trial basis as soon as the safari season ended. After three or four months, if he liked it, he would ask for a two-year contract.

"Well, the park is in a remote area. There is no school. No town, in fact. I already checked."

So while Patrick was in Togo for three or four months, Thomas and I were going to be clear on the other side of Africa, some three thousand miles away. And if in the end we decided to move to Togo, Thomas would have to go to a boarding school.

Early one morning, as the sky was lightening, Mesuli came around the wall of bougainvillea that separated our two houses and called "Hodi!" from the veranda. We invited him in, but Mesuli preferred to discuss business matters in the open air, informally, so we went out. "Sorry to dis-tub," he said and then, looking out over the front lawn and rubbing the top of his head slowly with one hand, he explained that we needed to hire someone to cut the grass. Mesuli himself had been arranging for the lawn to be mowed on an ad-hoc basis, by letting the grass grow knee-high and then inviting the neighbors to chop it down with their scythes and weed whackers and cart it away for their goats. It was a pretty good system except that the neighbors took only as much grass as they needed, leaving behind a very patchy lawn. Besides, the richest man in Sekei and his tenants should have a proper gardener, so Mesuli proposed that the gardener spend two days a week at our house and two days at his, and that we each pay him ten thousand shillings per month, or a total of about twenty dollars.

Mesuli already had somebody in mind for the job. "He used to work for an English lady, but she died," said Mesuli. "He goes to my wife's church. He needs a job." Those credentials seemed adequate so we nodded our agreement, and Mesuli said he would introduce us to our new employee maybe tomorrow.

The next day, Mesuli brought Loto to our house. The former gardener of the now-deceased English lady spoke no English and was extremely bashful. He smiled uncertainly as he shook my hand. "What is his name?" I asked Mesuli. Mesuli didn't know so he asked the gardener and the gardener said, "Loto."

I really had no idea what the bashful new gardener would do all day, since we had never had a gardener before and had never seen the need of one. The first thing he did was to make himself a broom out of twigs, which he used to sweep the square of packed earth behind the house, where Jenni hung the laundry. How very resourceful, I thought.

That is how we ended up with a part-time daytime askari. It was good to have an extra pair of eyes keeping watch over the place. We did, however, take the precaution of moving our cash to the top of the water heater in the bathroom after I caught Loto peering in the bedroom window just as I was reaching behind the matador's cape.

The gardener soon proved himself to be more of a groundskeeper than a grower and nurturer of plant material, his true talents being sweeping, raking, cleaning, and burning the trash. He particularly loved washing the cars. When he washed the cars, Patrick gave him a small tip. Loto took to washing the cars almost every day. He even snuck over on the days he was supposed to be working for Mesuli, to give at least one of our cars a good rinse.

The daily car washing was draining our cash reserves at an alarming rate, so the tips became less regular. Loto began appearing at the door on various pretexts; often it was to return to its rightful owner some piece of junk he'd found lying about in the yard—an old Bic pen, a plastic lighter, Thomas's filthy sneakers. The combined sight of him on our doorstep, grungy car-washing rag in hand, and in the driveway the sparkling results of his handiwork was supposed to remind us to give him his tip.

I was backing out of the driveway one day when he appeared from behind the house, where he had been sweeping the bare earth with his homemade broom. On his way to open the gate for me he paused beside the car; I rolled down my window. He spoke a few words of Swahili, accompanied by gestures, then, seeing my blank look, switched to English and said, "Please may have peep."

"Peep?"

Loto nodded vigorously. "Peep!" he repeated several times. Then he added, "For wah-tuh," and after a good deal more effort on both sides I ascertained that a peep was a pipe, and that a peep for water was a garden hose. So Patrick got him a nice blue one, which Loto used mainly on the car.

The top of the water heater was up near the ceiling, so to get at our few remaining hundred-dollar bills we had to carry a chair into the bathroom from the dining room, close the bathroom door, which was visible from the garden, to avoid being spied on, and stand on the chair to retrieve the cash, then reverse the process, all the while wondering how Loto might explain to himself the chair routine if he happened to observe it. Fortunately, we had plenty of chairs, and after a few trips to the cash-hiding place, we just left a chair in the bathroom, right under the heater. Gradually, however, I developed the feeling that Loto did a lot more observing than we really wanted him to do.

Shortly after Patrick got the job in Togo but before he left town, Thomas came trudging up the steps of the Mambo, wan and disheveled after another long day at St. George's, slumped into a chair at the table next to us, dropped his school bag, and thrust his leg in my direction.

"Sara, look at my knee." He pulled up a leg of his navy blue trousers; the knee was slightly pink and blotchy. "The other one's just like it." He raised the other pantleg. "They itch."

"Don't scratch," I said, dispensing the only medical wisdom that came to mind. For good measure, I promised to put some cream on the knees the minute we reached home. Then Ambrose brought a Fanta Orange and a brownie and Thomas opened his math workbook with a loud sigh and proceeded to cast bored glances in every direction except the workbook, which he only looked at whenever Patrick swung around in his chair and said, "Are you doing your homework, *mon grand*?" Each time, Thomas responded with a defeated sigh and an unconvincing yes, then he'd slump over the workbook for a while until his pencil accidentally hit the side of the bud vase, making a pleasant little chink, to which he added a few more pleasant little chinks, very lightly, to see how long he could keep it up before Patrick swung around again and told him to cut the crap.

The next morning, Thomas got out of bed and came into the living room, where Patrick and I were drinking coffee and reading. "My knees still itch," he said. "I didn't sleep all night." The knees were redder and puffier than the day before, and there were also a few spots on his torso that looked like mosquito bites.

"What do you think it is?" I asked Patrick.

He looked up from a dog-eared Tom Clancy novel and glanced at Thomas's knees. "Dunno," he said. "Some sort of rash, I guess." And he went back to his book.

That afternoon when Thomas came trudging up the steps of the Mambo he was accompanied by a small herd of schoolteachers, themselves headed for a stiff drink after a hard day at school. In the lead was Mrs. Valentine, the headmistress. She paused on her way to the bar long enough to draw our attention to Thomas's rash and suggested we "run him over to Dr. Patel."

The rash was definitely spreading, so as soon as we'd finished our drinks and Thomas had eaten his brownie and drunk his Fanta Orange, we climbed into the Land Rover and drove over to the doctor's office.

Whether Dr. Patel was a good doctor or not I can't say, all I can tell you is that among his patients, who included just about every muzungu in town, the question was routinely debated. It seemed natural that people would complain about him, the same way people feel obliged to complain about the food in the company cafeteria, since he was the only doctor available. We had no choice; we were stuck with Dr. Patel, and to simply accept the situation would not be right. We were morally obligated to criticize him. Stories therefore circulated about his flagrant misdiagnoses, about how he had been known to confuse the early signs of pregnancy with cerebral malaria and vice versa, about how you were lucky to escape from his office alive, but the fact is he had never yet killed anybody that we knew about and he even managed to come up with an appropriate cure at least fifty percent of the time. He took one look at Thomas and said, "Have you been playing in the bushes?"

"I guess," said Thomas, doubtfully.

"Have you seen a plant that looks like this?" Dr. Patel drew a picture of a leaf that looked a lot like marijuana.

Thomas studied the drawing. "No," he said. "I don't think so. Maybe. I don't remember."

"I'm sure that's it," said Dr. Patel. "You look around and see if you find that plant in any of the places you've been. It causes the sort of rash you have."

The doctor told me to put some calamine lotion on the itchy spots until they went away. Patrick gave the big German woman who did Dr. Patel's billing five thousand shillings, and we left.

The next day we were back. By now, Thomas was covered with itchy pink welts, from his scalp to the soles of his feet. His lips and eyelids were swollen, and his eyes were bloodshot.

There was no more talk of bushes or leaves. "It's a food allergy," said Dr. Patel. "Have you eaten anything unusual?" Thomas, who was sporting his normal orange-soda-and-brownie mustache, shook his head.

"Shellfish?"

"He's allergic to eggs," said Patrick, "but he can eat them in food, like cake or mayonnaise. He hasn't had a reaction since he was three."

The reaction resulted in anaphylactic shock. Patrick warned Thomas never to eat another egg, but he forgot to warn Wife Number Three, the Argentine painter, who cooked breakfast one morning while Patrick was on safari.

"I can't eat eggs," Thomas informed Three. "They make me sick."

"You eat those eggs like a good boy."

"No," said Thomas. "Daddy told me not to."

"Thomas," said Three, very stern, "eat, your, eggs."

So Thomas ate the eggs, and had to be rushed to the hospital.

But that was a long time ago, and Dr. Patel was baffled—he was pretty sure this was a food allergy, but none of us could figure out what food was causing it. So finally Dr. Patel scribbled something on a prescription pad and handed it to Patrick. The prescription was for prednisone, a steroid. "This will stop the itching," he promised. "One tablet twice a day for six days." Within a couple of hours, the itching had stopped and the redness had subsided. By dinnertime, Thomas was cured.

Patrick left for Togo in the early morning. I drove him down the hill to the Novotel parking lot, where we waited for the bus that would take him to Nairobi. From there, he would get a flight to Lomé, the capital of Togo, on the coast. Some two dozen other passengers were waiting, their duffel bags and suitcases clustered on the ground. The bus pulled in and the driver got out while two young men loaded the luggage, one climbing on top of the bus and deftly catching the bags as the other tossed them upward with impressive force. People began boarding. "I better find a seat," said Patrick. "Good-bye, darling. I'll send you an email from Lomé," and he was gone. I watched the bus pull away with a sinking feeling, already lonely. Then I drove back up the hill and entered the silent house, where Thomas was still asleep.

Our first year as a family ended with Patrick on one side of Africa and Thomas and me on the other, three thousand miles apart. Thomas coped with the separation silently and stoically, I in a rather whiny manner, tapping out desperate-sounding SOS-type emails at Max's Patisserie and Cyber Café, harassing the servants and the neighbors, and giving Thomas good reason to wonder why his latest mother was turning out to be so substandard when he clearly deserved better after all he had suffered. Not that he ever made such an accusation. Thomas would never do that. Despite the remark about wishing he had "a real mother, one who would stay home with me," he scrupulously avoided hurting other people's feelings. Besides, that innocent wish had been granted: There I was, at home with him, as real as real can be.

Roadside encounter with a native inhabitant.

Chapter Six

From the tatty mustard-yellow cotton cardigan that served in its later years as Patrick's housecoat, you would never guess that its original owner was always impeccably groomed. The sweater was a favorite of Maurice's; Mireille gave it to Patrick after the funeral. She also gave him, from Maurice's wardrobe, two pairs of socks: One was taxicab-yellow and had the smiling face of Mickey Mouse emblazoned on each ankle; the other pair was similar but done in earth tones, and the face was that of John Wayne.

The John Wayne socks, purchased by Maurice himself in a whimsical moment, were a reminder of the day his rental car sputtered and died while making a tour of America. Maurice went to the nearest house and rang the doorbell. Moments later he heard footsteps, the door opened, and there stood John Wayne. Maurice explained his predicament, and Mr. Wayne invited him in to use the phone. Once arrangements had been made for Maurice's rescue, the two men shook hands and parted company. Why a big American movie star would open his door without hesitation to a stranger is never questioned by those who knew Maurice. The two men were only acting as gentlemen do under the circumstances, and Maurice was nothing if not a gentleman. Anybody could see that right away. From such stories and from Patrick's father's extant wardrobe I pieced together a portrait of a man for whom things tended to fall into place, often aided by charm and an iron will.

To this day, Patrick can sit down and draw in a flash the caricature of Maurice he perfected as a child: the Roman nose and jutting chin, the cigarette in its ebony holder, the Clark Gable mustache and pomaded hair. He made a study of his father; the two men were never close.

Maurice came from a long line of military men who had served in exotic places; one had fought with Napolean all the way up to the general's Hundred Days as emperor of France and was probably still fighting at Waterloo; his medals were displayed under glass in the Texier parlor, along with his Meerschaum pipe. Maurice himself was a flight navigator in the French army before the German occupation. He navigated by looking out from the cockpit and comparing what he saw on the ground with the map spread across his lap. Sometimes he instructed the pilot to fly low enough so he could read the road signs—the towns all looked alike, with their stone cottages, schoolhouse, and church set around a village well.

After the war, Maurice sold tires for Dunlop and then earth-moving equipment for Richier, not just around Europe but all over the world—Russia, China, Africa, South America. He was a traveling salesman of the most glamorous kind, crossing the Atlantic several times in a propeller plane before the dawn of the jet age. Often he returned from these trips with fine clothes, purchased as souvenirs: His hat collection represented five continents. He spoke four languages fluently and a few others with difficulty, and his passports filled a drawer—Mireille saved them, bundling them with rubber bands. Patrick remembers him as always between two planes.

When Maurice was home, he sat in a corner of the parlor, smoking and rustling the pages of *Le Figaro* or *France Soir,* and everyone had to be quiet. The children were not allowed to have their friends in—too noisy. They were not allowed to speak at the dinner table unless asked a direct question. They had to sit up straight and hold their fork and napkin just so—a moment of forgetfulness might cause Maurice to reach across the table, middle finger curled behind his thumb, and give the small hand of the offender a painful flick. As soon as he left on a business trip, the household relaxed.

Maurice was a man who understood machines, probably better than he did people, and he was proud of his aptitude; in postwar France, men with his skill and training were sorely needed. Patrick understood machines, too, intuitively, without any training. As a child, he loved to take broken clocks apart to see how they worked and then put them together again; sometimes they ended up back in service. Years later, he liked watching the African fundis tinker with his broken-down vehicles. He admired their ingenuity. "They're actually making a part they need, in the back of the shop," he informed me excitedly one afternoon as I waited, bored, for the mechanics to finish up so we could drive away. "Come see!" Two guys in blue jumpsuits were soldering bits of metal together for some obscure purpose. Secretly, I wondered why this interest in car repairs didn't extend to such obvious defects as windows that didn't go up and down and doors that only opened from the outside. The window cranks of his old Nissan were kept in the glove compartment when they weren't in use, the windshield wipers under the driver's seat. When it rained, Patrick unrolled his window, retrieved a wiper from under his seat, and reaching out, swiped at the windshield with one hand while steering with the other.

Maurice drove big smooth cars, parking them in a garage with a long and winding ramp at the end of which was a perilously tight parking space—it took skill to ease a big car into it without rubbing up against one's neighbor. Whenever he went out for the evening and drank enough to merit extra caution, he would leave the car on the street, rather than risk the garage. On one such occasion, he woke up the next morning and couldn't find the car. He searched the neighborhood, walking up and down the small streets. This went on for a couple of days, during which he said not a word to anyone about the misplaced vehicle. Then he had an idea. He checked the garage, and sure enough, the car was there, immaculately parked. When Patrick, in a similar condition, tried to drive his MGA sports car home from a party in Abidjan, he got halfway round the France-Amerique carrefour and crashed through the glass door of a perfume shop. In Sierra Leone, he tumbled off a bridge and cracked three ribs. In Ivory Coast, he slid his motorcycle under a truck. In Cameroon, he flew his brand-new Dornier into a flock of birds and landed in a yam patch.

In the Texier family library were several shelves of *National Geographic*, the text of which was in English. Among the first words Patrick learned to recognize were "Terra Incognita"—the blank spaces on the maps were what interested him most. The more he read, the larger Africa loomed in his imagination. From a very young age, he resolved to go there, and to see as much of the world as possible. Then, on the coast of Spain where the Texier family spent summers, he met a man who actually lived in Africa. Denis was a park warden in the Central African Republic. His job, as Patrick understood it in his twelve-year-old mind, was to wander around in the forest, having adventures. For the two weeks or so that they spent at the same resort on the Costa del Sol, Patrick dogged the man's heels, peppering him with questions. After he met Denis, he knew with absolute certainty that he would go to Africa someday.

He was a city boy from Paris, twenty years old, when he stepped off a plane into Africa for the first time. A young man on holiday from a job with Air France, he was wearing a navy blue blazer with gold buttons, wool slacks, and a tie — air travel was still a luxury in 1964, and you did not board a plane in shorts and sneakers. His first impression was of tropical air gusting up his pantlegs as he stood on the gangway above a steaming tarmac.

The next morning, he checked out of a Douala hotel and boarded a small plane bound for northern Cameroon. The plane looked so rickety, he walked around it twice before deciding to board, despite the puddle of oil underneath. The woman beside him had a chicken on her lap. Once they were airborne, he concentrated on the scenery, a sea of green: The rain forest, at last.

As the plane hopped from outpost to outpost, a disturbing pattern emerged: The vegetation was getting thinner. Instead of heading into the forest, the plane was speeding away from it. By the time Patrick reached his destination, he was in a sort of wooded savannah. The rain forest he had come to see was hundreds of miles away.

In the northern outpost of Garoua, he stopped at a hunting-supply store to get his bearings. The person he was looking for was an army buddy whose father owned a hunting camp. Patrick and Jean had met in Tours, during their eighteen months of military service, required of all Frenchmen at the time. That Jean was born and raised in Africa didn't get him off the hook. He was a French citizen and he had to serve, like everyone else. His parting words to Patrick were "Come to Cameroon. You're welcome anytime."

The Lebanese shopkeeper told him the camp was some three hours by car. "They are expecting you?"

"I wanted to surprise them."

The man studied him for a moment, then made a decision. "I can take you," he said. "I have a delivery to make. We can go there this afternoon."

So he arrived with the groceries. The shopkeeper drove very fast over the bumpy road, talking nonstop, yelling over the roar of the diesel engine; Patrick gave up straining to catch his words after a while and gazed out the window in a kind of trance. They passed through a few small villages, fields of maize and beans and onions: slender women in bright sarongs chopped at the earth with handmade hoes; men drove donkeys loaded with sacks of grain. Tiny goatherds ran toward the truck, waving and shouting, while the goats scattered every which way. Dust drifted up through the floorboards.

After two hours of driving, they passed the last small village. Without warning, the shopkeeper turned off the main road onto an unmarked dirt track and struck out across the shimmering plain. Under a sky big and blue, antelope raised their heads and stared, tails swishing mechanically. Birds darted up the road ahead of them, up-down-up, like tiny speed-boats skimming the waves. A jackrabbit zigzagged into the bushes.

It was late afternoon and the shadows were long when the truck rumbled to a stop in the grassy parking lot of a small compound, a collection of stone buildings in a clearing in the woods. The shopkeeper killed the engine. Out of the sudden silence, a screen door creaked open and slammed, and from the main house emerged a sturdy, freckle-faced woman, her bouffant hair-style lacquered to withstand the stiffest breeze: Jean's mother. "I wasn't expecting you till tomorrow," she said to the shopkeeper.

Two men had come running at the sound of the engine; one was on the truck throwing packages down to the other: bags of onions, crates of ammunition. Patrick's duffel hit the ground with a thump.

"I brought you a visitor," said the shopkeeper.

The woman looked the new arrival up and down. "From Douala?"

Patrick smiled his most charming smile. "From Paris. Jean said to come anytime, so I did."

Cameroon in 1964 was famous among big game hunters for its giant eland, a magnificent 2,000-pound antelope with four-foot antlers that spiral upward like corkscrews. It was also one of the few places in the world where one could hunt the tiny royal antelope, the size of a hare. Elephant were plentiful then, and so were bongo, bushbuck, and forest hog.

Jean's father, Yves, held exclusive hunting rights to an area of some two hundred square miles, much of it lightly wooded savannah, traversed by several rivers edged with gallery forest. Father and son guided the hunts with the help of at least one other PH, as the professional hunters, or guides, are called. That year it was Jeff, a young Rhodesian who had learned to hunt on his father's farm in a country where the safari industry had been eclipsed by civil war—in a few years, Jeff would no longer be a Rhodesian but a Zimbabwean. From November to May, Yves employed some two dozen drivers, trackers, skinners, and camp cooks, in addition to the year-round mechanics, gardeners, and houseboys.

Patrick had arrived at the busiest time of the year, the height of hunting season. Everyone was working twelve-hour days, every vehicle and cool box and cooking pot was in use. But Jean's parents were kind people and used to the spontaneous habits of young men. Marie Petit showed him to a spare bungalow, invited him to help himself to beer and cigarettes from the bar, and informed the kitchen to set a place for one more at the communal table.

The next morning Patrick arose at dawn and was already having his breakfast when the first of the hunters appeared. He gulped his coffee and croissant and then hung around the parking lot, watching as the staff loaded the newly washed cars with guns, machetes, axes, cartons of ammo, picnic hampers, cool boxes, whiskey. He was still standing there when the last car drove away. Each held four or five passengers: a guide, a tracker, one or two skinners, and the client—most often a wealthy businessman from France or Spain. A hunting car was no place for a freeloader, and a big-game safari cost more than twice what he made in a year.

At dawn the next day, before anyone but the kitchen staff was stirring, there was a soft and persistent knocking on the bungalow door. Patrick opened it to find a small, very thin, and very wrinkled African standing on the doorstep. He was wearing a pair of ragged cutoffs that had patches on top of patches, a shirt several sizes too big (one of Yves's castoffs), and a pair of canvas shoes laced with twine. He smiled, revealing several missing teeth. *"Salut, patron,"* he said, extending a leathery hand to the sleepy and hung-over kid who stood blinking in the doorway. "You are ready?"

Fetnat was the camp's senior tracker. Born on July 14, which on many French calendars is abbreviated Fet Nat for Fete Nationale, he was everything you'd expect a game tracker to be. The man could follow a trail blindfolded. "Lion been here," he'd say, sniffing the forest air, deconstructing its bouquet of leaves, soil, grass, wood, and dung with the deftness of a sommelier. He spent most of his time in the bush by himself, returning to camp now and then to report his findings. Yves would then assign a younger tracker to accompany a hunting party to the spot where Fetnat had last seen a solitary bull elephant, or the fresh scat of a leopard, or a herd of warthog that included a nice male.

That day, and every day thereafter for the next two weeks, Patrick trailed Fetnat. By evening he was so exhausted that he went to bed before the hunters, and asked Yves for an alarm clock, which he set in a saucer filled with coins to make sure it woke him up, so as not to keep the old tracker waiting. The two went alone, Fetnat carrying his old 12-gauge shotgun, less for protection than for food. At midday, they'd build a small fire and roast a francolin or a hare, then rest under an acacia for an hour or so. The rest of the day they spent on foot, following animal trails through the bush. "Lion been here," Fetnat would say, sniffing the forest air. Inevitably, they'd come upon a paw print, fresh scat, or a bit of fur on a twig.

It was Fetnat who showed Patrick how to gauge the freshness of a buffalo patty by taking its temperature with a poke of his forefinger. It was Fetnat who patiently explained to him, several times, the difference between the prints of two types of mongoose, marsh and Egyptian, an explanation that went right over his head and confounded even Yves. From Fetnat, he learned how to sniff out a lion, which isn't that hard once you know what a lion smells like. I saw him do this on safari in Longido as we sat just outside our tent watching the sun set behind Kilimanjaro. "I smell a lion," he said, and I laughed, knowing he was teasing, trying to scare me. The next morning, there were fresh tracks less than a minute's stroll from the camp.

When, at dinner one evening, Patrick announced with a long face that he had to leave soon, Yves looked startled. "Leaving!" he barked, as if he'd forgotten that Patrick was merely a visitor. Patrick muttered something about having to go back to work. Yves extended his brawny, sunburned arms to take in the general surroundings. "Hell," he said, "we've got work. Plenty. If you wanted to work, why didn't you say so? Stick around, we'll put you to work."

The next day, Patrick sent a wire to his parents: He was staying. His new job, he explained, was as a ticketing manager in Douala for the airline UTA. He threw in the "manager" bit because it was a step up from his job as a clerk at the Air France ticket counter on the Champs-Elysées. When I asked him why he hadn't simply told them the truth—that he'd been offered a job in a hunting camp—he had to think for a moment, as if the idea had never occurred to him. "They wouldn't have understood," he said finally.

❧

In 1961, when Patrick was sixteen, his father told him he was old enough to have a summer job. Patrick was devastated. For a boy who didn't like school, summertime had always meant three solid months of freedom. His father advised him to get a job in a factory. Such experience, he pointed out, would be useful later on, for it was Maurice's intention that his son develop into a mechanical engineer like himself. Patrick didn't want to be an engineer, and he didn't want a summer job. However, one did not argue with Maurice.

Then Patrick had an idea. He went through the Paris yellow pages, and under the heading "Bois Tropicaux" he found a listing of companies that sold tropical wood. He jotted down the names and addresses, and the next day he took the metro to Quartier de la Republic.

At the first place he visited, he stated his business succinctly: "I'm looking for a summer job; I want to go to Africa." A secretary took down his name and phone number and said she would give the message to the *directeur general*. The same thing happened at the next place. At the third, he was ushered into the director's office and introduced to a pleasant man behind a great big desk of dark gleaming wood — mahogany, Patrick thought with satisfaction, imagining the giant tree that had produced it. The man came out from behind the desk long enough to shake his hand, and invited the young job seeker to have a seat.

"Well, well," he said. "So you're interested in the timber business."

Patrick didn't give a damn about the timber business. He wanted to see gorillas, pythons, and Pygmies. Day-Glo reptiles with bulging eyes, moths big as cabbage leaves, vines you could swing on. He wanted to see spotted tails twitching in the leafy shadows, and groves of trees with branches in motion, dancing under the weight of a hundred monkeys.

"Yes, sir," said Patrick, nodding eagerly. "The timber business. Very much so."

The director spent a good half hour with him, describing the dreadful conditions that came with living in a rain forest timber camp. He talked about snakes and scorpions and mosquitoes and something called a tumbo fly, whose larvae burrow deep into human flesh and have to be dug out with a scalpel. He talked about the incessant damp and eternal twilight of the rain forest; about soil that is wet like a sponge; about walking for days, marking trees; about being away from camp and having to sleep in the forest with only bush meat and a few rations for dinner.

It sounded wonderful.

The director offered him a job in the Gabonese rain forest for three months, including free passage on a freighter from France to Gabon and back. They shook hands, and Patrick walked out elated.

He did not deliver the news to his parents right away. The director had said he would send an offer letter; Patrick should receive it within a week. Each day after school, he anxiously checked the pile of letters that the building super left on the doormat in the hall.

The day the letter came, he read it carefully, several times, then mustered his courage. When Maurice came home from work, he gave Patrick a few centimes, as usual, and sent him to the *marchand de journaux* on the corner for the evening newspaper. All the way down and back Patrick prepared himself, rehearsing his side of the argument that he and his father were about to have. On his return, he handed Maurice his change and the folded copy of *France Soir.* Then he retrieved the letter from his room.

"Papa," he said. "I have found a job."

Maurice read the letter in silence, then he folded it, placed it next to his ashtray, and held out his hand. Congratulations, he said. Well done.

A few days later, the postman delivered another letter from the timber company.

"Cher Monsieur Texier," he read, "we regret . . ."

They wouldn't need him after all. They were sorry.

Patrick knew what had happened, knew it before he had even finished reading the catastrophic letter: His father had intervened. But he had no proof, and besides, no good ever came from a confrontation with Maurice. So Patrick barely mentioned the retracted offer, pretending he didn't care. Nobody would know how crushed he was, least of all his father. That summer, he went to work across the street in a car factory.

❧

As an assistant PH, Patrick was given a bunch of odd jobs that nobody else had time for. One was to make the supply run to Daloa, an outpost of Greek- and Lebanese-owned shops, African beer joints, a few third-rate restaurants, and one dingy hotel thirty-five kilometers south of the camp. Once every week or so he drove there with a shopping list: two drums diesel, three cans cooking oil, ten kilos rice, tomato sauce, beer, soda.

On one of the grubby town's littered side streets, two young Africans approached him; one was holding a bundle of dirty rags. The youth lifted a corner of the fabric and beckoned him closer: two small leopard cubs raised their heads and blinked in the sudden glare of sunlight. The female emitted a plaintive squeak.

Patrick pulled about two dollars' worth of change from his trouser pocket and swapped it for the female. Her scrawny little legs splayed stiffly as she was lifted into the air by the scruff of her neck and handed over. Settled in his arms, she picked at his shirtfront with her tiny claws and nosed around for a teat.

All the way back to camp—two hours over a bumpy road—she lay shivering in his lap, too weak from hunger to lift her head. In his bungalow, he prepared some of the baby formula he had found in Daloa and fed it to her from a bottle. She sucked greedily, then puked it all up on his bed.

"Go back to town," instructed Marie Petit, handing him a few bills. "Visit every shop, and buy every brand of formula available. And get a few more bottle tops, of varying sizes. We'll see what works the best."

Patrick returned from Daloa with half a dozen different formulas, which Marie herself prepared, one by one. Each formula produced vomiting and diarrhea.

"Try condensed milk," Yves suggested. By now, everyone in the camp was involved in rescuing the starving cub. "Condensed milk!" exclaimed Marie. "This is no food for babies. It's loaded with sugar. She will become diabetic."

Ignoring her, Yves instructed the cook to warm a can from the pantry. Then he took the cub in his burly arms and, holding her like a human infant, fed her a good big dose. The milk stayed down.

Condensed milk is what kept her alive until a better remedy could be found. The cub loved it, awakening Patrick three or four times during the night to let him know it was time for a feeding. During the day, Marie took charge of the feedings, often assigning Fetnat or one of the kitchen helpers to administer them.

A livestock veterinarian who lived nearby heard about the cub and stopped by one day for a visit. "You might try dog's milk," he said. "Cats love it."

The dog's milk was air-shipped from France at considerable expense; Yves advanced Patrick some money to pay for it, then seemed to forget about the debt. When Patrick reminded him, he said, "Don't worry about it." Adequately nourished, the cub grew bigger every day. Within a few weeks, she had quad-rupled in size, growing strong and sleek. The entire camp was devoted to her. Patrick called her Chita.

His first week on the job, he drove into the parking lot wild-eyed, trembling, unable to speak; the truck had a set of empty hinges where the driver's-side door should have been. The hinges themselves were ripped apart, the steering wheel was bent, and just behind the driver's seat was a gash that had ripped the wall of the truck wide open. Yves circled the vehicle once, survey-ing the damage, then walked his new employee straight to the bar and poured him a Cognac.

Patrick had been driving back from town with a load of supplies when storm clouds began to gather overhead. He hustled along, both hands on the wheel, working it back and forth as the road, deeply rutted in places, tugged at his wheels. The sky darkened and rumbled. Camp was still many miles away when he felt the first few drops; within seconds, the rain was coming down in sheets. The truck had no roof, and he hadn't so much as a hat brim to shield him from the blinding downpour. Soon, he and everything else in the truck was drenched. The road was a blurry tunnel through the leaves, and he eased up on the accelerator to avoid driving into a tree.

He had a clear path in front of him when the car exploded, struck with megaton force by something dark and massive in his peripheral vision. It burst out of the foliage to his left, rammed the vehicle broadside, then picked it up and carried it into the bushes. When the truck came to rest, he was still in the driver's seat, hands on the wheel, foot on the accelerator, head down. Cringing, he opened his eyes. It took him a moment to register what he was seeing. Meanwhile, he felt pressure on his legs. Looking down he saw, resting on his thighs just below the steering wheel, a long white tusk.

There was another tremendous jolt as the elephant raised its head. The other tusk was behind him, grazing the back of his seat. Both tusks had pierced the body of the truck; now the elephant was trying to extricate itself. The truck shuddered, rose slightly, and then fell with another bone-jarring crash as the tusks ripped through it. The driver's-side door, impaled on the forward tusk, came off its hinges with a metallic shriek. The same tusk caught the edge of the steering wheel, bending it upward like a paper clip.

The elephant backed up several feet. Patrick's foot was still on the accelerator, and the engine was still running. He had a clear path through the trees. His legs were so weak that for a moment he couldn't work the gas pedal. Then he floored it, sending most of his cargo out the back.

When he dared look over his shoulder, the elephant was shaking its head from side to side, trying to rid itself of the door, which was skewered like an olive on a toothpick. "That could have been me," he thought.

The boxes that had fallen off the truck were still there the next day; they never found the door. He apologized for the truck. "No big deal," said Yves. "These things happen in the bush. You're okay, that's what matters. You handled yourself well."

As a professional hunter with many years of experience, Yves must have been a shrewd judge of character. Anyone responsible for taking armed strangers into the bush should be able to size up a person's strengths and weaknesses pretty fast. But what Yves saw in Patrick is a mystery. At twenty, Patrick was headstrong and undisciplined. The only thing he really excelled at was getting into mischief. Even the army, when it tired of his antics, had given him an early discharge without penalty just to get rid of him. But to say he had no qualifications for the job would be wrong. He had a keen eye and a steady hand. He was patient, able to sit quietly for long periods, waiting for game to appear. He had physical endurance, tolerating thirst, hunger, mosquitoes, sore muscles, and bad weather without complaint. Above all, he loved the bush, from day one.

At his Grandmother Louisa's house in Continvoir, he had spent much of his time in the woods, making bows and arrows out of sticks and imagining himself as an Apache warrior. Once he told his little sister, Hélène, to throw an apple into the air and he would shoot it. The arrow passed right through the core. It stunned him so, he never tried it again, unwilling to spoil his perfect record.

One morning he asked Yves for a bow, saying he wanted to do some bird hunting. At midday the hunters found him standing beside the road, empty-handed. "Swing around by that cottonwood," Patrick said as he climbed into the back seat; the tree was some distance from the road. At the base of it was a hundred-pound warthog with a single arrow in its heart.

Perhaps Yves saw talents that others had missed. Or perhaps he saw only a young man's enthusiasm. Either way, having decided to give Patrick a chance, Yves followed through, standing by his young protégé when he fumbled. Under his mentorship, Patrick, for the first time in his life, became a model student. He read the books Yves gave him, about animal behavior, from cover to cover. He asked questions and listened to the answers. He even took notes.

ઢ

To become a certified professional hunter, an apprentice must fulfill a long list of requirements. He must demonstrate to his mentor that he can tell at a glance whether an animal is a male or a female. He must be able to judge its age from a distance, and to pick the best trophy out of a herd. He must know all about hunting weapons, of course, and how to shoot when the wind is blowing, and how to track a wounded animal through thick vegetation. He must know all about animal behavior: mating, parenting, and social habits, diet, and so on. And he must know by heart the rules and regulations governing his conduct, codified in the game department manual, a dog-eared copy of which Yves loaned to Patrick, instructing him to study a little at the beginning and end of each day. Once his scope of knowledge is well established, the PH-in-training has to pass several field tests. For one, he must kill a dangerous animal on a charge. This test must be performed three times.

Around the edges of the hunting area were a few small settlements, hardly big enough to be called villages, where subsistence farmers eked out a living. The farmers had frequent complaints about elephants that raided their millet fields and lions that carried off their goats and chickens. It was not unusual for a representative of the game department to visit Yves's camp on the farmers' behalf and request that the hunters rid the people of a particular nuisance.

For months, an old male lion had been bothering a nearby settlement. A small delegation made the trek to Daloa to discuss the problem with the game department's representative there, who in turn drove out to see Yves. The next morning, a hunting party drove to the settlement. The party included Yves, Fetnat, the game department official, and the designated lion killer, a novice who, not so very long ago, had been struggling to fathom the mysteries of airline billing codes.

Word of the "hunt" had spread, and some two hundred men and women had come to serve as rabateurs—the people who, making as much noise as possible, drive the game toward the hunters. When the hunting party arrived, the old lion was lying in a small depression, head raised, eyeing the crowd, which was spread out on a ridge at a cautious distance. He was nobody's idea of a trophy. Despite the farmers' goats, he was skinny, subsisting mostly on field mice. Too decrepit to hunt his natural prey, he would continue to bother the farmers, who had no weapons of their own with which to hunt him down or even ward off an attack. The goats, not to mention the little goatherds, were certainly in danger, and the lion himself was miserable.

A handful of men from the game department, armed with cheap rifles insufficient to do the job at hand, had positioned the crowd on the ridgetop. The hunters took up their positions on the other side of the lion, Fetnat on Patrick's left, Yves on his right, ready to fire a second shot if the first one missed. On a signal from Yves, the rabateurs began banging on the pots and pans they had brought with them, and singing at the top of their lungs as they slowly descended the ridge. The old lion rose to his feet. His ribs were clearly visible, his tail drooping.

"Wait for him to charge," Yves instructed. The licensing requirement was very specific: The animal had to be charging when it was shot.

The lion gave the hunters a brief appraisal, then turned his back and passively studied the rabateurs. The clamoring crowd inched forward and stopped. The crosshairs of Patrick's site were now centered on the lion's rump. The line of rabateurs shouted and banged in place. The lion stared. The seconds ticked by.

Yves signaled again, and the crowd moved forward, more slowly this time, another ten paces. The lion's tail twitched. He began turning in circles.

Patrick's gun, a .500-express that weighed about twenty-five pounds, had begun to feel heavy. His arm trembled. He tried to relax.

"Get ready," Yves said. "I'm going to make him charge." Yves fired, grazing the lion's rump. The lion snarled, turned to face his attackers, and rushed toward them. At fifteen meters, Patrick pulled the trigger. The lion fell. Nobody needed to fire a second shot.

The elephant was supposed to belong to a client, but the client missed. Missed an elephant at one hundred feet, which is almost impossible. They never found the bullet. Patrick was just there to watch and learn—it was his first elephant hunt. He stood to the client's left; Yves was several feet away on the right. Yves was again providing backup, which meant he would fire an automatic second shot immediately after the client pulled his trigger.

The elephant was grazing in a small clearing among the trees that lined the riverbank; lining up a shot was tricky. They waited until the elephant turned its left side toward them, and then Yves signaled "Go," jabbing the air with his right forefinger. The client fired. In his sight, Patrick saw the elephant, unharmed, turn to face him, ears back. The client ran for cover. The elephant charged.

"Shoot!" yelled Yves, whose line of fire was now obscured by the trees. "Shoot-shoot-shoot-shoot!"

Patrick fired. Then he took a step backward, tripped, and fell. He and the elephant went down together, sprawling on the ground within feet of each other, he on his back and the elephant on its side. The tip of its trunk was inches from his feet.

The third animal was a wounded pregnant female buffalo, shot without a permit by a Spanish duke who was supposed to be hunting warthogs. Patrick was so mad he punched the client, then sent him back to camp with the skinner. The man stalked off, holding his nose with a bloody bandanna, while Patrick and Fetnat went after the buffalo. For two days they tracked her through grass eight feet high, Fetnat in the lead. A wounded buffalo will lead its pursuer around in a circle; once it has gained enough distance, it will attack from the side. Patrick's T-shirt was soaked through, his arms ached from the weight of the .500-express, and his guts were in such turmoil he had trouble holding himself upright. He was squatting in the grass, relieving himself, when his eye caught something off to the right. Looking hard, he could make out a shadow, a dark patch in the dappled green light. Still crouching, he reached for his gun.

The rifle exploded and the buffalo appeared—it flew upward, partially rising above the grass, flipped upside-down, and crashed. Only Fetnat saw it; Patrick had been knocked off his feet by the .500-express and was on his back, staring at the sky.

They were still examining the carcass when they heard a shout. It was Yves, coming to find them. The skinner, arriving at camp with the bloody-nosed client just before sundown the previous day, had told him the whole story. Yves had set out that morning before sunup.

Back at camp, the duke was demanding to be seen by a doctor and threatening to go to the police. Finally Yves had had enough. "You want to file a complaint?" he shouted. "Your nose is broken? I don't think so!" He drew back his right arm and let the man have it. "There! Now it's broken—go file your complaint."

At the end of the hunting season, the Petits closed the camp; they would be taking a long vacation in France. The beds were stripped, the food lockers cleaned out, the trucks put on blocks, the guns locked in the walk-in safe off the master bedroom. Just before the camp emptied out, Yves produced a blue sheet of paper certifying that Patrick Maurice Texier had fulfilled all the licensing requirements of a professional hunting guide in Cameroon. He instructed Patrick to take the paper, which bore Yves's signature, to the game department's office in Yaounde, and exchange it for an actual license. Then the two men parted company, promising to see each other again in six months. Thirty years later, the blue paper was still making its way around Africa in a battered canteen. It quickly became worthless as an official document, and was kept only as a souvenir, but the knowledge it certified stuck. By the time the canteen was stolen in Sierra Leone, and the blue paper with it, Patrick had traversed thousands of wilderness miles on three continents, much of it on foot. But trophy hunting was not for him, and he never saw Yves again.

His favorite client never fired a shot. "Look," said the man when Patrick, mortified, tried to refuse his tip, "you should see my place; it's full of trophies. I enjoyed myself these past three weeks. Keep the tip. You've earned it." On their last morning together, they got lucky, coming upon a herd of eland that included a magnificent male. The hunters crawled toward the grazing antelope until they were close enough to hear the grass being ripped from the turf. They lay on their bellies, absorbed in the beauty of the scene before them as the sun inched across the sky. Finally, the client gave the signal, and the two men rose to their feet. The herd whipped to attention. Hunters and hunted regarded each other for a long moment. Then the client brought his hands together with a loud clap and the entire herd bounded away.

By the time Patrick finally confronted his father about the summer job in Gabon, he had been knocking about West Africa for three decades. His decision to go there had shaped his life more than any other single decision he'd ever made. No one could say that Africa hadn't proved a risky choice. Still, it had been his choice, and he didn't regret it.

But as far as Maurice was concerned, Africa was one of the bigger mistakes in a life filled with bad decisions. Now an old man, he still had the power to get under Patrick's skin. He rarely missed an opportunity to let Patrick know he was wasting his life running from one backward country to another when he should long ago have come home to France and found a proper job.

It was on one such occasion that Patrick blew. "You've never cared what I wanted," he said. "You've never listened to me."

For evidence, he came up with the earliest reference he could think of: the summer job in Gabon, three decades earlier, that had mysteriously disappeared.

121

"Why didn't you want me to go to Gabon?" he demanded.

"What do you mean?"

"The timber company—why did you tell them not to hire me?"

"How did you know?" It was a rare faux pas.

"You just told me."

Maurice was nearing the end of his life, and there was little fight left in him. Propped in his favorite chair, a frail figure surrounded by medical paraphernalia, he looked at his son.

"I was afraid you'd never come back."

Patrick was still struggling to recover from the Sierra Leone debacle when Maurice went into the hospital for the last time. The two men joked throughout their farewell visit while Mireille hovered. A comfortable, respectable middle-class life was what Maurice had wanted for his son. He couldn't understand why Patrick refused to settle down. What was the point of so much shifting about, from country to country, job to job, marriage to marriage? How could a man's life add up to something without continuity? Knowing how his father felt about the choices he'd made, Patrick could not bring himself to tell Maurice about many of the most important events of his life. He guarded them, so sure his father would not understand that he never gave him the chance. When Patrick kissed Maurice's hollow cheek and whispered, "Au revoir, Papa," as if they might see each other again, he did not walk through the door with the sense that his father had confidence in him. Instead, he left the hospital with the feeling that the unsaid things were better left unsaid.

Jenni at work.

Chapter Seven

With Patrick away, the days passed slowly, especially the weekends, because there was so little to do. I waited for the school bus. I went to the gym (three thousand shillings) and sometimes a yoga class (also three thousand). I wrote. Sometimes I went to the pool at the Novotel (2,500 shillings). I read. On Tuesday and Thursday mornings, I went to a little school run by the French consulate, where I was one of two students studying beginner French (way, way too many shillings). This was in case we did move to Togo, a French-speaking country. The class was taught by a Tanzanian. "Yoo ek-sent is veddy goot!" he said.

I went to Max's to send and receive email (500 shillings for fifteen minutes). Three days after Patrick's departure I got an email saying he had arrived in Lomé. "Don't expect to hear from me again for a while," I read. "There is no phone line at Fazao. I love you, darling. I miss you big deal."

Thomas and I played table tennis. We made Halloween costumes. We practiced wheelies. We painted a mural—a leopard lounging in a tree—on his bedroom wall. We did kitchen experiments, nearly burning the house down when Thomas tried making caramel the way Mami had taught him one summer in France, and turning a package of gelatin dessert with Arabic instructions into something so rubbery and hard that it couldn't be pierced with a fork. Sometimes I took Thomas to play pool at the Discovery Club or the Mambo Café (hemorrhaging shillings), but I didn't much like going there without Patrick.

A week or so after Patrick's departure, the Prednisone wore off and Thomas's spots returned. I eliminated the most suspicious foods from his diet—shellfish, tomatoes, chocolate, eggs—but Thomas remained blotchy and itchy and had trouble sleeping and Dr. Patel didn't know what to do, so one day we drove over to the Forresters' house so that Sue Forrester could have a look at the spots.

Sue opened the gate and escorted Thomas and me into the house. We wound our way through the maze of stuff that had collected in the Forresters' front room— towering stacks of books and magazines, tables and chairs piled high with all sorts of junk—for this was the way the Forresters were, they collected things. The house was an archivist's dream, a regular vault of Forrester paraphernalia—nothing like our own collection of household stuff, which was as meager by comparison as our own family history was brief.

Sue was a cheerful, bossy mother, firm in her opinions: Children need fresh air; children need exercise; children need routine; a packed lunch is better than cafeteria food; all children benefit immeasurably from dance lessons and horseback riding; the BBC is the voice of sanity in a lunatic world. "Bicarbonate of soda is the single most useful item you can have in your first-aid kit," she had informed me, leaning across the big slab table at Masai Camp the night we were introduced. "It will safely and swiftly cure a multitude of ailments." At the Forresters', the after-school routine included a healthy snack and homework at the kitchen table under Sue's scrutiny. When Thomas was there, he submitted to the same routine, resentfully. In his universe, homework was a form of torture invented by mean-spirited adults who only pretended to like children. These malevolent adults had brainwashed the world's parents into thinking that homework was good. These same gullible parents then applied the same twisted bad-is-good, good-is-bad logic to all manner of things, including vegetables, which are inherently disgusting, with the exception of radishes, carrot sticks, and French fries. Tomatoes occupy a neutral zone between good and evil. At Sue's house, Thomas had to eat his vegetables, good and bad, no exceptions, but Sue said he did so without complaint. In fact, she seemed surprised that I was surprised. "Even broccoli?" I said. "Oh, yes. You mean to say he doesn't eat broccoli at home?"

Sue sat us down at the dining room table, and the family clustered around—Derek and Andy and Kaykay, and various dogs and cats, the dogs flopping under the table, disturbing our feet, the cats milling about on top. I offered what scant information I had. "Dr. Patel says it's a food allergy."

"That's all very well," said Sue, "but the question is, what food?"

If anyone could get to the bottom of this, it was Sue, with her very practical, no-nonsense ideas about nursing. She disappeared into another room and returned with a small box, which she set on the dining table. Inside the box was a smooth crystal the size of a thimble. A string was attached to the crystal. "Lay your hand flat on the table in front of you," she instructed. Gently, she lifted the crystal from the box by its string and dangled it above Thomas's blotchy hand, swinging it back and forth like a pendulum. The cats came closer to investigate.

"Get down, Nuisance," said Derek. He picked up the two cats, one by one, and plopped them on the floor. The cats, whiskers stiff with indignation, exited.

The rest of us watched the crystal swing back and forth, back and forth.

"I'm getting wheat," Sue said.

I glanced at Thomas. His face was without expression as he watched the pale pinkish-purple crystal.

"And possibly dairy," said Sue.

After a few minutes, she shook her head: The reading was unclear. It happened with crystals; crystals were moody, subject to atmospheric conditions. Some days they were more cooperative than others.

"Take your time, dear," said Derek.

But the crystal remained indecisive. "It's just possible that he has a contact allergy instead of a food allergy," said Sue. "There are so many toxic substances around nowadays. We should try again this weekend—normally it takes at least three readings." Just in case, she advised me to have Jenni launder all of Thomas's clothes, bed linens, and towels in the mildest soap I could find.

We got in the car and drove home. As we bounced over the deeply rutted road to the highway, past open fields sprinkled with gated compounds, Thomas was silent. When we reached the main road, I braked to a stop and looked over at him. "Sara," he said, carefully. "I don't know about you, but I think I'm not really allergic to wheat."

ॐ

The short rains were late that year, and all over East Africa, crops   failed. By mid-November the dust on our road was six inches deep, as fine and soft as flour. A choking cloud followed the Toyota; on our hill, people on foot gestured for me to slow down even as I inched along. The women pulled their long kangas over their faces and the men stepped into the bushes to protect their clothing.

In the countryside, people began pouring into relief camps and the cattle were left to die.

For Jenni, the dusty road made the daily walk up and down the hill a trial. She arrived just before noon each day, stamping her feet three times on the threshold, chook-chook-chook, then removing her shoes before entering the house. "Muchi dusti," she complained. Much dust.

Daily she swept and mopped the floors, carefully going around my feet with the broom as I sat pecking at the computer in a corner of the bedroom. Sweeping done, she took an old T-shirt of Patrick's from a peg in the store room and, bending from the waist and walking backward, wiped from side to side across the polished cement floor. Floors done, she straightened up and swatted at the computer keyboards with another rag and polished the stereo console, the bookshelves; an hour later, you could write your name on every surface with your index finger.

Loto, too, waged an all-out offensive against the dust, driving it with his blue hose deep into the Toyota Tercel's nooks and crannies, clogging the works. Soon the windows wouldn't roll up or down, the locks wouldn't lock, the windshield wipers wouldn't wipe.

When he was finished with the car's exterior, he tackled the interior, polishing every knob and crevice. One day I went out to start the car and the battery was dead. I checked the dashboard: The light switch had been turned on. Odd. Then I realized: Loto.

It cost a dollar to get the battery recharged at a hole in the wall between the Bull Cheka Hair Cutters and the ChiChi Beauty Saloon at the foot of the hill. Mesuli disconnected and then reconnected the battery, which he seemed to understand better than he did the fuse box.

"But *why* did he turn on the headlights?" asked my friend Pat, shaking her head. She worked in the office at St. George's International School; we had lunch and went to yoga class together every couple of weeks.

"He's very thorough," I said, in Loto's defense. "He cleans the entire dashboard, every knob and switch. It takes him hours."

Pat looked skeptical.

"He doesn't know about cars, or batteries, or anything like that."

But she had planted a small seed of doubt—did he do it on purpose? Did he harbor some sort of grudge? What could it be?

At Max's Patisserie and Cyber Café, I checked the email almost every day, hoping for something from Patrick. To send and receive email, he had to drive fifty miles to the town of Sokodé. The round trip took at least half a day and tied up a vehicle and a driver, so he went only about once a week. His infrequent emails were short and not very informative—he missed me, he hoped everything was okay, give Thomas a kiss for me, and so on. My emails were full of complaints, which I tried to disguise as news: Thomas's spots are back; the car is busted; the power is out. I didn't want him to think of me as a fusspot, but

I did want full credit for the many inconveniences I was enduring in his absence.

Then, disaster struck: Jenni got sick. Two days in a row she failed to show up for work, there was no comforting chook-chook-chook on the doorstep, and on the third day Moses, her husband, came to explain, pulling up to our gate at the wheel of a freshly washed white Nissan four-wheel drive with a U.N. sticker on the side. When nobody answered his horn, he opened the gate and let himself in. "You have no askari?" he asked.

"We have a gardener," I said, "but it's his day off."

The nature of Jenni's illness was uncertain—not unusual in Tanzania, where illnesses are often as mysterious as they are lingering. It seemed that she might be ill for some time. Moses suggested that we think about hiring another housegirl in her absence. Then he got in his shiny white car and drove away. I closed the gate behind him.

I did not want another housegirl. I wanted Jenni. If I couldn't have Jenni, then I wanted no one. I spent the major portion of the afternoon hunkered in the shower with two plastic buckets and a scrub brush, doing laundry. The next day, I did a bit more, and the day after that, and the day after that, slowly working my way through the huge pile that had collected in the short time Jenni had been laid up. In accordance with Sue's advice, I conscientiously laundered all of Thomas's clothing and sheets and towels in mild soap. The powdered soap we normally bought was not mild—it was cheap African detergent, ferociously blue and probably toxic by Western standards. So I went to the market in Kijenge and came back with some "baby soap," with a picture of a smiling baby with pink cheeks on the box, which made no discernible impact on Thomas's filthy socks, or his rash.

With the onset of Jenni's illness, everything started to go. The power outages became more frequent. When the power was out, the meat went bad and we didn't have water because the electric pump was also out. The only good thing about this was that it meant I couldn't do laundry.

Meanwhile Patrick's paycheck, which he had said was being wired from a bank in Switzerland to a bank in downtown Arusha, had not arrived. Each day I went to the bank and the same clerk looked at me sadly and shook his head: There was no sign of the money. "These African banks like to hold your wire transfers hostage so they can make interest off them," said Emilio, emerging from his office sanctuary inside the Mambo Café, where I had gone at ten o'clock in the morning to fortify myself with a vodka and orange juice. "Sometimes they'll hold your money for weeks. They say they don't know where it is, they just play dumb, but all along they're making money off your money. For them, it's a free loan. They just borrow it for a while without asking."

After that, whenever I went to the bank to ask about my money and got the same apologetic response from the same bank clerk, I thought, "You are lying and I know you are lying, you evil lying liar." Then, after I'd given him a long look that I hoped conveyed my utter contempt for him and the entire Tanzanian banking system and all its personnel, I said, "Thank you. I'll see you tomorrow then," and I left.

When the power was out we went to bed early, and I listened to the drums from the neighborhood church, which closed up shop at about eleven. Then I fell asleep, to awaken a few hours later and lie in the darkness, listening. Sometimes the noise that woke me was the barking of the neighborhood dogs on their nightly rampage through the garden. Sometimes I heard the askari, coughing and circling the house, his footsteps crunching on the gravel. Often I heard Mesuli's rooster, which began crowing at 3 A.M. The muezzin's call from a distant mosque at 5 A.M. And then, at first light, the clank of the garden gate as the askari left. If burglars come, I told myself, I will grab Thomas and we'll crawl under the bed and be very very quiet while the burglars ransack the house. Hopefully, the askari will run away in time to avoid being killed, so he can rally forces to come rescue us before the burglars, who will no doubt be armed, think to look under the bed.

Patrick in the elephant grass.

Chapter Eight

Patrick's first African odyssey extended south from Cameroon, around the tip of the continent, and back up the other side. Leaving Yves's camp, he hitched a ride to Douala with a weekend hunter, sliding into the backseat. The front seat of the car was occupied by Chita. How he was going to travel around Africa with a full-grown leopard he hadn't yet figured out.

Halfway to Douala, the road began climbing up into mountainous rain forest and passed a few scattered houses. At the entrance to one village, three sticks were pounded into the earth beside the road; on each stick was mounted a human head. Atop each head was the French military cap known as a kepi, worn by the gendarmerie. Patrick was in the driver's seat, taking a turn at the wheel. "Have you seen what I've seen?" he asked. "Just keep going, keep going," urged his friend. They drove on, passing through the village, where all appeared normal. People were going about their daily business just as if they knew nothing about any severed heads.

For the next few months he and Chita lived in a rented second-floor apartment on the edge of a quiet residential neighborhood in Douala. Chita was a housecat, used to spending most of her time in a one-room bungalow; from her standpoint, Douala wasn't so very different from life in the bush. Patrick bought a mini-Moke and took her on weekends to a park in the rain forest, where she roamed around while he sat under a tree, reading, watching the birds, and waiting for her to come back. During the week, she slept a lot.

The cool cement floor of the hallway just outside the kitchen was one of her favorite resting spots. From there, she could keep an eye on the houseboy. Bienvenu, whom Patrick judged to be somewhere in his forties, came to work every day wearing a navy blue business suit, a white shirt, a tie, and eyeglasses with thick black plastic frames. His shoes were polished to a high gloss, and he carried a smart faux-leather briefcase, which he parked on a chair in the pantry until it was time to leave. Over the back of the chair he draped his jacket, and under the chair he set his shoes, going about the house barefoot and wrapped in a long white apron. The eyeglasses went inside the briefcase.

Bienvenu was responsible for keeping all corners of the small apartment neat and clean, yet he spent most of his time in the kitchen. With a 160-pound leopard stretched across the floor, blocking his exit, Bienvenu invented many chores for himself there—ironing sheets and pillowcases till they were smooth as cardboard, scouring pots and pans till they shined like silver.

With his hunting tips and wages, Patrick bought a single-engine Dornier VSTOL—the initials stand for "very short takeoff and landing"—and on the strength of an army pilot's training, he began making regular flights to a small airstrip just outside Victoria. The airstrip where he landed two or three times a week was a mere 350 meters in length, squeezed between the steep slope of a volcano and a palm tree plantation. He had to hug the mountainside and clear a deep gulley before he could set his wheels down, then brake hard to avoid crashing into the palms. The takeoff was equally difficult: Facing the sixty-foot palms with the wind at his tail, he had to be airborne within three hundred meters, for that was the point at which a railroad track intersected his path, as well as his last hope of avoiding the trees.

In the interval between landing and takeoff, he drove to the docks where a speedboat was moored, motored across the bay to the island of Fernando Po, a well-known hub for smuggling operations that extended all across Africa, and picked up a consignment of duty-free merchandise—watches, cameras, perfumes. This he brought back to Douala concealed in a couple of fuel tanks. Within a month, he and his two partners were filling orders from as far afield as Gabon, Benin, and Nigeria.

Chita was almost fully mature; soon she would go into her first heat. Patrick knew he couldn't keep her much longer. Each time they visited the rain forest outside Douala, he hoped she would leave him, disappearing into the forest for good. She always returned, sometimes with a present—a monkey or a duiker, which she'd drop at his feet, too well fed at home to have any interest herself in such food.

Once she vanished for most of the day while he hiked along a riverbank. He was sitting on a rock, wondering if he would ever see her again, when a family of picnickers on the opposite bank jumped to their feet, gesticulating and shouting at him: "Leopard!" Silently, Chita came up from behind him, nosed his arm in greeting, and sat down beside him. He put his arm around her. "It's okay!" he shouted to the picnickers. "She's mine."

He loved her to despair. The furniture and the woodwork in his rented apartment were covered with the marks of her claws, and she was so jealous of other females that he was unable to invite women home. He tried it once. Chita broke down two doors trying to get at the intruder, who escaped out the back way.

"What am I going to do with her?" Patrick moaned to a friend.

"You've got to make a choice, man," said the friend. "It may seem heartless, but you're gonna have to let her go if you want a life of your own."

"But she doesn't know how to be a real leopard. What if something happens to her?"

"Maybe I can help you out. Give me a few days, and I'll let you know."

He was flying toward Douala with the usual load of merchandise when he plowed into a flock of large birds, probably storks. One or two lodged in the propeller, damaging the shaft and the blades, and at about three thousand feet, the engine quit. The Dornier was now essentially a glider, though far clumsier than the light and graceful aircraft he had mastered in the army. As it sailed noiselessly through the sky, coasting on banks of air, he searched the ground for a smooth spot large enough for a landing. Below, the forest had been mostly cleared to make way for small vegetable plots. He came down in a plowed field and bumped along through hillocks of yams for fifty feet before a wheel caught and the plane veered violently to the left. There was a loud crack as the wing snapped in two.

The crash attracted a cluster of villagers. The owner of the destroyed yams arrived, and a palaver ensued, the yam farmer demanding compensation for his ruined crop. Patrick offered him a box of the plane's cargo. He covered the remaining miles to Douala in the front seat of an old Peugeot pickup.

Shortly after, one of the lumbermen who frequented his favorite restaurant—a bachelor who lived alone in the rain forest—drove away with Chita in the back of his pickup. Chita, happy to be going for a drive, climbed in willingly and didn't look back. A couple of weeks later, Patrick paid her a final visit, making the four-hour drive in his mini-Moke to see how she and the lumberman were getting on. She was out when he arrived; the man proudly showed Patrick the entrance he had carved for her in his front door, so she could come and go freely. When she returned a few hours later, she walked right past her visitor, without so much as a glance in his direction, as if he didn't exist.

Just before Patrick left Douala, he bumped into the lumberman, quenching his thirst after a day of errands in town. Patrick settled himself on the adjacent bar stool and ordered a beer.

"How's my leopard?"

"She left me."

Soon after Patrick's good-bye visit, Chita had disappeared. The lumberman was taking it hard. They sat for a moment, quietly sipping their beer, reflecting. Chita might have encountered a hunter or some other threat, but he preferred to think not.

"I expect she found a more suitable mate," Patrick said. "No offense. She was ready for that."

"Aye-yuh," said the man. He stared down at his glass and sighed. "I suppose it's for the best."

❧

Zambia, formerly Northern Rhodesia, was barely a year old in the waning months of 1965. Arriving in Lusaka, Patrick exited the plane to find dozens of khaki-uniformed soldiers, rifles in hand, stationed inside and outside the airport. Military convoys rattled through the streets.

Zaire, Zambia's northern neighbor, had been embroiled in civil wars since the Belgians pulled out four years earlier, and in the south, rebel soldiers from white-ruled Rhodesia had crossed the Zambezi to set up their training camps in Zambia's southern forests. The Zambian army was poorly trained, the government in the hands of novices and a few British advisors.

After a run of bad luck in a Swaziland casino, Patrick was nearly out of money. He was on the verge of returning to Paris when his Lusaka host came up with an alternative. Within a fortnight, Patrick was the owner and operator of an export business with a staff of three. His base of operations was a lakeshore cabin west of Lusaka, his only client a Swiss company that imported exotic leather.

The first night on the lake everybody was tense. Isaac, standing in the stern, poled the boat along close to shore; February stood in the prow holding a makeshift headlight, borrowed from an old automobile. Zachariah sat in the middle of the canoe with a rope coiled at his feet, Patrick beside him with a rifle across his knees. The air was warm; the water shimmered with starlight. In the distance, they could see the lights of small fishing boats, far out on the lake. In the trees, owls hooted softly, and nightjars called.

Coming to a freshwater inlet, Isaac turned the canoe, then nosed it forward. The trees closed in on either side, blotting out the sky, and the steady thrum of cicadas crescendoed as they entered the channel. There was a rustle on the bank to their right, followed by a splash. "Light," said Patrick. February leaned down and touched the wire to the electrode, then straightened and searched with his beam. It swept across the water's surface and stopped, arrested by two red coals: a pair of eyes. More red coals glowed in the shadows. The beam skimmed to the right, then to the left. The place was teeming with crocs.

"That one," said Patrick, pointing. Medium-sized crocs—two to three meters in length—were young enough to ensure that the belly skin, the only part of the carcass they were interested in, would be soft and unscarred, the scales small.

February trained the light on their quarry as the boat closed in. A shot rang out over the lake.

Zach hooked the noose with the pole and lifted it out over the water. When it was directly in front of the floating carcass, he dipped the pole, dropping the noose in front of the animal's snout. The idea was to slip the noose over the head and release the rope from the pole. The next step was to pass the pole to the nearest set of hands and pull the noose tight.

The maneuver wasn't particularly dangerous—the animal was shot at point-blank range, and there was little chance of accidentally roping a live one—but it required dexterity and speed. Although the crack of the rifle was enough to send all nearby crocodiles scurrying, you could count on them returning within minutes to feed on their dead relative. Second, crocodiles routinely swallow stones, which remain in their stomachs and act as ballast. So once the dying crocodile had expelled the air in its lungs, it would quickly lose its buoyancy and sink to the bottom of the lake. At that point, they could forget all about retrieving it.

It took about a week, during which they shot and lost perhaps a hundred crocs, before Zachariah finally got the hang of it. By the end of the second week they were averaging ten to twelve skins per catch, working from ten in the evening to about one or two in the morning. Every few days, in the late afternoon or early evening, when the sun was no longer hot but there was still enough light to work by, they'd prepare the drums for export. When they had twenty skins or so, they'd lay them out flat, one on top of another, roll the stack into a bundle and pack the bundle in a solution-filled drum. Then Patrick would seal the drum: First, he'd place an inner lid a foot or so from the top of the drum and weld it shut. Then, he'd pack a layer of dirt on top of it—the "soil sample" indicated by the drum's label. Finally, he'd weld the outer lid into place.

When he had two filled drums—forty to fifty skins in all—he'd load them into the back of the Land Rover and drive to Lusaka. At the airport, he'd drop off his consignment of "soil samples," and present the required papers to the clearing agent—always the same man, whose name had been given to him by the customs manager. Once the papers were stamped, he'd swing by to say hi to the customs manager. They'd while away a quarter of an hour in his office, chatting, and when it was time to leave Patrick would reach into his shirt pocket, draw out an envelope, and slide it across the desk.

Each time a consignment was received at the other end, his Swiss bank account would grow by several thousand dollars. Every week or so, he'd arrange for a wire transfer to an account in Lusaka, from which he'd withdraw enough money to pay weekly salaries and other expenses.

He was never 100 percent sure what went wrong. The lake that night had been calm, as usual, and they were making good time. After a couple of hours, they had five skins, about half their evening quota. With three months' experience behind them, they were confident and efficient.

Five hundred yards from shore, near one of several streams that flowed into the lake, Patrick picked out what appeared to be a moderate-size croc, swimming a few yards off to starboard. Isaac poled the boat forward. The croc, blinded by February's light, didn't move. When they were about five feet from their target, Patrick fired, and saw the bullet enter exactly where it should, between the eyes.

Using his pole, Zach guided the rope around the croc's snout; when it was in place, he handed the pole to Isaac and began pulling the noose tight. Patrick had his eyes on the carcass. Just as the rope went taut, the dead croc plunged below the surface, tugging on the rope as if it were alive. The boat lurched, and there was a scrambling motion, followed by a splash. Patrick caught only a glimpse of Zach in February's light: One arm was outstretched, and the other appeared to be holding the rope. In an instant, he was gone.

There was a moment of confusion, and then Patrick and Isaac sprang forward with the same instinct. Each of them grabbed the rope, one end of which was tied to the center bench, and began pulling. It was no use—the weight on the other end was too great, and the rope slipped through their grasp, burning the skin from their palms. Very quickly the slack was taken up, and the boat swung violently around. Then it began to move swiftly forward, pulled by an unseen force.

The boat quickly picked up speed, headed toward the riverbank. They could see nothing in February's light except the rope, stretching out over the water at an angle and then disappearing below the murky surface. Was Zach still entangled in it? Or had they left him behind? Patrick's mind raced as he tried to figure out what was happening. Then a small noise came from the center of the boat and quickly crescendoed: the crackle and pop of splintering wood. As the bench gave way, breaking under the strain of the rope, it flew up in three pieces, one of which struck Isaac in the face. He crumpled and went down as the boat abruptly lost its momentum.

With no sign of Zach, February and Patrick knelt over Isaac, trying to revive him. When he came to, he could barely breathe, much less talk. Blood gushed from his nose and mouth. They made him as comfortable as they could, then Patrick picked up Isaac's pole, stepped into the stern, and pushed the boat back in the direction they'd come. February stepped forward into the prow, picked up the lamp, and skimmed the water with its beam, calling Zach's name.

By now, however, Zach had been in the water nearly a quarter of an hour. The chances of finding him alive were practically nil. They drifted for a moment in silence, and then Patrick spoke.

"We should go back."

There was nothing more they could do. His concern now was for Isaac, whose injuries were severe; he needed to be seen by a doctor. Without a word, February disconnected the light from the battery. Patrick waited a moment for his eyes to adjust to the darkness. Then he turned the boat toward shore.

"You say you were hunting." The sergeant glowered from behind his desk. Outside the window, Lusaka baked in the sun. In a corner of the small office, a junior officer was taking notes, struggling to get everything down in longhand with a stubby pencil.

"That's right."

"Crocodiles."

"Yes."

The sergeant, a burly man with jowls, shifted in his seat. "Your friend said you were fishing."

Overhead, an ancient ceiling fan turned, rustling the papers stacked in untidy piles on the desk. The room was stifling, the air thick with the fine red dust that drifted in through the window. Patrick's head pounded, and his eyes smarted with fatigue.

He wasn't supposed to be here. The plan they'd made while driving Isaac to the hospital in Lusaka was for Patrick to leave the country as soon as possible. Once he'd had a couple of days to get away, the other two would report the accident to the police. They were fishing, they'd say, and a man fell overboard. If the police wanted to blame somebody, they could blame the white man.

At the hospital, however, February babbled on nervously to the woman at the front desk. It didn't take long for hospital personnel to learn that there was a missing man. A police cruiser arrived with four cops inside, leaving just enough room for the two suspects, one in front and one in back. The cops drove to the nearest precinct house, confiscated wallets, belts, shoes, and papers, and escorted the prisoners to a crowded cell, its centerpiece a brimming latrine.

February was the first to be questioned. He was gone for over an hour, and when he returned, setting off a chain reaction of shifting bodies as he squeezed in next to Patrick, his face and arms were covered with bruises the color of eggplants. One eye was swollen shut, and a gash on the side of his head oozed blood. Patrick made a quick decision to cooperate with the police, sticking to the truth and divulging as much of the story as possible without implicating the friends who had helped set him up in business.

"Poaching is a serious crime." The swivel chair squeaked angrily as the sergeant rose.

"I'm sorry."

"Poaching is stealing." The sergeant came around the desk and stood directly in front of the prisoner, his holster at eye level. He motioned to the stenographer to hand over his tablet. "Sign it."

Patrick penned a shaky signature.

"Now you will tell us the real story."

Patrick's belly began to twist itself into a knot. "But sir, I have told you the truth."

The first blow knocked him off the chair. He tried to get up but a kick sent him sprawling.

The other detainees fell silent when the guard returned Patrick to the cell. He slumped to the floor next to February and rubbed his wrists where the cuffs had been. He could feel the eyes of the men as they took in his bruises.

So far, he hadn't been officially charged with any crime, although he'd confessed to several. The sergeant appeared to be tormenting him for sport. He wondered what the punishment was for illegal possession of firearms. And what about bribing a public official? That hadn't come up yet in the sergeant's random, often illogical line of questioning.

His thoughts shifted between anxiety over his predicament and flashbacks to the accident. He had shot the croc dead, he was sure. It could not suddenly have come alive again, dragging Zach overboard. Besides, it wasn't big enough to tow the boat at the speed it had been traveling. Another, much bigger croc must have been on the end of the rope. It must have grabbed the dead one as it floated in the water, and dragged it under, pulling Zach with it. Then it headed toward its nest in the riverbank. Over and over he replayed the sequence of events: Zach's shout as he was dragged overboard, the splash as he hit the water, the sight of him going under, the burn of the rope as it slipped through his hands, the crackle of splintering wood.

ॐ

"I am French, Patrick heard himself say. His voice sounded far away. "I have never been to Rhodesia." All was black outside the window behind the police sergeant's desk, and the street was deserted. Patrick had lost track of time and no longer knew what day it was. His wrists and ankles were raw from the metal cuffs that anchored him to the wooden chair. He figured his nose was broken and maybe his jaw too, and he had a bloody hole in his gums where there had been until yesterday a front tooth.

"I want to contact the French consulate."

The two deputies in the room looked sleepy and bored, and the sergeant's balance was unsteady from many hours of slow tippling, his speech at times incoherent. Unsatisfied with having caught a mere poacher, the man had convinced himself the prisoner was a member of the Rhodesian army, his presence in Zambia evidence of a foreign conspiracy to overthrow the government. "I'm tired of your boo-sheet," he slurred.

"I wish to see a lawyer."

"You will see nobody!"

The sergeant retreated to his long-suffering swivel chair and closed his eyes. For a brief but hopeful moment he appeared to be asleep. Then he stood, fumbled with his holster, and drew out his gun. Confused and agitated, he paced about, brandishing his weapon and shouting angrily. The room began to spin as Patrick saw the barrel swing this way and that, pausing as it aimed at his groin. There was an explosion, then blackness.

ॐ

When Patrick came to, he was on his back, lying on something soft—a cot? The room was dark and still. He tried to raise his head enough to look around. Then he tried his arms, legs, fingers, toes. Nothing moved and nothing mattered; he drifted off on a cloud of nirvana. As the effects of whatever drug he'd been given wore off, he felt a burning in his right knee. He tried to bend the leg and a searing pain shot through him.

It was nighttime, but whether the same night or a different one he couldn't say. As his eyes adjusted to the faint light coming from the street, shapes appeared in the room: a desk, a chair, another desk—the cot was in the center of a small office. Familiar sounds in the corridor told him he was still at the police station.

When he was alert enough to raise his head, he discovered the knee was encased in a thick white bandage, professionally wrapped. He touched the gauze lightly with his fingers, then pressed gingerly, wincing. Lying back, he tried to raise the leg, but was brought up short by another jolt of pain.

For the next few hours he slipped in and out of consciousness. As the sky lightened he became aware of noises: loud voices in the hallway, banging doors, the murmur of pedestrians on their way to work, the rumble of morning traffic through the window.

He was wide awake when the door opened and a tall man with a blond handlebar mustache entered the room. The man looked very colonial in his khaki shorts, knee socks, and polished black shoes. An advisor—an officer, presumably, though he wore no badge. Probably held over from the colonial regime. The man pulled a chair over next to the cot.

"How are you feeling?"

The anesthesia had worn off and the knee was throbbing; Patrick was quite sure it was broken. He hurt all over, and he was terrified—of losing his leg, of going to prison, of what his father was going to say.

"I was in my office when I heard the commotion," the officer was saying, "and by the time I reached the room, it was filled with people. You were lying unconscious on the floor. The bullet grazed the knee before hitting the leg of the chair in which you were sitting. You've been quite lucky. The chair was blasted to smithereens."

Patrick had a sudden image of the chair exploding underneath him, sending pieces flying into the air and himself crashing to the floor, as the sergeant stared in slack-jawed amazement, unable to comprehend what had just happened.

"We called in a doctor to dress the wound and give you something for the pain, and then left you here to recover."

"Will I be able to walk?"

"That's what we need to determine. Eventually, yes, of course. But I'd like to know if you can walk now."

"Now?"

"As soon as you've had a bit more rest and some food. First I want you to try standing, and then, if you're able, to walk around the room a bit. I'll see you tomorrow and you can tell me how it goes."

The next morning two guards took him to a sunlit office that smelled of fresh coffee; they set the stretcher on a couple of chairs and left the room.

"How are you feeling?" said the officer.

"Okay, I guess. A bit tired."

"Did you try walking?"

149

He had made it around the perimeter of his chamber, leaning on the walls for support. Now, however, he hesitated, unsure how to answer the man's question. No matter how much authority the officer might have, he couldn't simply release a confessed lawbreaker. And why was he so anxious to see Patrick back on his feet? Was he readying him to stand before a judge?

"It went okay. More or less."

"Can you show me?"

Patrick took a few steps; the pain had lessened considerably since the day before.

"Can you walk across the room and back?"

He did, limping and grimacing only somewhat more than necessary.

From a desk drawer the officer extracted some neatly folded articles of clothing. "These are for you. Go ahead and put them on. I think we're about the same size."

Patrick stripped off his filthy T-shirt and shorts and pulled on the clean clothes, gathering up a good portion of the trousers' waistband and clutching it in one hand to prevent the trousers from slipping to the floor. The officer solved the problem with a length of twine. Then, offering Patrick a razor, a pot of shaving cream and a brush, he invited him to use the sink and mirror in a corner of the office. "Don't shave your mustache," he instructed.

Patrick studied his reflection in the mirror above the sink: One eye was half-closed, his lip was swollen, and one of his front teeth was missing. The other was broken in half. His hand shook as he slid the razor over multi-colored bruises and worked around cuts.

"Rest, eat, and sleep," said the officer. "Practice walking, but don't let anyone see you. I'll send for you again at the end of the day."

At dusk, the stretcher returned. "Tell me," said the officer, closing the door behind the bearers as they exited the room. "What really happened?"

On an impulse, Patrick told him everything. When he reached the part about Zach going overboard, his voice started to quaver.

The officer rose from his chair. "Well," he said brusquely. "You mustn't stay in Zambia. I have a duty to attend to; I'll be gone about one hour." The words were slow and distinct.

"Do not escape through the window."

Patrick's eyes flew to the window. It was large, close to the ground, and completely unsecured.

"Do not open my center desk drawer, where I've put your papers, watch and money. I'll lock you in," the officer said, and he left the room.

Hopping on one leg, Patrick went around the desk and opened the drawer. Directly in front of him were his wallet, passport, and watch, as well as about half the money he'd had on him at the time of his arrest. He hopped to the window: The alley was clear. It was by now after seven o'clock, and quite dark. He drew open the window and stepped easily over the sill and onto the ground.

Two days later he flagged down a Rhodesian army convoy south of the Zambezi and got a lift into Salisbury, where he was dropped first at the hospital, then at the police station, then at Salisbury's finest hotel. He had his knee X-rayed and stitched, his passport stamped, his pillow fluffed. The hotel concierge recommended a dentist, who removed the painful roots of the missing tooth. He had a steaming hot shower. He lay on a thick mattress and breathed in the scent of clean sheets. He picked up the receiver of the bedside phone and a pleasant female voice said, "Room service!"

Within a couple of weeks his leg was much improved. Waking up one morning in the Salisbury hotel, he felt ready to move on. When he stopped by army headquarters to say his good-byes, the officer in charge of his case tried to recruit him. "We need men like you," he said.

೫

When Patrick returned from his first trip to Africa, he was missing two front teeth. Parts of his face were purple and swollen, and he walked with a pronounced limp. His three-week vacation had lasted more than a year.

"And what did your parents say," I asked him, "when they finally found out you were not working for UTA during this time?"

"I never told them."

We were sitting on the living room sofa at the house in Njiro; from the kitchen came the noisy rustling of a small mouse, which nightly came out of its hiding place in the pantry to look for food. I had heard the Zambia story several times, but I wanted details.

"So you didn't tell them you'd just come from a Zambian prison."

"Jail," he corrected me. "Not prison."

"Jail then."

"Certainly not."

The rustling grew louder and, not liking the direction this interview was taking, Patrick went to the kitchen to investigate. Soon I heard a loud clack. A tiny figure darted from the kitchen and, hugging the wall, shot down the corridor toward the bedrooms. Patrick was right behind, wielding a broom. Several times a week they played this game. The mouse made a sudden U turn, and, dodging the broom, charged toward the living room, then changed its mind and streaked back into the kitchen. Patrick made another swipe with the broom before giving up and returning to the living room, a bit winded. When he saw me standing on the couch, he burst out laughing.

"Leave that poor mouse alone," I said.

"Don't worry. We're just playing. He knows I won't hurt him."

When we were both settled on the couch again, I asked him one more question. "How did you explain the missing teeth?"

"Car accident."

That closed the subject for the evening. It was my first clue to the secrecy with which he protected himself, but I didn't give it much weight. To decide not to tell your parents that while visiting a foreign country you were arrested, handcuffed, and thrown in jail, and that you left as a police fugitive, crossing the Zambezi in a rowboat under cover of darkness—this didn't strike me as particularly odd behavior. Little by little, however, I discovered how much of his story he had never told before.

"So why tell me?" I finally asked him. By then I knew that silence was his best defense.

"Because when I told you, I didn't know you very well" was his answer.

"So?"

"So it didn't matter what you thought."

We both knew this wasn't true. It mattered a lot.

"But you kept talking," I pointed out.

"I found out you were a good listener."

This was a little closer to the truth. I wasn't there to judge him; maybe he knew that. Or maybe he just figured it was time to take a chance. He was fifty-two years old when we met and nobody—nobody who mattered—knew who he was.

"What happened in Zambia" was the rather innocuous working title I gave to this episode as I labored over it, tapping away at my dusty laptop while Thomas was at school and Patrick was chasing poachers through the bush three thousand miles away. I didn't know what to make of such a screw-up, nor any of the other screw-ups upon which so many of his stories hinged. I tried. Oh, how I tried, writing out lists of questions, recording the answers, then mulling over all the bits and pieces, arranging and rearranging them in a mind-boggling attempt to come up with a telling narrative. I was never satisfied. All through our courtship and into our marriage, I grilled him. He answered with remarkable patience and little insight, leaving interpretations to me. His reticence was a challenge, but one I found interesting. After all, I was a reporter; getting information was my job.

But the man I had married remained a mystery. What had driven him to take so many risks? And how had he survived? I don't mean physically—dumb luck could explain that. But what was the secret of his resilience? "No brains, no headaches" he would say, quoting one of his shabby old T-shirts.

"What's wrong with your knee?" I asked, and our courtship began. Of all his stories, what happened in Zambia is the one he chose for me. That he chose it, I have no doubt. Was it really his knee that prevented him from climbing Lengai? Or might it have been his ruined lungs, perhaps, or his damaged feet? It doesn't matter. For some reason, he wanted me to hear about Zambia. I took it as an invitation of sorts. He had been all over this dazzling continent by the time we met, and he had made some bad mistakes, but if I wanted to see Africa, then here was my guide.

Thomas with his fishing pole at Lake Duluti.

Chapter Nine

The weather turned cooler, clouds gathered, and finally the rains began. With the first shower, the jacarandas burst into color, and the dust on our road
turned to mud. Most days it rained twice, once in the
early afternoon and again in the middle of the night.
Often the rain thundering on the tin roof woke me up.
Warm in my bed, I fretted about the poor askari huddled in the dark, waiting for somebody to attack us,
with only a thin blanket to protect him from the cold
and the damp. Where did he take refuge from the
rain? On the back porch? In the stone shed under the
cistern, with the spiders and the scorpions? I told myself I should get him a chair, a rain jacket, a flashlight,
a thermos for his tea. Then I rolled over and went
back to sleep.

At night, the askari covered the Toyota with a
tarp—one that he found balled up on the porch where
Patrick had thrown it at the end of a safari. He put a
few rocks from the garden on the tarp to keep it from
blowing away in the wind. This was to protect the car
from the rain. The Toyota's windows had gotten stuck
in the down position, a problem that I was sure was
the result of Loto's assiduous car washing.

The car washing may have had another unfortunate result, for Loto had recently acquired, perhaps

with the help of his tip money, a small radio that blasted out rasta hits as he puttered about the yard. When it rained, he retreated into the tool shed, where he had arranged two overturned red plastic crates, one for him and one for his radio. When it was time for him to leave, he sometimes knocked at the door and asked me for a plastic bag, to keep the radio from getting rained on during the walk home.

One day Loto failed to show up for work; bright and early the next morning he came hodying up to the front door to explain. He said a few words in Swahili and then looked at me, waiting, hopefully. I shook my head. He tried again. I made out the word *mgonjwa*: sick. I murmured my condolences. But there was more, something about shillingi for the daktari. I gave him five hundred shillings and he went away. Pretty soon I heard the swish of his broom and the voice of Bob Marley singing "Buffalo Soldier."

The next day Loto was back, and this time it seemed that the sick person we had been discussing yesterday was no longer mgonjwa (sick) but kufa, dead. I had a terrible feeling that he was talking about his wife. He needed more shillingi—for the funeral, perhaps?—so this time I gave him a thousand.

The third time he came I told him to follow me and we walked next door to Mesuli's house. "Mesuli," I said, "Loto has a problem. Somebody in his family is sick, I think. He needs money."

Mesuli and Loto had a brisk conversation, the gardener nodding the whole time, and then Mesuli turned to me and said, "Okay."

"Okay what?"

"I told him not to ask you for money any more."

"But what does he need the money for?"

Mesuli and Loto exchanged a few more words, and Mesuli said, "His wife was sick but now she's better."

"Are you sure? He said somebody is kufa."

So Mesuli and Loto conferred again and then Mesuli turned to me and said, "That was somebody else. That was"—he squinted at the treetops with the calculating look of somebody doing long division in his head—"his wife's . . . brother's . . . cousin."

He waved his hand, as if banishing a mosquito. "A long time ago," he added.

After that, whenever I heard the scritch, scritch of Loto's rake on the gravel drive or the spray of his blue hose on the hood of the car, I hid in the bedroom with the curtains drawn, pretending to be asleep.

I laundered everything in the house, but Thomas's rash got worse. In desperation, I took him back to Dr. Patel, who said, "There is nothing I can do. You need to take him to Nairobi." So I borrowed some money from friends—the money Patrick had sent was still lost in the international banking system—and early one morning in mid-November Mesuli drove us down the hill, past the Big Y Club, the bicycle-repair tree, and the Masai women's vegetable pyramids; past the ChiChi Beauty Saloon and the mud-puddle car wash to the Novotel parking lot to catch the bus.

Nairobi was a cramped and jostling five-hour ride away, unless the bus broke down. The road itself was narrow and straight, the bus hot, the air close, the route not very scenic—conditions that tended to induce drowsiness, a worrisome aspect of the journey from a driving standpoint. Fatal bus crashes were alarmingly commonplace on Nairobi Road—Thomas himself had once seen an old man flying through the air on the outskirts of Arusha after being struck by a bus that never stopped or even slowed after the fatal impact.

By the time we reached the Kenyan border, three hours from Arusha, Thomas looked like he'd stumbled into a hornet's nest. His feet were so swollen he could barely get his shoes on. "Listen, Sara," he said.

He drew a few raspy breaths. I listened, my eyes on his puffy lips.

"Does your asthma pump help?"

"Not really."

He leaned against me, then against the window, trying to get comfortable. He was hot and sweaty but unusually quiet, too sick to complain.

In Nairobi, a taxi dropped us off at a bright and cheerful building, its reception room filled with picture books and educational toys. The doctor, an avuncular white-haired pediatrician who had treated many of our friends' children, looked Thomas over. Within half a minute he had reached a diagnosis.

"You've got hives," he said.

I was speechless. So this was the mysterious malady that had flummoxed Arusha's best medical minds—I had consulted three different doctors about the affliction, as well as an assortment of unlicensed experts. None of them had mentioned hives.

"It's an allergic reaction," the doctor continued. "Probably to a protein—could be milk, could be eggs, could be fish, could be a lot of things. You'll have to avoid certain foods until we can identify the cause."

"I'm allergic to eggs," said Thomas. "If I eat eggs, I blow up. I could die."

"But he hasn't eaten eggs," I said.

"Hives can be brought on by stress," said the doctor. "You can eat a food one day and be fine, and the next day the same food might cause a reaction. Sometimes the difference is stress."

I looked at Thomas, stretched out in his underwear on the examining table. He looked remarkably composed, but still—I knew that I myself had been feeling stressed lately, and I didn't think I looked any different from usual.

"His dad is away," I said. "Maybe that's a factor."

The doctor gave me a long list of things to avoid, and prescribed another dose of prednisone. The list included spices and anything with food coloring and other food additives.

"If he's symptom-free, you can add back foods from the list one at a time. Wait three days, and if he's still symptom-free, add another. If he has a reaction, you'll know which food is responsible."

He patted Thomas's arm and told him he could put his clothes back on. "You're a fine young man," he said.

"Thank you," said Thomas.

The doctor gave me his email address. "Call or email me if you have any questions."

The prednisone started to work immediately and by dinnertime Thomas was feeling much better. At the hotel restaurant, he ordered steak and potatoes and a Fanta Orange. "No Fanta Orange," I said.

"Why not? That's not on the list."

"Food coloring is on the list."

"Fanta Orange has food coloring?"

"Tons of it."

Thomas stared at me in disbelief. "Then what can I drink?"

"You can drink water. Or seltzer."

Various emotions flickered across his face—shock, panic, doubt—before he settled on pure outrage. "Not fair," he howled.

"Cheer up," I said, laughing. "It's not so bad. It's better than hives."

But Thomas just looked at me as if I had suddenly grown fangs. As if not being able to drink Fanta Or-

ange was not only worse than hives, it was worse than
death, and anyone who could laugh about such a punishment must have the soul of the devil. If I were a
good person, a kind person, a person who wanted to
take care of him, I would make this list of banned
foods go away. I would burn it, or tear it into little bits
and let the wind scatter them. Only a person with a
heart of stone would drag him all the way to Nairobi
in order to obtain this new instrument of torture. But
he will show me. He will resist, not only that, he will
fight back, with all the power in his small being.

Back in Arusha, faced with yet another mountain of
dirty clothes, many of which were splotched with mud
produced by the twice daily downpours, I got a brilliant idea: Loto could help with the laundry. I set him
up in the backyard, where there was an outdoor tap.
He was happy—he had something new to clean—and
the results of his laundering were far superior to mine.

Mesuli came, stepping through the bougainvillea-
covered hedge and summoning me with a soft "Hodi."
Emily, a chubby and bow-legged toddler, was in his
arms. Setting Emily on her feet, Mesuli asked politely
how we were and stated his business: "Sara," he said,
"you must hire a housegirl. I will see if I can find you
one."

The little hen, disturbed by the intrusion, had
hopped off her hat and was strutting nervously
around the veranda. "I Shot the Sheriff" emanated
from the garden shed. I struggled to think of a way to
explain that it was bad enough having Loto outside,
with his peep and his radio and his shidas great and
small, and that I didn't want anybody lurking about
inside, that I needed my space, my privacy. Jenni I
didn't mind, but nobody could replace Jenni. Unfortunately, there was no way of explaining all this to
Mesuli without sounding like just another stubborn

and disagreeable muzungu, so I simply said, "Not yet." Mesuli lifted Emily with a sigh and walked back through the hedge, I went into the house and shut the door, and the little hen returned to her hat.

Loto, meanwhile, was doing a first-rate job on the laundry. He had also learned a few new English words and phrases, one of which was "salari advanci." No matter how hard I tried to avoid him, I couldn't stay in the bedroom with the curtains drawn all the time. Whenever we encountered each other, he uttered the magic words and I gave him a few shillings for the doctor, the pharmacist, the whatever. By the end of the month, he'd received so much of his salary in advanci that he had almost nothing left to collect. That meant he was going to be stalking me until he got his next paycheck, a month from then. The only solution was to give him a raise.

Mesuli came. "Why did you do that?" he asked. Now Loto expected Mesuli, too, to give him a raise. I hadn't thought of that.

"He knows you are soft," said Mesuli. "That's why he comes to you. Next time he asks for money, send him to me."

❦

I began my campaign to get to the bottom of Thomas's food allergy, and he began his campaign to thwart me. From one of the other mothers who waited for the school bus every day I borrowed a book about homeopathic remedies. Under "food allergies," I read about how to ferret out the dietary culprit; the approach was far more radical than the Nairobi pediatrician's. Instead of starting out with a list of unsafe foods, you started with a list of safe ones. It was a very short list. On day one, you could have lamb, rice, soy, and peas. You were allowed to add one new food every three days; if the hives returned, you'd know that the most recently added food was the guilty one.

The first morning of the new regimen, I presented Thomas with his breakfast: a bowl of rice porridge with soy milk. Patrick always served him breakfast in bed, setting the bowl of sugar-frosted cornflakes on his nightstand. I followed the same routine. Thomas opened his eyes, raised himself up on one elbow, and stared at the bowl of porridge.

"What's this?"

"Cereal."

"Where's my cornflakes?"

"No cornflakes yet."

"Cornflakes are not on the list!" Here was clear proof of evil intent: Not only was I strictly adhering to the list of banned foods, I was adding to it.

"You have to eat this for a while. Try it. It's good."

He took a small taste and shoved the spoon back in the dish. "It's disgusting," he said, flopping back down. He glared at the ceiling.

When we left for the school bus a half hour later, the porridge was still cooling on his nightstand like a stiff, clammy cowpie. Round one ended in my solid defeat.

The next day I tried again, and the next, and the next, hoping to wear him down, but Thomas held strong. Meanwhile, I sent him to school with a packed lunch that I had prepared the night before, cooking lamb and peas and rice on the gas burner by candle-light. In the afternoon, I examined the lunch box like a forensics specialist, extracting candy wrappers and the crusts of his friends' sandwiches, which they had been sympathetic enough to share. The lamb had dis-appeared, the rice and peas had not. I switched back and forth between promises ("If you eat your porridge today, you can have cornflakes next week") and threats ("If you don't do as I say, we're going to end up on the bus to Nairobi again"). But Thomas held his ground.

Moses returned. "Your road is very bad," he accused, eyeing the mud on his white U.N. car. He told me that Jenni would come the following Monday. It seemed she had recovered. "That is very good news," I said.

Jenni arrived not on foot, as usual, but in Moses' car. She looked healthy and a bit plump. "Welcome back, Jenni," I said, giving her a hug.

She set right to work and did a thorough cleaning, starting with the mud that had been tracked in from outside. When all the rooms were clean and tidy, she picked a lily from the garden, found a glass vase in the pantry, and set the lily on the coffee table. Then she came to where I was working and knocked softly on the bedroom door, which was wide open. She had already been in and out of the bedroom several times without knocking. "Come in, Jenni," I said, pausing at my computer.

She took a few steps into the room, stopped, and cleared her throat, as if she had been rehearsing what she was about to say. "I have been to doc-tah," she said. "He say I must not work for some time. He say I must rest-i."

"Oh, Jenni, I'm sorry. I didn't know. You shouldn't have come today. Don't worry about us, we can manage. We'll be fine. Does the doctor say what the problem is?"

"Yes." Jenni paused, overcome with shyness. "He say, I going to hev beh-bi."

I walked her to the garden gate, where Moses was waiting in the shiny white Nissan. As we walked, I noticed she was carrying the small leather handbag that Patrick had brought her as a gift from New York; she was hardly more than a scrawny teenager when Patrick hired her. It had been well over a year since she and Moses got married; they had been anxiously waiting for this baby for many months.

"Well, Moses," I said, shaking his hand, "this is good news. I'm happy for you."

I gave Jenni a hug, and she climbed into the car. "Come at the end of the week," I told Moses. "To collect Jenni's pay."

And then Jenni left our house for the last time.

The rest of that lonely season is mostly a blur. I remember (with a shudder), running out of the house just before dawn in my nightgown, crazed because somebody was playing the radio. I rushed toward the noise, throwing open the garden gate and picking up a wooden bench outside the little shanty that sold kerosene and Coke at the end of the lane, then hurling the bench against the shanty wall and screaming at the man who emerged, ordering him to turn off the goddamn radio. The man, who turned out to be Mesuli's younger brother, quietly apologized; the radio went silent, and I, shaking, went back to bed.

I remember Thomas asking me for money to buy a leopard tortoise that some neighborhood children were tormenting and, a few days later, after the tortoise had escaped from our garden, being approached by a boy who wanted to sell it back to us. I remember Loto, coming up to me as I walked from the car to the house, blocking my path, and then, when I stopped to see what he wanted, reaching out his hand and, to my astonishment, lifting a single strand of hair from my face and smoothing it into place, leaving me to wonder what such a gesture could possibly mean. "Asante sana," I said, thanking him. "Karibu," he said: You're welcome. And I went into the house.

And I remember a stranger in a greasy blue jump suit opening the gate one afternoon and announcing, to my surprise, that Putschi had sent him to repair the Toyota. I hadn't seen Putschi or Penny since before Patrick left, but no doubt my troubles were much talked about in the neighborhood. The stranger lifted the hood of the Toyota, which was parked in the drive next to the bougainvillea, shiny clean and useless, and looked inside. Curious neighbors gathered at the gate and Loto hovered, jealously keeping an eye on the precious source of so much of his income while the stranger tinkered with her innards. After a few minutes the stranger nodded and I tried the ignition; the Toyota came to life. I thanked the stranger profusely and asked him his name. "Saidi," he said—the Swahili word for "help." My helper smiled, and when I offered him some of my few remaining shillings, he shook his head.

It was Mesuli's eldest daughter, Beatrice, who came to introduce the new housegirl. "This is Esther," she said. Esther, wearing a pretty flowered skirt and clean shoes despite the muddy road, smiled and offered her hand. "She doesn't speak English," said Beatrice.

"No," said Esther, apologizing.

"That's okay," I reassured her. "Hamna shida."

We went through the house together, and I explained what needed to be done; Beatrice translated. The next morning, Esther arrived in another pretty dress and took charge. She tiptoed around the house in her bare feet, cleaning, dusting, sweeping, straightening. The quiet sound of her dust cloth and broom, the clink of the dishes in the sink, the sozzle of the laundry bucket, were familiar and comforting. It was almost as if Jenni was back.

At the end of the course of prednisone prescribed by the evil Nairobi doctor, Dr. No Fanta, I went on red alert, watching for signs of another attack. But despite all the banned foods that were finding their way into Thomas's digestive tract, he remained spot-free. It was as if he had willed away the hives, as he had willed away all evil—the evil porridge, which had morphed into cornflakes, the evil soy milk, which had morphed into good old Parmalait. The spell that had turned me into such a monster had been broken, though I remained vulnerable. "Sara," he assured me repeatedly, "you don't have to worry. I don't have hives anymore."

The money transfer arrived, and soon after, an email from Patrick: Come to Togo. He had already met with the director of the school in Lomé—they were holding a spot for Thomas—but he wanted me to see where we'd be living before he signed a long-term contract. He told me to bring Thomas when St. George's Christmas break began. It fell to me to explain about the boarding school.

"You would stay there during the week," I told Thomas. We were sitting together on the living room couch, where we'd been catching up on our reading of *Harry Potter and the Sorcerer's Stone*, which had been slowed by the power outages.

Harry went to a boarding school.

"You'd share a room with another boy your age, and eat all your meals with your friends. Then, on Friday afternoon, you could come by car to Fazao and stay with us."

"How far is it?"

"From Lomé to Fazao? About four hours."

In other words, an eternity. Thomas was silent.

"Or you can stay at school with your friends."

168

Thomas fidgeted with the book, open on his lap to chapter eleven.

"Maybe *you* could come visit *me* sometimes."

"Of course."

"Look," he said, pointing to an illustration, "that's Harry on his broomstick." He handed me the book. "Your turn. You read."

"What do you think of this idea?"

"What idea?"

"Moving to Togo, going to school there, all the stuff we've been talking about."

He shrugged. "It's okay I guess."

A few days later, Mesuli arrived in the early morning to drive Thomas and me to the bus stop. We were to spend the night at a hotel in Nairobi before boarding the flight to Togo. Standing in the Novotel parking lot, I dug in my pocket and fished out a wad of bills.

"These are the salaries for everybody," I told Mesuli. I handed him the entire wad—no need to explain who got how much since it was he who had done the hiring. "You'll pay them at the end of the month?"

"Hamna shida," said Mesuli. "Don't worry, Sara. I'll look after the house. I'll look after everything."

The two cars were at a friend's house for safekeeping. With no cars to wash and the vegetable plot in ruins, there would be little for Loto to do while we were away; he could blast rasta tunes from the garden shed as much as he wanted. Esther would come once in a while to check on the house, taking the key from its secret hiding place under the plant pot. Our neighbors would know we were away, of course, making the property vulnerable to burglars. There was little of value for them to steal, but I feared for the askari, the nameless askari, wrapped in his blanket under the porch roof each night, guarding an empty house.

A West African highland village.

Chapter Ten

In 1960, the year Patrick turned sixteen, Britain's prime minister Harold Macmillan addressed the South Africa Parliament on a tour of African commonwealth states: "The wind of change is blowing through this continent," Macmillan said, "and whether we like it or not, this growth of national consciousness is a political fact." The greatest issue of the twentieth century, the prime minister went on to say, would be which side of the cold war the newly independent African states would support, and whether these new alliances would "imperil the delicate balance between East and West on which the peace of the world depends." For the remainder of the twentieth century, the continent would be a bloody cold war battleground. Patrick stepped off the plane in Douala in what would become known as "the Decade of the Coup."

In 1967, he was in a Douala bar called the Hayman when a stranger approached him. Early forties, tall, thin, gray mustache, well-dressed, French. He introduced himself: David Tournier. Later Patrick discovered it was one of several aliases.

The stranger knew where and when Patrick was born, who his parents were, where he had been to school. He knew about his military training. He knew about his recent marriage, and the identity of his current employer. His information was almost 100 percent accurate.

David Tournier, who had presented himself as a health-care specialist in charge of setting up bush hospitals, turned out to be a high-ranking officer in the French army, a coordinator of military intelligence. He and Patrick met several times over the next few days. Over cheap beer in an African bar that was quieter than the Hayman and more discreet, David explained that he needed someone who could relay messages to French officers in remote areas. So, first off, this person had to be someone who wouldn't get lost. Then, this person had to be someone who wouldn't die of thirst or starvation, alone in the wilderness, if the unit he was looking for wasn't where it was supposed to be. He had to be willing to risk getting shot at, or captured, by guerrillas. And he had to be willing to travel.

Patrick was twenty-three, newly married, about to be a father. He had a good job with the French airline UTA, in PR. David wasn't offering him any money; the incentive was presumed to be something intangible. A sense of patriotic duty, perhaps. Or just the possibility of excitement.

"Okay," Patrick said. "What do you want me to do?"

For his training, he was assigned to a mentor—a massive six-footer with a cue-ball head and the Samothrace Victory tattooed on his back. Richard was fortyish, a former army intelligence officer who had spent his entire career in the field: Indochina, Korea, Vietnam, Algeria. His cover, like David's, was to look for possible sites for bush hospitals to be run by French doctors. Conducting this research necessitated extensive tours through rural areas, during which he casually questioned the locals to find out who had passed through recently, what business they had been on, and so forth.

Patrick accompanied Richard on half a dozen of these intelligence-gathering missions, some of which lasted more than a week. They drove, in Richard's car, to the western highlands, the arid northern country, the lowland forests of the southeast. David arranged things with UTA so that Patrick's absences from home could be explained as business trips. UTA continued to pay him his regular salary while allowing him the necessary time off.

In the hills of western Cameroon, he and Richard discovered a German fort, four hours by foot from the nearest road. The villagers who lived nearby hadn't seen whites since the German colonialists left in 1918; at the sudden appearance of these two Europeans, the old schoolmaster lined up the children to sing "Das Lied der Deutschen."

He saw some stunning landscapes, in parts of the country where he'd never been before. The ones he described to me were like secret worlds: a small pepper farm on the floor of a steep-walled canyon that was "like a paradise" with a lazy river running through it; a sea cliff with a cavelike opening through which a canoe could pass, twisting through the rock tunnel and emerging in a natural amphitheater inhabited by many kinds of colorful birds; an island that looked like a big rock in the sea until, flying over it in a helicopter, he saw that it was actually a volcanic crater with a lake at its center, on the shore of which was an African village.

For two months, Richard taught his young protégé what to look for in the bush, how to question the local people, all the basics of his new line of work. At the end, he delivered Patrick back into David's hands with a good report.

His first assignment was to deliver a parcel to a renegade band of mercenaries who had run amok in the eastern Congo. The Congo had been a bloody cold war battleground since 1960 when, as a fragile, newly independent state, it became suddenly vulnerable to a slew of foreign interests that swarmed over it, fighting each other for control of its vast resources and threatening to carve up the republic into fiefdoms. In the south, they fought over copper, cobalt, and uranium; in the east, gold. The country descended into chaos and madness as first the southern and then the eastern provinces threatened to secede.

The trouble in the east was ignited by the assassination in 1961 of Patrice Lumumba, the first democratically elected president of the country. The coup was followed by an uprising of Lumumba partisans, known as the Simba Rebellion. The Simbas, many of them armed with bows and spears, took over the eastern provincial capital of Stanleyville and named it the seat of a provisional government. They did so without a fight: The Congolese army, convinced that the Simbas had been rendered impervious to bullets by powerful witchdoctors, fled in terror at their approach. Army chief Joseph Mobutu called for help, of which there was no shortage, so eager were outsiders to get in on the action.

Commando units of Kantangan soldiers headed by white mercenaries from France, Belgium, and South Africa moved into the eastern provinces of Kivu and Orientale. The CIA backed them up with air power, supplying WWII fighter planes flown by anti-Castro Cuban pilots. A few small commando units and a handful of old planes was all it took to wreak havoc with the Simbas, even after the Soviet Union and its

African allies began supplying them with modern weapons.

By 1967, the rebellion in the east was over, and the mercenaries who had suppressed it were no longer needed. The government ordered them to leave. With vast stretches of valuable territory under their control, however, the mercenaries refused. So the CIA ordered its Cuban pilots to bomb them.

Patrick's role in all this would be to deliver a shoebox-sized package containing money and written instructions to Commando 6, which was camped in the bush near Bukavu, just west of the Rwandan border.

One morning instead of going to the office, he kissed Huguette good-bye, drove to the airport, boarded an Air Afrique DC4, and flew from Douala to Libreville, in neighboring Gabon, to meet David for two days of mission-specific training. It wasn't until he arrived at the French army base outside Libreville that he discovered the training included a brush-up course in parachuting. Jumping out of planes had been a mandatory part of his army pilot training, but he had never gotten used to it. The very idea of falling through the air from a great height made him weak with terror.

Five times he jumped, each time more scared. Twice the instructor had to throw him from the plane; after that, he managed on his own. Four of his landings missed the helicopter pad by a considerable distance. The fifth was a direct hit, which he attributed to sheer luck. After that, the instructor said, "You're okay." He was flown back to Douala to await further instructions.

A couple of weeks later, he went back to Libreville. When he arrived at the base, at midday, David was waiting for him. David handed him a parcel the size of a shoebox, wrapped in oilcloth, and gave him his instructions: He would be dropped in a field near the main road to Bukavu. He was to make his way, on foot, toward the lake region just east of the drop zone. He would be looking for a commando unit of about one hundred soldiers, French and Africans. He was to deliver the package to their commandant. Then he was to continue on to Kigali, in Rwanda, where the pilot would be waiting for him.

David had Patrick repeat his orders twice to make sure they were set in his mind, then he told him to get some rest. He would be summoned for dinner, by which time he should have all his gear in order, as the plane was to leave soon after.

It was then that Patrick realized he was about to do a night jump.

"I've never done that before," he said.

"Don't worry," said David, who himself was an enthusiastic jumper. "There's always a first time."

The plane was an old two-engine used for military transport; during the four-hour flight he dozed a bit. When he awoke, the jumpmaster was checking his chute—black, he noticed with a sinking feeling, to avoid detection in the night sky. Just before they reached the jump zone, at around 2 A.M., the pilot stepped out of the cockpit.

"When I tell you to jump," he said, "you jump. I'm not going to circle back. I've barely enough fuel to make it to Kigali, and I can't do this twice."

They opened the door. The jumpmaster said go.

It was a cloudy, moonless night. Patrick plunged through the darkness, tense as a bowstring. He had an altimeter with an illuminated dial to tell him when he was about to land. He never looked at it. He had no idea where he was in the sky.

Somehow he managed to make his fingers work enough to release the rope that tied his rucksack and the dismantled crossbow to his waist; they fell away, then caught with a jolt so that they dangled below him. The rope was about five or six meters in length. The idea was that the impact of the rucksack would warn him a split-second before he hit the ground, giving him just enough time to pull himself into a tuck.

He drifted down through the darkness and the stillness, no clue what sort of terrain he was headed for, or what would eventually break his fall—water, rock, tree, turf.

Some three minutes after he left the plane, there was a crackling below him as the rucksack struck something. He felt leaves whipping past. Then his harness gave a violent jerk, and he stopped falling.

He stayed like that, suspended in midair, feet dangling, for the rest of the night. Shortly after six, the sky lightened enough so that he could finally see the ground. It was less than three feet below him.

Miraculously, he was unharmed. His only injuries were a few small scratches, not even serious enough to require a bandage. He peered upward, straining to see in the faint light, and made out the silhouette of the crossbow, solidly lodged among the branches. The chute was tangled in the upper branches. It took him a couple of hours to get everything down out of the tree and to bury his chute.

Thick forest lay before him in every direction. The road he was supposed to follow was to the east, so he walked toward the rising sun.

ॐ

Patrick knew next to nothing about the tangled political drama that was being played out in the Congo at the time, nor did he give it much thought. Who could hope to follow such madness? Politics was for others to worry about. His instructions came from the French military, and that was good enough for him.

His little package was addressed to a French soldier of fortune by the name of Bob Denard. When Patrick found Commando 6, Denard's unit, some thirty hours after disentangling himself and his chute from the tree, they were camped about two kilometers from the main road south of Bukavu. He heard them well before he saw them—men shouting, engines revving. Cautiously, he went closer, stuffed his rucksack and crossbow in the bushes, and climbed a tree.

Through the leaves, he could see a little of the camp's interior, and several men guarding the perimeter. There were three or four jeeps, two of them mounted with machine guns, and two or three trucks. From the number of white soldiers, he knew it was the unit he was looking for.

The sun slipped toward the horizon and the thrumming of cicadas died down; a late-afternoon hush settled over the bush. Then, as the night sounds of the bush started up and the lanterns in the camp were lit, he dropped to the ground.

Leaving his rucksack in its hiding place, he started working toward the camp on his belly, just as Fetnat had taught him to approach wild game a few years earlier. From the tree, he had picked out the two guards he would sneak past. The first was a black soldier; the second, a bearded and long-haired white man who was alternately smoking and dozing with his back against a tree, legs sprawled.

It took him nearly two hours to pass the first sentry. Approaching the second, the crackling of twigs obliterated by the rustling breeze and the thrumming of insects, he saw that the man's gun was on the ground. It was a Mat-49, French issue—he knew how to use it from the army. He could have grabbed it easily, but he was afraid the guy would shout. Instead, he put his knife to the sentry's throat and whispered, "Keep quiet and don't move."

The sentry did as he was told.

"I'm a friend. I have a package for the boss. He's expecting me. I need you to take me to him: I don't want to get shot by mistake."

The guard nodded, and the two walked slowly toward the camp, the guard leading the way, Patrick following with the Mat-49. He could feel the eyes of the soldiers on them, and the tension in the air.

From a tent emerged a tall, gray-haired Frenchman with a gray brush mustache and a slight limp: Denard. He regarded Patrick suspiciously.

"What do you want?"

Patrick held out the parcel; Denard took it and disappeared into the tent for a few minutes. When he reemerged, he asked Patrick how he had found his way to the camp.

"I just followed the noise."

Denard looked displeased. "And how did you get past the sentries?"

"On my belly. It wasn't that hard. Several looked drunk; one was sleeping."

"And this one?" Denard indicated the guard he had jumped.

"I asked him to bring me to you and he did. He didn't have much choice — I had his gun."

Denard motioned for the guard to approach. When the man was standing directly in front of him, Denard clocked him once, in the jaw, knocking him out cold. Two soldiers carried him away.

Patrick spent a nervous night in the camp. Early the next morning, the troops packed up their tents and equipment and loaded it onto the trucks. The men were sullen and edgy, and even the simple routine of breaking camp led to arguments. Everybody, which is to say nobody, seemed to be in charge, and the work was sloppy and disorganized.

Patrick couldn't get away from Commando 6 fast enough, but as he prepared to head out alone while the men finished packing up, Denard stopped him. "You'll come with us to Bukavu," he said. "You can go on to Kigali from there."

As the convoy rolled along the main road, making very slow progress, Patrick grew increasingly anxious. He could go twice as fast alone, and an undisciplined unit of combat soldiers on a march through hostile country was the last sort of company he wanted to keep, so after a few miles, he made a hard right and walked off into the bush. The next day, he crossed the Rusizi River south of Bukavu, met the pilot in Kigali, and flew home.

Commando 6 went on to Bukavu and took the town with the help of other commando troopers. The troops then went north to Kisangani, where they encountered government forces. Denard's men suffered heavy casualties; Denard himself was wounded in the head. Thirty Commando 6 troopers were executed; others, Denard included, fled to Rhodesia on hijacked C-47s. The mercenaries' rebellion ended shortly thereafter, when the last of the mutineers surrendered at Bukavu.

Denard would soon resurface in Angola and go on to have a long career as one of the world's most notorious mercenary soldiers.

Patrick went home to his wife and baby and his job with UTA.

From that time on, Patrick led a secret life that Huguette knew nothing about, much of it government classified. Nobody outside the secret service and the organizations it did business with knew about his night jump into the eastern Congo, nor any of the other missions that followed, roughly a dozen in all. That was the rule—tell no one.

It was easy enough to camouflage his absences from home as marketing trips for UTA. That the airline allowed an employee to moonlight for the government on its dime gives a small idea of the influence of the secret service under De Gaulle. The Service de Documentation et Contre Espionage (SDECE), a branch of the military, exerted its influence all over West and Central Africa in the latter half of the century, becoming a tool for maintaining control over France's former colonies and their treasure troves of natural resources, particularly oil. Working hand in hand with the state-owned oil company Elf Aquitaine, it squeezed as much oil as possible, using whatever means necessary, out of petroleum-rich and cash-poor African nations.

The Nigerian civil war began with ethnic strife. Nigeria was a federation of three regions dominated by three different ethnic groups, all scrambling for the upper hand in the new republic: the Yoruba in the west, the Hausa-Fulani in the north, and the Ibo in the east. In January 1966, six years after independence, the government was overthrown in a military coup instigated by a group of Ibo army officers. Ministers who survived the coup appointed a new president: Major-General Johnson Aguiyi-Ironsi, an Ibo. Ethnic tension mounted until, in September, people went berserk. Thirty thousand Ibo living in the north were massacred by their Hausa neighbors in a wave of spontaneous violence. A million terrified survivors of the attacks fled to the Ibo's traditional homeland in the east. The region, known as Biafra, announced that it was severing its ties with Nigeria. The world took notice, because Biafra had the lion's share of Nigeria's oil.

The Nigerian army attacked the outlaw state. Other countries rushed to take sides. The United Kingdom and the Soviet Union allied themselves with the Nigerian government, France with the rebel state. Everyone was gambling on the war's outcome: When the dust had settled and the troops had gone home, who would control the oil?

A few weeks after his return from the Congo, in the waning months of 1968, Patrick flew back to Libreville. The airport was a hive of secret-service activity—the Gabonese president, Omar Bongo, was a friend of the French, to whom he owed his job, the result of a 1967 French-sponsored coup. Every evening just before sundown, planes loaded with wooden crates labeled "army rations" would begin lifting off from the airport runway. The planes were unmarked DC4s; the crates contained food, medicine, and guns. The pilots were both military and civilian, a mix of characters—some were mercenaries who had recently been flying over the Congo, others were veterans of Algeria's war of independence, still others were "bus drivers" for Air France.

Each night, two or three planes would leave the runway and head north, flying between the Cameroonian mountains and the island of Fernando Po to avoid radar detection. They would come in low over

Nigerian airspace—or sometimes high, dropping down at the last minute—and land some ten minutes apart at Uli airport, in the newly declared People's Republic of Biafra. The so-called airport—an airstrip lit by car headlights, its air-traffic controller a guy with a radio—was landing dozens of planes every night, most of them loaded with food from aid organizations, and traffic was increasing as smaller airstrips in Biafra were shut down by advancing Nigerian troops. Getting in and out was hairy, not so much because of antiaircraft fire as the danger of colliding with another plane.

The Nigerian army was held back from Uli by the Niger river, but some of its shells landed close enough to warrant extreme caution. The pilots didn't take any chances; the cargo hatch was opened even before the plane touched down, and the crates were unloaded as the aircraft was moving. The plane made a swift U turn at the far end of the runway—and usually another U turn at the opposite end, depending on the velocity of the wind—and took off again, without ever coming to a halt.

Patrick's job was to help unload the cargo, some ten tons of it, shoving the crates through the hatch with two or three other guys, bailing as fast as they could while rockets lit up the western skyline.

As the fighting continued—through 1968, '69—so did the airlift. Even so, Biafran men, women, and children were dying by the hundreds of thousands, most of them from starvation. Photographs of hollow-eyed children stirred pity around the world, and food poured in. So did guns, most of them from France, which had signed the international arms embargo against the warring parties and was thus obliged to keep its weapons contributions a dark secret.

After half a dozen weekend flights to Nigeria, Patrick accepted a job from David that was both more lucrative and more dangerous. It would mean going back into the war zone, but this time he would be on the ground. He was to be paid with oil money, its source the various drilling companies whose equipment was stranded in the war zone. It would be Patrick's job to retrieve it.

He and Huguette moved to Lagos; David arranged for him to work with a French travel agency under the same sort of agreement he'd had with UTA. Every couple of weeks he would receive a call from the Lagos headquarters of Elf Aquitaine: The oil company was coordinating the salvage operation. A De Gaulle creation, brand-new in those days, Elf was the French government's main source of intelligence in Africa, its director a former secret-services big shot.

The caller would tell Patrick where in the oilfields to go and when, and what to bring back. Before he left Lagos, he would stop by the Elf office, where he was given a sealed package and a code (something like "Are you John from Port Harcourt?") with which to identify its intended recipient, an African who would meet him at the drilling site.

Patrick made half a dozen trips into the war zone from Lagos, driving a fifty-ton armored truck with bulletproof tires, paid for with a loan from Elf. In a pocket of his trousers was a handgun; in the cooler that held his food were several grenades. He drove as fast as he could, the quicker to get in and out. Each trip took two days; he slept a bit in his truck and smoked cigar-sized joints to keep himself going, feeding tapes into the truck's cassette player: Deep Purple, Santana Abraxas, the Who, sixties psychedelic rock. As the weeks went by, his hair grew down to his shoulders—he wore it in two ponytails that looped out over his ears, and waxed his handlebar mustache until it stuck out so far you could see it from behind.

The checkpoints were his only real problem. He dreaded them. Stories of drivers being held up and robbed, even murdered, circulated in Lagos. Each time he approached a blockade his heart began to pound in his chest. It was often impossible to discern whether the guards were federal troops, Biafran soldiers, or bandits. Not that it made much difference: They were all nervous and trigger-happy. He rarely stopped to find out who they were. Instead, he approached each checkpoint at a modest pace and then floored it, ramming his way through the thin wooden barricades as Nigerians leaped right and left.

One day as he was approaching the battle zone, he came to a blockade that was constructed with oil drums. He slowed, studying the situation from a little distance. The drums were a worry—sometimes they were filled with concrete. He drove slowly up to the barricade and stopped.

A man approached the cab, weaving slightly, pistol held casually by his side, and leaned in close to the window. His breath stank of alcohol. "The road is closed," he said.

"I have permission from the army," Patrick replied. He reached into the left pocket of his vest and pulled out an army-issued pass, authorizing him to enter the area. In his right pocket was a pass issued by the Biafran side. Often the choice of pass was a gamble, but this man was clearly an officer, a captain in the Nigerian army.

The captain squinted at the pass. "Not today," he said. "We are turning back all vehicles."

"This pass is from army headquarters in Lagos."

"You must have approval from the local headquarters." He wasn't aggressive, merely stubborn.

"Where is the local headquarters?"

"That way." The captain waved the gun vaguely in the direction Patrick was headed.

"How far?"

"One mile, then you turn off the main road and go another twenty miles. I'll show you. We'll go together."

Patrick sighed—the detour would cost him a full day.

"All right," he said. "Get in."

Pistol still in hand, the captain climbed into the cab. His two subordinates rolled the drums aside—they were empty—and the truck passed through the checkpoint. Within five minutes, the captain was slouched in his seat, eyes shut, mouth open. Keeping one hand on the wheel, Patrick reached over with the other and plucked the gun from the captain's lap. Then he stopped the truck.

The captain opened his eyes.

"Get out."

A blank stare.

"Go on. Fuck off."

The captain opened the door, rolled to the side, and half-fell out of the truck.

Patrick put the truck in gear, drove a few hundred meters, and stopped. In the rear-view mirror, he could see the captain waving his arms, his shouts barely audible above the din of the truck's engine. Taking the gun, Patrick removed the bullets from the magazine and threw them out the window to his left. He threw the magazine and the pistol through the opposite window. Then he continued on his way.

With every assignment, his fear of the checkpoints escalated, and when some unidentified assailants opened fire on him from a hill overlooking a barricade, he was ready. They launched the first mortar before he was within range; it struck the road some fifty meters ahead of him. He hit the brakes. The next few hits were closer. Then one struck the bulldozer that was loaded on the back of his truck. He reached for the picnic cooler.

He attached the two hand grenades to his vest, eased open the cab door just enough to squeeze through it, and slipped into the tall grass. Slowly, he worked his way around to the far side of the hill and began climbing as mortar fire rained down on the truck and the dozer.

The attackers were in a small depression with their backs to him. From their clothing, he couldn't tell who they were; they didn't appear to be uniformed soldiers. He stood and lobbed the grenades. There was a double explosion, and the mortar fire abruptly stopped. In the silence, he walked back to the truck and drove away.

৵

Patrick's final mission for David began in the waning days of August 1973, in the Bolivian capital of La Paz. It ended on September 11 in the Chilean capital of Santiago. He was a military observer this time, assigned to follow troop movements. The troops were Chilean army soldiers under the command of General Augusto Pinochet.

His briefing, as usual, had missed a few points. For instance, it wasn't until after Patrick met his contact in Bolivia that he realized he was supposed to walk to Chile. In between were the Andes. He crossed them on foot, wearing a thin pair of moccasins, in four days, chewing coca leaves, miserable from the cold and the altitude, telling himself whatever awaited him in Chile couldn't possibly be worse than this. A few days later, he was in Santiago, surrounded by machine-gun fire; planes were dropping bombs on La Moneda, and the roof was in flames. The officer he was with handed him an automatic rifle that he barely knew how to use, said, "Stay close," and dashed through a palace entrance, up a broad stairway, then down a long corridor, past blasted walls and the bodies of several guards.

In the palace he saw a body that he later identified to David, in his debriefing, as Allende's. The corpse was on the floor in a room where there were soldiers. Patrick was in the room for less than a minute before someone told him to leave. A Chilean officer debriefed him before he left the country.

"What did you see in the palace?" the officer asked.

"Nothing," said Patrick. "I was there a few seconds, that's all. Everything is a blur."

"You know that the president committed suicide," the officer said — it was not a question.

"Yes — that is, I have heard the reports. I wouldn't know anything about that myself."

The official report was that Allende had shot himself with a gun given to him by Fidel Castro, blowing his head apart. The family wasn't allowed to see the body, nor was anyone who might have contradicted the report. The body Patrick had identified as the president's, however, was intact, and he recognized the face from newspaper photos. The purported suicide weapon was nowhere in sight. This is what he told David.

Years later, he was less sure of what he had seen. When I asked him for details, he couldn't give any: He had long since forgotten the way the room looked, the number of people in it, the name of the officer whom he had been trailing, what the president—if that's who he was—was wearing, and so on.

I myself recalled little about the fall of Allende. "What were the French doing in Chile?" I asked.

"Nothing. I was sent as an observer. They wanted me to report what was going on, that's all."

"Well, what did they think was going on?"

He shrugged. "A coup."

"The French knew there was going to be a coup? Weeks before it happened? Are you sure?"

"Sure I'm sure. That's what I was told."

"Were the French backing Pinochet?"

"He didn't need the backing of the French; he had the backing of the CIA. The French weren't involved. But we knew what was going on."

Whether Allende shot himself or was murdered, the role of the CIA, these were unanswerable questions. Whatever happened in Chile, it left him drained—the trek through the mountains, the firestorm in Santiago, the scene at La Moneda, the whole Chilean experience. He was tired of the senselessness and the brutality of war, and he had a feeling that if he didn't quit he might soon be dead. So after Chile, he retired from the business, telling David, I've had enough. I can't do this anymore.

❧

Patrick was married with two small children when he finally saw the Gabonese rain forest, and instead of working in a timber camp he was an assistant manager in the spare parts division of a company that sold bulldozers. As a sideline, he purchased a mining concession and began looking for gold. The mine was in the forest, miles from his home in the capital city of

Libreville, and he loved it. He loved the mechanics of setting up the mine, and he loved anticipating what it would feel like when he and his partner finally struck a rich vein of ore.

Only there was no rich vein of ore. Almost every sample the two novice prospectors had taken before buying the concession had contained gold, but once the concession was theirs, it stubbornly refused to produce. Instead, it gobbled up money, demanding a steady stream of cheap labor and expensive equipment. There was the truck, for instance, which, due to arrive from Libreville on a certain day, failed to show. Patrick went back and forth along its supposed route several times, expecting to find it stranded on the side of the road with a flat tire or a seized-up engine. Nothing. Then he had a thought. He stopped looking for the truck and began looking for the driver instead.

The driver was at his house. He claimed to know nothing about the missing truck. Patrick pointed out that the man had been driving the truck when it was last seen. Little by little, they progressed to the point where the driver admitted he might possibly know where the truck was. Patrick asked the driver to take him there.

The truck was deep in the bush, several yards from the road, with its wheels mired in the mud and its nose wedged in the underbrush. Patrick studied the scene for a few minutes, then turned to the driver, who was lagging behind by several paces. How did this happen?, he asked.

"It is not my fault, sir," said the driver, his apologetic expression suggesting otherwise. "It is the fault of the mango."

The mango, he explained, was the one he had been eating, or trying to eat, as he hastened toward his destination. The mischievous fruit leaped out of his hands, dodged between his knees, dropped to the floor of the truck, and rolled out of reach. The driver lunged for it, and that's when the truck, disturbed by all the activity going on inside it, decided to leave the road.

After many episodes of this sort, the mine closed, a bust. For a while, Patrick occupied himself with his job in spare parts. Then one day, while Huguette and the two children were on a summer holiday in France, he packed up his kit, got in his truck, and headed for northern Gabon.

The Bee Forest is a dense, tropical rain forest that covers some ten thousand square miles in northern Gabon; when Patrick saw it, there were neither roads nor maps. It was an almost mystical place, inhabited by Pygmies and forest gorillas. There had long been rumors of gold.

In a small village on the forest periphery, Patrick inquired about a guide. The chief of the village presented Mamadou. Leaving his car in the care of the chief, he set off on foot at sunrise with Mamadou leading the way. By noon, they were completely lost. Mamadou, Patrick now discovered, had never been more than a half-day's walk from the village. The forest terrified him with its unfriendly beasts and evil spirits. At least he made a pretty good porter.

Patrick took the lead. For the next three weeks, he cajoled, coaxed, pleaded, bribed and threatened Mamadou to keep him moving forward. They spent several days with a group of Pygmies, who insisted they sleep indoors; Patrick spent half the night in a small hut made of leaves, crowded among a family of four, his legs sticking out the door, before suspending his hammock near a smoking fire in the hope of warding off mosquitoes. He met a wild gorilla for the first time, a huge male silverback, who came lumbering out of the bush with a sudden whirl and whoosh of the leafy underbrush. "Sit down, shut up, and don't move," Patrick instructed Mamadou. "And don't look at him." They crouched in the middle of the clearing, trying to make themselves small and unworthy of a gorilla's attention. The gorilla knuckled its way toward them and crouched next to Patrick, its enormous head inches away, puffing hot, sweet gorilla breath into his ear. Then it turned and, with a dismissive grunt, scooted into the bush.

The bag of soil samples that Patrick brought home revealed no trace of gold whatsoever. Which was just as well, since his recordkeeping was hopeless. He had practically no idea where any single sample had come from. Whether he found gold or not didn't matter; it was enough just to look for it. What he found, instead, was the jungle of his childhood dreams, a paradise where you didn't have to wear clothes.

What he couldn't explain to Maurice, or to anyone else, was that the gold was unimportant, a mere pretext on which to strike out. Any reason was a good one, as far as he was concerned. Perhaps it was the same with the shoebox wrapped in cellotape, and even the stuff he dragged back from the Nigerian oil fields. Everything was an excuse, a reason to go, the nudge that set him in motion. At the end of the journey there were some parts that made better telling than others, but it was the long stretches when nothing remarkable happened that he went for. How do you explain that you risked everything—your life, your limbs, your sanity—for a chance just to walk through the dusky forest or drive toward the place where the blue sky touches the land.

Patrick on an anti-poaching patrol.

Chapter Eleven

At the airport in Lomé, Thomas and I were greeted as
VIPs, whisked past passport control and into Patrick's
arms with an assist from a dark-suited stranger. "Bonjour, Madame Texier," Patrick said, enveloping the
two of us in a bear hug. "*Ça va, mon grand?*" Normally
shy about public demonstrations of affection, he
kissed me on the lips, in full view of everyone, our reunion made all the more joyful by the awfulness of the
separation.

"This is Monsieur Gaumieau," Patrick said, indicating the man in the suit, our benefactor. It was a
nod from him that had prompted airport officials to
usher us to the head of the queue. "He is in charge of
forestry and national parks." Monsieur Gaumieau
smiled politely and extended a bony hand. "He wishes
to welcome you to Togo and hopes you will let him
know if there is anything you need and all that stuff."

His excellency, I couldn't help but observe, looked
awfully thin for a high-level bureaucrat, but then,
Togo itself was awfully thin, a long sliver of land that
extended inland from the merest scrap of coastline.
Indeed, studying an online map at Max's Patisserie
and Cyber Café, I had estimated that an able-bodied
person might cross the entire country on foot between
sunrise and sunset, especially if one started out with a

hearty breakfast and a good pair of shoes. It was hard to see how such a skinny little country could contain enough wealth to fatten up even a few of its luckiest citizens. No wonder the minister was wispy.

"Give me your passports," Patrick said. I handed them over, and he presented them to Monsieur Gaumieau, who walked off with them. "He's going to get them stamped."

At a circular plastic table in the airport bar, we ordered two gin-and-tonics and a Fanta Orange to celebrate our arrival. Thomas plunged a straw into the Fanta Orange and happily inhaled his first orange soda in weeks.

"Next time you go away for three months," I said to Patrick, hoping the lightness of my tone conveyed something of the valor with which I'd carried on in his absence, "we're coming with you."

Monsieur Gaumieau joined us and ordered a 7-Up. He was eager to hear my impression of his country. What did I think of Togo so far?

At Max's Patisserie and Cyber Café, between sending and receiving email, I had done a tiny bit of reading about Togo—a place I had never even heard of until recently—on various Web sites. I knew that it was about twice the size of Maryland, and that it had been successively colonized by the Danes, the Germans, and the French. Togo, I read, had distinguished itself early on in Africa's postcolonial history by becoming the first newly independent country to experience a coup d'etat—an event widely copied throughout the continent. Its first democratically elected president was shot and killed by a Sergeant Etienne Eyadema in 1963 as the head of state tried to scale a wall of the American embassy in an effort to gain asylum. After this incident, Sergeant Eyadema was promoted to the rank of lieutenant-colonel, in which role he led another successful coup in 1967. He appointed himself president, suspended the constitution, and disbanded all political parties except his own. He also made himself a general and changed his name from Etienne to Gnassingbè. He had been president ever since, for thirty-three years and counting, a record among African rulers, topping Gabon's President Bongo by ten months. I knew that in the first multiparty presidential election since the last coup, held in 1963 and widely considered fraudulent, Eyadema had won 96 percent of the vote. I knew that after that, the European Union blacklisted Togo, cutting off economic aid. And that Eyadema's 1998 reelection provoked violent protests in the streets. I also knew that while there were thirty-seven different ethnic tribes in Togo, all the ministries, including the one that oversaw the national parks, were headed by members of Eyadema's tribe, the Kabye. My own observations, however, were slight, since I hadn't yet left the airport. From the plane, the most distinguishing feature of this part of the continent had been a thick layer of brown smog that stretched as far as the eye could see.

"That's the Harmattan," said Patrick. "The wind that blows this time of year."

At the word *Harmattan*, Monsieur Gaumieau's face brightened and he said a few words to Patrick, who translated.

"He says the Harmattan brings dust all the way from the Sahara, thousands of miles — a huge cloud of dust. It covers all of West Africa for months."

This startling information was punctuated by a loud slurp as Thomas sucked the last of his Fanta Orange up through his straw. I thought I had heard all about West Africa's remarkable climate, with its mon-

soons and 200 percent humidity and plagues of lo-
custs, but this was something new.

Patrick, ordinarily meticulous about table manners, ignored the slurp, too happy to care, even in the
company of a dignitary. Everything was falling into
place. He had a job he liked, with a respectable salary,
and free lodging in the park's hotel, and free meals in
the hotel's restaurant, and a car and a driver. And a
motorbike. And a swimming pool, not that he ever
swims, but Thomas and I do. Best of all, this great
good fortune had brought him back to the part of the
world he loved most, to West Africa, home of the
world-famous Harmattan.

"What about our passports?" I reminded Patrick
as we thanked Monsieur Gaumieau for his assistance
and rose to leave—the documents were still in the
minister's possession.

"He's going to keep them," Patrick explained, "so
that he can get us extended visas."

The arrangements would all be taken care of by
the middle of January, a month hence, he assured me;
that's when we were due to return to Arusha just long
enough to pack up our things for the big move.

At the open-air reception desk of the Hôtel de
Fazao, our soon-to-be new home, we were greeted by
a committee headed by Antoine, the bright-eyed
young Togolese front-desk attendant. Arranged behind him were the bartender, the headwaiter, the cook
and his helper, and a sultry young woman who turned
out to be the cocktail waitress. Hovering in the background was a twitchy little man in coveralls—the
bellhop.

Antoine stepped forward and nodded courteously.
"Bonjour, mon directeur," he said to Patrick and "Bienve-
nue," to me. Then he added a bit stiffly, as if he'd been

practicing, "Welcome, madam." He motioned to Gaspard, the bellhop, to take our bags.

Little Gaspard, shoulders hunched, lurching slightly from side to side under the weight of our two duffels, marched off down a concrete walkway at an energetic clip, whistling breathily as he went. The entrance to our suite was past a burbling fountain, its trellis-shaded stone pool laced with aquatic plants, and through a small walled courtyard that offered privacy but no shade—in fact, it was hot as an oven. Gaspard opened a set of glass double doors that let us into the living room.

Our not-yet-official new home was a two-bedroom apartment crowded with furniture, much of it oversized, as if to make up for the meager dimensions of the rooms themselves. In the dining alcove was a massive circular table with just enough room around its edges to squeeze in a few chairs; the enormous bed in the master bedroom could have accommodated a family of six. The rooms were bare of personal belongings except for the few articles of clothing Patrick had brought with him, neatly folded and placed in the bedroom wardrobe, and a small collection of familiar items huddled in a corner of the living-room wall unit—Patrick's binoculars, his long-handled police torch, and three books: a history of Lewis and Clark's famous expedition (chosen by me for its considerable length as much as its subject matter), and two text books on park management, on loan from a friend in Arusha. The kitchen was similarly bare, except for a tin of sardines and some instant coffee. The liquor cabinet, however, was well stocked.

"Look here," said Patrick, opening the cupboard door to show me the bottles of whiskey, gin, and vodka inside. "Pastis," he said, removing a bottle and offering it for inspection.

The apartment had until very recently been occupied by a scowling Frenchman whose job was to run the hotel. When the hotel manager arrived from France, shortly after Patrick came on the scene, one of the first things he did was to call a meeting. Those present were Patrick, the pilot in charge of air reconnaissance, and the young woman in charge of the park's office in Sokodé. Everybody was on the payroll of the same Swiss foundation that had hired Patrick. The new guy announced that he was now the boss. I beg your pardon, said Patrick: You are the boss of the hotel, yes, but I am the boss outside the hotel. After that, they didn't speak to each other. Within a month the hotel boss, who rarely emerged from his apartment, was taken to the hospital in a state of general collapse. From there, he went to the airport and boarded a plane for France, never to return.

With no one to run the hotel, Patrick shouldered the job, like a good soldier. He also took over the departed hotel boss's apartment. In it, he discovered a large collection of empties, which he disposed of, and a few bottles that still had something in them, which he kept. So now, in addition to antipoaching, he was the one making sure the beds were made and there was butter for the croissants.

As the hotel's decidedly underqualified fill-in manager, Patrick had little to worry about for the simple reason that there were no guests. Few people knew that the hotel had recently reopened after sitting idle for many years, and fewer cared. Leisure travelers were not exactly beating a path to Togo, described by the U.S. State Department as "a small, economically stagnant country in West Africa in a state of political uncertainty" where "tourism facilities are limited." So Patrick's services were barely needed; the cook was able without much assistance to rustle up meals for the pilot, a thin and gray-haired Italian by the name of Paganelli, and us, and the few guests who wandered in; Hussein, the headwaiter, oversaw the dining hall and made sure nobody was stealing the booze.

We had dinner that evening—and every evening thereafter—with the Italian pilot. Spurning the air-conditioned dining hall, which felt big and empty, we sat on the patio overlooking the pool and slapped at the mosquitoes. Hussein, gracious and dignified, served, assisted by a young woman with platform sandals and hair extensions, whom he introduced as his cousin. Hussein didn't yet trust her to take the orders (even though there was only one table, ours, to keep straight), so she was assigned to bring the plates and remove them while Hussein hovered, watching her every move.

Paganelli lived in one of the bungalows and patrolled the park from the air. Twice a day he rode la moto—the company motorcycle—over to the airstrip, a quarter mile away, and took the Cessna for a spin. He was a shy and solitary creature, who spent most of his time in his room, reading, sleeping, and playing folk songs on his guitar. He emerged only for meals, to conduct aerial surveillance, and when the generator broke, as he was also the resident mechanic.

Paganelli spoke French and a little Spanish in addition to his native language, but alas, no English, so conversation was awkward. Patrick translated a little, but mostly he and Paganelli talked to each other, with small contributions from Thomas, while I listened, straining to catch a familiar word. As Patrick had so sensibly pointed out, if I relied on him to translate, I would never learn French.

"It's how I learned Spanish," he explained. "I never studied it in school—I just picked it up."

"Yes, but you were nine years old," I reminded him. "It's different."

"How is it different?"

"It just is. Your brain is wired different at nine than it is at forty-six. It's naturally programmed to acquire language."

"I always been able to do that," he said.

Secretly, I had doubts that I was capable of learning French through osmosis, or that merely by living in a French-speaking country I would begin to "pick up" French. However, eager to show that I was prepared to give his method a try, since it had worked so well for him, I listened intently as he and Paganelli discussed, among other mysteries, "*les braconniers*," and by the end of the evening I was fairly sure that *braconniers* were poachers. An awful lot had failed to percolate, however, such as who the poachers were and what they were up to, and when, and where, and why.

Not that I didn't know a lot of words already. I did. If you were to put together all the words I knew and leave out the ones I didn't, the conversation that first evening would have gone something like this:

Paganelli: Many poachers more or less elephants forest on the trail and tomorrow me the plane two times you later elephants please pass the salt.

Patrick: Me also by truck in the forest poachers always in the forest elephants elephants always something very interesting elephants elephants elephants but not I and not always.

Paganelli: Exactly.

Often the effort of keeping a conversation going proved too much for the four of us and we fell silent. Nobody seemed too concerned; the silences, in fact, were welcome. Why talk just to make noise? It was peaceful on the terrace, in our little pool of light with darkness all around and no sound except for the chink of metal on china, the flutter of moth wings against the overhead lights, and the intermittent whine of mosquitoes.

The reserve that was the main topic of our dinner conversation—our new backyard—was the largest of Togo's three national parks, comprising some two thousand square kilometers of grassland, swamp, and semi-deciduous moist tropical forest. Foret de Fazao was considered "frontier forest"—part of the original forest that covered West Africa eight thousand years ago, once temperatures had warmed up enough from the last ice age to resemble today's climate. As a frontier forest, Fazao was also big enough—at least in theory—to sustain its biodiversity. Not only could it regenerate naturally, but it could also support such wide-ranging animals as lions and elephants.

Despite this, nobody had reported seeing a lion in Fazao National Park for years, or a leopard, or a giant eland, or a bongo. The reason, of course, was *les braconniers*: Like most of Togo's so-called protected areas, Fazao was not very well protected. For starters, it had what in conservation terms is known as a porous boundary, meaning there was nothing to keep people out (or animals in). And it was surrounded by towns, villages, farms, roads. The villagers considered the parkland to be community property, stolen from them by President Eyadema and his Kabye friends; they continued to use it for growing yams, for pasturing their goats, for firewood, for meat for the cooking pot. Large chunks of the perimeter had been taken over by villages and couldn't reasonably be reclaimed; to prevent further encroachment and to keep out game and timber poachers would require a ten-foot-high chain-link fence some three hundred miles long.

The fence was by far the most expensive item on Patrick's rapidly expanding wish list, which also included shoes for the rangers, some of whom were wearing rubber flip-flops. Their government-issue guns, for those who had guns, dated back to World War II. They had no radios, so they couldn't communicate with anyone outside their own post. They had only two vehicles—they needed four more, one for each ranger post—and no tents, so to camp in the bush they had to sleep outdoors, where they risked nasty encounters with insects, scorpions, and spiders.

Clothing and personal equipment for the forty rangers would cost about twenty thousand U.S. dollars, according to a quote Patrick had received from a British vendor who dealt in army surplus.

"And the rangers need training," Patrick pointed out. "Training costs money. And ammunition, don't forget ammunition."

"Where is all this money going to come from?" I asked the not-yet-official new director.

"The foundation will have to raise it. That is the old man's job."

The foundation was the life's work of a Swiss philanthropist, now in his seventies, whose projects tended to favor such sympathy-rousing animal species as baby seals and wild mustangs. The big boss, as we called him, had a twenty-year contract with the Togolese government to run the park. It was he who held the purse strings.

"Has he seen your list?"

"Oh yes, he's seen."

"And?"

"We will talk when he comes next month."

Among the resident species that had survived over the years was a small herd of elephants. One of Patrick's duties as warden was to visit the farmers whose fields and vegetable plots the elephants had plundered and dole out compensation. Standing with the unhappy farmer in the rows of trampled corn, he would reach into his pocket and extract a wad of bills, then peel off a few notes and hand them over slowly, counting. Then the two would shake hands and Patrick would drive away. These encounters happened almost daily when the herd was in the area.

One big male had fallen into the habit of helping himself with such regularity to the sorghum, millet, and yams that grew on the park's fringes that he had become an expensive nuisance. The male had also made a daily habit of coming to eat the fruit of the mango tree that shaded the little beer garden just inside the park boundary, but there he was welcome. One day, he stopped coming. Soon the rangers discovered why. The big male had been felled by an assassin's bullet. The shooter had never been found.

Patrick had yet to encounter the herd, which tended to roam the northern sector. It was not good to lose the park's only real mascots. "They should have radio collars," said Patrick, "like the rhinos at Ngorongoro, so we'd know where they are at all times."

Sitting by the hotel pool in the heat of the day when he might reasonably have been taking a siesta, the not-yet-official park warden worked on his lists of things to do and things to buy. The lists grew longer every day.

As Christmas approached somebody rustled up some tinsel and a tree, and Hussein decorated the dining room. At the front desk, Antoine showed Patrick the growing list of reservations, some from as far away as Ivory Coast. The park's chief warden grunted and, setting aside the question of how he was going to outfit his troops, went off to discuss with the cook how we were going to feed the guests.

It was hard to tell, given their symbiotic relationship, which should receive our primary attention, the park or the hotel. The answer seemed to be both. The hotel needed the park to help lure its guests, and the park needed the hotel not only to provide food and shelter for its visitors but also to help raise money for its many expensive needs. This was a problem, since the hotel was running at a deficit. At least it was serving another of its functions, which was to provide jobs for local people. Not that there was much for them to do. Sometimes the captain of the local gendarmerie wandered over from the outpost down the road with a buddy or two to buy drinks at the pool bar in the evening; the rest of the time Martine, the solitary cocktail waitress, sat in the shade, fanning herself in boredom. At lunchtime, when it was too hot to even pretend to work, the staff sat around a stone table under the grape arbor and played a game called kala, in which several players moved little pebbles around a board, scoring points, while a half-dozen others looked on. This was not a good time for a siesta, as the grape arbor was within a few feet of our apartment and the game was way more exciting than you might suppose, judging from all the shouting. So instead of napping, I sat by the pool in a soporific daze, a book of French bedtime stories that Thomas had long outgrown in my lap, pausing now and then to look up words in my French-English pocket dictionary. Patrick worked on his lists or read a few pages of the book about Lewis and Clark.

I was trying to follow the adventures of a roller-skating sheep when Antoine hurried over from the front desk one afternoon to say, his voice hushed with urgency, that the reservations list had grown substantially since the morning's count.

"How are the rooms?" I asked Patrick. The sounds of victory and defeat emanated from the grape arbor where the midday kala match was in progress. A small black and white goat drank from the edge of the pool, which was empty of bathers. Patrick glanced toward the row of bungalows, where another goat was munching what remained of the shrubbery.

"I don't know. I've never seen them." He went back to his reading. After a moment, he added, without raising his eyes from the page: "I gunna make an inspection."

It sounded for all the world like the sort of statement with which one files away a good intention firmly and forever, but a moment later, he raised his head again, looked over his shoulder toward the grape arbor, and gestured to Martine, who clopped over on her platform sandals, beaded hair extensions swinging apart and colliding together in an explosion of small clicks.

"Have you seen Gaspard?"

"Non, mon directeur."

"Find him," said Patrick. "Tell him I want to see him."

"Oui, mon directeur."

Gaspard was located, and came hustling over.

"Now Gaspard," Patrick began, "I would like you to prepare the rooms for an inspection. Make sure"— and he gave Gaspard a list of make-sures: Make sure the wastebaskets are empty and the soap dishes are filled, make sure the beds are properly made and the light bulbs work.

"At ten o'clock tomorrow morning, I will do an inspection."

"Every room, mon directeur?"

There were twenty-five rooms.

"Every room."

"Oui, mon directeur."

Gaspard hurried off, a man on a mission.

The next morning the three of us went from room to room together, flushing toilets, flipping switches, peering under beds and into closets. Patrick, armed with a legal pad attached to a clipboard, took notes. We inspected all twenty-five rooms.

The rooms had recently been given a new coat of paint, applied in a very untidy fashion, particularly around the edges. Most had something wrong with them—a broken light fixture, a cracked window, a toilet that didn't flush unless you reached into the tank. The flowerbeds were weedy and stubbly, nibbled down by the goats. At the end, Patrick ripped several pages from his legal pad and handed them to Gaspard.

"So," he said to Gaspard. "You know what to do."

"Oui, mon directeur."

"Next week, we have another inspection."

Gaspard went off to ponder his marching orders, a little less bounce in his step.

Thomas, meanwhile, was beginning to miss Arusha, having felt the full impact of our change of locale the moment his Game Boy died. With the nearest set of replacement batteries miles away in Sokodé, he looked around really carefully for the first time in days and discovered there was nothing to do and nobody to do it with. The day we arrived at Fazao, one of the village boys had come wandering up the hill to stand under a tree a few feet from where Thomas was trouncing me at the outdoor Ping Pong table. The boy watched silently, curious but shy, until Thomas invited him to play, showing him how to hold the paddle. The boy's first few whacks sent the ball sailing toward the treetops, but it didn't take him long to catch on. I began to have hopeful thoughts of making a quiet escape. Just as I was preparing to sneak away, however, the guard who'd been watching us from the front entrance came over and told the boy to leave. "But he's my friend," Thomas protested.

"He is not allowed here," the guard retorted. "That is the rule."

After that, we sometimes heard giggles coming from the bushes. The children were almost always around, but we rarely saw them. We heard them, rustling twigs, murmuring to each other. They especially liked to hide behind the shrubbery by the pool. Sometimes the braver ones would call out; they might even step out where we could see them if there were no guards around. But they did not venture very far into the open, aware of what would happen if they were caught.

I was whiling away the siesta hour on a chaise, having tossed aside the book about the roller-skating sheep with a sigh of sympathy for the departed hotel manager, who I now theorized may have collapsed from sheer boredom, when I heard a sharp whistle and, raising my head, saw a small boy emerge from the hedge. He stood looking down at his bare feet as the guard who had summoned him approached, carrying a stick a foot and a half long and pencil-thin. The guard stopped a few feet from the boy and spoke, and the boy came forward. Still looking down, he held out his hand. The guard raised the stick and brought it down on the boy's palm. The boy jerked his hand back and grimaced. The guard spoke again, shook his finger, and the boy beat a hasty retreat.

Still the village children continued to come around, sometimes calling out to Thomas in a friendly way from the sidelines, as if he were a prisoner or a particularly interesting zoo animal.

At least at the boarding school in Lomé, he'd have friends. For now, I was his sole playmate, a situation that was wearing on us both. We had visited the school, between our family reunion at the airport and our departure for Fazao. At the campus in Lomé, a couple of old men were sweeping the bare ground with ancient brooms when we arrived; the children were away for Christmas break. So was the headmaster—a grizzled history professor showed us around, leading us through a well-stocked library, a student lounge with modular furniture and a big TV, a well-equipped science lab. Thomas seemed impressed, particularly by the science lab.

"I like biology," he informed the history professor, causing me to glance over at Patrick, who shrugged. "Do you have a rugby team?"

Walking around the deserted campus, perhaps populating it in his mind with future friends, Thomas had seemed, as Patrick noted to me in a whisper, "very okay," with the prospect of boarding school. The only person he knew who attended one was Harry Potter, and he would have preferred Harry's school, where they taught magic and potions, and where the groundskeeper had a pet dragon. But Harry was a fictional character and, unfortunately, his school was also fictional.

The history professor handed us a sheaf of papers—itemized tuition and fees, syllabus, packing list, medical forms. Then he told us that before the start of the next semester, Thomas would have to take a placement test.

Instantly, Thomas was transformed. "A test!" he yelped.

"No problem," said Patrick. "We'll be back in Lomé in a few weeks; he can do it then."

210

Thomas's stricken countenance suggested there was a very big problem indeed. "How long is the test?" he asked in a small and slightly quavering voice.

The professor smiled apologetically. "About one hour, maybe one and a half."

Thomas glowered and said nothing.

We thanked the history professor and left, heading toward the highway that went north to Fazao. From the backseat emanated a powerful silence. The road was a straight strip of laterite through open fields and stands of teak. Along its edge, neat squares of multi-colored beans had been left to dry on the blistering-hot pavement in the sun. In one spot, a brush fire burned and two small boys were beating around its edges with sticks.

"What are they doing?" I asked Patrick.

"Clubbing mice." I looked more closely and saw that one of the children was dangling a small rodent by the tail.

"What for?" The boy tossed the mouse onto a small pile and returned to the fray. The other boy was running back and forth, stick raised.

"They're going to eat them."

"You're joking."

"Certainly not."

"But . . . why would they do that?"

He looked at me. "Because they're hungry."

After a few miles, Thomas decided to speak again. "I can't believe I have to take a test," he said. "Not fair."

"What did you think of the school?" I asked.

"I dunno." The question was too vague, too big, too complicated. "It's okay, I guess. Whatever."

I waited to hear if there was more.

"They have a rugby team."

So in addition to the hotel that nobody wanted to manage, we now had the boarding school that nobody wanted to discuss. By now, I knew that both Patrick and Thomas were apt to throw up an impenetrable wall of silence whenever a difficult subject presented itself. Just recently, for instance, I had learned that while Thomas loved bugs, he had a great fear of spiders, and was loath to walk through our new apartment in the dark of night because of the many large gray ones that clung to the walls, the very walls that he might encounter as he felt his way to the bathroom in the pitch-darkness. For two weeks, he had been avoiding the midnight trek to the toilet, a windowless closet that was well known to be a spider hangout. Upon learning of Thomas's fear, Patrick suddenly admitted that he hated spiders too—something I never would have guessed. The solution was simple: I gave Thomas a flashlight. But the spiders were a good example of how much anxiety a small boy could keep locked up. Especially if he was away from home at boarding school and had nobody to listen to his concerns.

A hammock bridge in Sierra Leone.

Chapter Twelve

Sierra Leone in 1988, the year Thomas was born, was known for its beautiful beaches—scalloped stretches of white sand protected by inlets and shaded by coconut palms. There were islands off the coast, some deserted, where sea turtles nested. Fishermen plied the waters with nets and sold langoustes on the beach, a big bag for a dollar—they used the shellfish as bait, and at the end of the day they'd just give it away. Patrick was in charge of water sports at a beach resort, hired to take people sport fishing, or boating, or water-skiing. On his days off, he drove into the interior, exploring. At first he went alone. After a while, he began taking clients with him.

He jealously guarded his turf. Would-be competitors had trouble just reaching the bush by car: The soldiers who manned the highway checkpoints on the edge of Freetown were his friends. "This road is closed," they would solemnly inform the driver of a rival's car. "Only authorized vehicles can pass until further notice." To maintain these alliances, Patrick took time on his trips to the bush to pull over, pass out cigarettes, and joke with the soldiers. Sometimes, for fun, he'd borrow a clipboard from one of them and step up to the highway barrier as a vehicle approached. "Good afternoon, sir," he'd say to the driver. "Vehicle inspection. Could you switch on your headlights, please." Then he'd launch into a straight-faced parody of checkpoint officiousness, politely asking the driver to sound the horn, turn on his wipers, go forward, go backward, while the real guards stood back, giggling.

Thomas's world was the beach resort of Tokey Village. The roof of the family bungalow was made of thatched leaves; the next-door neighbor was Elias, a Greek sailor who used to lift Thomas up and set him down on the deck of his boat. Years later, Thomas would tell me about Elias, whose chest and back were as hairy as his head. He would tell me about Elias's pet monkey, and the rock pythons that Papa used to bring home from the bush. Each snake in turn was given a name — Adelaide — and kept for a week or two before being released. Thomas would remember draping the various Adelaides around his bare shoulders and walking through the resort compound, scaring the clients and the African staff.

After Chile, Patrick had stopped running after trouble, preferring to wait until it found him. His first marriage had ended ten years later in a determined bout of wild spending designed to burn through as much communal property as possible rather than lose it in a divorce settlement. On Christmas Day 1984 he woke up in Abidjan with the equivalent of seventy-five cents. The children were in France with their mother, who was no longer speaking to him. He bought a bottle of cheap wine and took it to a friend's house for dinner. "Were you scared?" I asked. He had gone through hundreds of thousands of dollars in a matter of months. "You can't imagine," he said. "I was so relieved." Freed from his moorings, he drifted, until he met and married a fun-loving girl from the south of France, fourteen years his junior. Anne restored him to sanity.

Thomas was born at a hospital in Toulouse and whisked in his mother's arms to Freetown, the capital city of Sierra Leone. That's where the trouble began. Anne was a young and inexperienced mother far from home, with too much time on her hands. Patrick was often away in the bush, and Sento looked after Thomas. There were servants to cook the meals, do the housework. Anne became listless and apathetic, sleeping all day and partying in the Freetown clubs all night. Patrick watched, uncomprehending, as the beautiful woman he had married collapsed before his eyes. One day the local drug dealer came to the house with a cop. "He says your wife owes him money," the cop said. "Owes him money for what?" Patrick shouted at the cop. "What did he sell her? Did he tell you that?" He sent the men away, then he checked his bank account for the first time in several weeks and found it empty.

They went through it all, the spying, the lying. In desperation, he bought a one-way ticket to France, where Anne's mother was living. Anne didn't want to go, and there was a big scene when Patrick told her Thomas was staying.

When Anne left Sierra Leone, Thomas was just learning to speak; he said very little for the next few years. Much later, he would be told that his mother had fallen ill. It would be left to Thomas to imagine what might happen to somebody who went off to the hospital and never came back. In an effort to ease the blow, Patrick destroyed all evidence of Anne, including every photograph of her and Thomas together. Neither did he keep the imploring letters she sent before disappearing without a trace.

For the next five years Sento was the most important person in Thomas's life. She taught him to speak Krio, and to love spicy African food, and to ride a bicycle. By the time he left Sierra Leone Thomas had no memory of Anne. Sento was the mother he left behind.

ই

The war began in the south, near the Liberian border, where the diamond mines are located. Patrick's Tiwai Island camp was right on the edge of the mining region; he had discovered the site while leading geologic expeditions. The island was a primate sanctuary in the middle of a river, its only human inhabitants a handful of Americans who manned a tiny research station. They were there to study the fauna: fluffy green colobus monkeys, chimpanzees, pygmie hippos. With a loan from a French bank, Patrick set up sleeping tents for twelve guests, a thatch-roofed mess tent, and showers. Six months later, he was leading a duck hunter through a swamp when he almost walked into a guerrilla encampment.

The chief of the Kuranko people was a worldly man who had served in the Belgian army; his people made up a substantial portion of the country's military forces. On his trips into the interior, Patrick often visited the chief in the highland village of Yifin. In April 1992, at the height of a busy tourist season, the chief warned his visitor that trouble was brewing; he would be wise to cancel all bookings and leave the country.

Anxious to increase army ranks, President Momoh had begun recruiting jobless young men from the cities. As the army grew bigger, the average age of the new recruits had steadily dropped, and their training had become increasingly rudimentary. Soon Momoh had on his hands an army of youths who not only lacked training and discipline, they lacked any reward for their services: The state treasury was dry.

A convoy of soldiers came to Freetown to demand their pay. Many were in their teens, and they wore their uniforms with style, unbuttoned over colorful T-shirts and accompanied by dreadlocks and scruffy beards; several of the jeeps had human skulls mounted on the grills. The convoy made a rowdy procession through the streets of Freetown, firing their rifles at the sky, before rumbling up to the presidential palace.

Momoh, however, wasn't in it. He had slipped out, leaving the country aboard the presidential chopper. The army entered the palace to find there was no president, so they picked a new one: Captain Valentine Strasser, twenty-five years old.

One day as Patrick was returning from the bush with some clients he got a flat—the second one of the safari, so he was already using his spare. While he was wondering what to do, a car passed—a shiny new Nissan Patrol with a government sticker on its side. In the backseat was a soldier he knew from one of the checkpoints, dressed in civilian clothes and aviator shades.

"Hey, Patrick," he said, leaning out the window and waving a huge joint. "What the fuck happened to you, man?"

"Got a puncture."

"Get in," said his friend. "I'll give you a lift."

They threw the tire in the trunk and, leaving the clients with the truck, went down the road to get it repaired.

"Nice car," said Patrick. "What are you doing with such a car?"

"Don't you know?" said the guy. "I'm the vice president now."

"No kidding," said Patrick. "Congratulations."

"Don't worry," said the vice president. "It won't last."

❧

At the statehouse in Freetown, a newly appointed minister opened a folder and pulled out a newspaper clipping: an article about Patrick in the local press. "This says you were a military observer in South America," said the minister. He was a young guy, like all of Strasser's men. "Chile. In . . ." his eyes scanned the smudgy print, "nineteen-seventy-three."

"That's right," said Patrick. He had seen the article, which had run as a business story and carried no byline. He suspected a competitor had slipped the info about Chile to the police.

"A military observer," the minister repeated thoughtfully.

A chill went through him, and he remembered Zambia. This could be much worse. From the folder, the minister pulled the résumé that Patrick had given to Immigration with his visa application. The minister and his deputy proceeded to ask about every country that Patrick had ever been in—what he had done there, why he was in Nigeria during the war, and so on. Their questions were polite, and Patrick waited for the interrogation to turn ugly. After several hours, he decided to take a risk.

"Listen," he said, "you really think I'm spying here? Okay, let's see what can be spied. Everybody knows you've got no planes. You've only got one helicopter and it belongs to the president. So, what about the navy? You've got two boats from the Chinese. One has got a Chinese crew and one has a local crew but they're not moving because you've got no money to buy gas. They're moored in the port where everybody can see them. What about the land forces? You've got three tanks, which are manned by East Germans. Two are in plain view, one in front of the prison, the other in front of the statehouse. The third is known to be broken down somewhere in the bush. Armored vehicles: You've got three and they're broken down. And everybody knows about it because they're in plain view with their guts out. Weapons: AK47s, RPGs, mortars, that's it. About the economic secrets: There is one refinery, one brewery, and one soap factory. The wealth of the country is gold and diamonds and fisheries. I don't know anybody in the government, only the tourist board, immigration, and income tax. Is there anything to spy there?"

The young minister laughed. "I think you are right, sir," he said. "There is nothing much to be spied." He rose, smiling, and offered his hand. "You are excused," he said. "I am sorry for the trouble."

ॐ

By the end of the rainy season, the number of army checkpoints had increased dramatically; they began just north of his camp and stretched all the way south to the Liberian border. President Strasser sent a few troops to quiet things down. Most people thought the rebels would quickly disperse. Patrick continued to make the half-day drive from the coast, once a month, to pay the staff: a manager and two watchmen. That was how he learned that a nearby village had been burned to the ground. He and the manager talked about it over lunch while the manager's little girl sat on her daddy's lap.

The meat served at lunch was not very fresh, and an hour later he was in the bushes, sick to his stomach. He was there again after sundown when he heard the first shout. About twenty men entered the camp. They wore makeshift uniforms and carried automatic rifles. He could see them clearly from the kerosene lanterns placed at intervals around the camp's perimeter. The magazines of their rifles were taped, one up, one down, for quick reloading.

At the first shot, the older watchman fell to the ground. The camp manager's wife screamed and turned toward the children. The attackers blasted the lamps, the chairs, the makuti roofs. When the firing ceased, Patrick heard moaning, then the thud of a machete. He was not even two hundred feet away, concealed in the brushy woods. He heard a voice say "the white man" in Krio: They were searching for him. There was a shout as somebody discovered the well-stocked bar. He heard the swish and crackle of shifting logs as something was thrown on the fire. Recognized the smell of burning flesh. Inching away from the camp, he slipped into the bush.

Three days later, he arrived at a highway checkpoint on foot, dirty and delirious. An army vehicle took him to Freetown. A week later, another army vehicle brought him back to the village where he had left his truck. The villagers confirmed what he already knew: The two watchmen, the camp manager, his wife, their son, and their little daughter were dead. The bodies of the children had been burned and cannibalized. The attackers had disappeared back into the bush.

Patrick got in his car and drove home. He never went back to Tiwai Island. At Tokey Village he didn't talk about what had happened, and he didn't write about it when he set down his life story during the rainy season that followed the attack. By the time I met him, the memory of that night in camp was like a small stone at the bottom of a very deep well.

❧

Patrick and Thomas stayed in Sierra Leone for two more years. The local press began to carry daily stories about rebel soldiers going into southern villages, slaughtering people and stealing food. The tales of their butchery and atrocities were stomach-turning—whole villages burned, people's limbs and lips and ears hacked off. Young boys kidnapped or lured with drugs into the movement, forced to commit crimes in their own villages that would make it impossible for them to return. Once they'd wrested control of the mines, the rebels had an unlimited supply of diamonds with which to buy arms. People were no longer talking as if this was a bush war that would burn itself out.

News of the war began to make the front pages of foreign newspapers, along with photographs of its victims: mutilated children, young boys toting rifles. The tourists left; Tokey Village shut down. Patrick had nowhere to go, and he refused to walk away from his investment—he still had his cars, five Suzuki Samurai convertibles and one Nissan Patrol. He stayed on at the resort as a caretaker, receiving a small stipend from the owner, who lived in France, to keep an eye on things.

A truck carrying soldiers came to the hotel; a young officer in a Chicago Bulls T-shirt did most of the talking. "The army needs your cars," he said. "You want to support the army, don't you?" Patrick refused to turn over the keys, so they jump-started all six vehicles and drove away.

He went straight to army headquarters in a taxi to make a complaint. "We're busy right now," said an officer. "Come back in fifteen days."

The next day, he tried again. They asked for names, but he had none. He tried to describe the young officer in the Chicago Bulls T-shirt, but the desk sergeant frowned and shook his head. "We don't have your cars," he said. "And we don't know who took them. It was not the army. These were private individuals." He tapped his ballpoint pen on the desk blotter, impatiently. "Thieves."

Patrick stayed in Sierra Leone two more months with nothing to do. The few employees who stuck around Tokey Village grew unfriendly; they hadn't been paid in months. The furniture began to disappear, along with the bed linens, the towels, the doors, even the hinges. When the workers realized it was over and that he was just there to keep them from stealing, two of the men came to him with a message: "Leave the country and go home. It is too dangerous here for a white man. If you stay here, you will be killed. Go now. But leave your things."

He and Thomas departed for the airport in a taxi. At the gate, there was a palaver. "I need to check your bags," said the hotel's assistant manager. He and his buddies went through each suitcase, looking for hotel property; finding none, they demanded a fee for opening the gate. Patrick would have paid up to save time, but he had no money; the palaver went on and on. Eventually the gatekeeper relented, opening the gate for free. A few hours later, Patrick arrived on his sister's doorstep in Paris with Thomas and two suitcases. He was fifty, homeless, and broke.

❧

While Patrick carried on a discouraging job search in Paris, Thomas boarded with a family in the countryside. Maurice and Mireille had sold their country home and were living in the old fortress town of Fontainbleau, in an elegantly appointed second-story apartment above a busy intersection. Every Friday afternoon, Mireille would pick Thomas up at school in Villebeon and drive him to Fontainebleau for the weekend. Patrick took the train out from Paris, arriving in time for dinner. He stayed through all of Saturday and part of Sunday, catching a train to Paris at around the same time that Mireille drove Thomas back to Villebeon.

Mireille fixed up the spare bedroom for Thomas; on his weekend visits, Patrick slept on the couch. When Mireille showed her little grandson his new room and said, "This is your room," Thomas sat on the edge of the bed and stared at the floor. "I have no family," he said. "I'm all alone."

Mireille tried to console him. "You have me," she said. "And Papi. And your father. You have your sister, and your brother, and your aunt and uncle, and your cousins. We are your family." But Thomas was inconsolable. What good was having this nice big family if he had to go live with strangers?

Maurice sat by the parlor window, a gaunt-faced old man, studying the street for hours. That's four," he'd say, and a few minutes later, "Five." He was tallying the number of black people among the pedestrians, for the benefit of anyone who would listen. More and more Africans were coming to France, immigrants from its former colonies, some of them fleeing the civil wars that had erupted there. Maurice, dying of cancer and in constant pain, didn't hesitate to wonder aloud why anybody would want to waste his life in such a place. The tension between father and son had steadily worsened ever since Patrick's divorce from Huguette after fifteen years of marriage. There had never been a divorce in the family before; Maurice didn't have to say much for his disapproval to be keenly felt.

"What are you going to do now?" he asked Patrick, over and over.

"I don't know," Patrick would answer, seething; his father never showed any confidence in him. "Don't worry. I'll figure it out."

At an unemployment office in Paris he presented himself: Patrick Texier, safari guide. Former airline ticket clerk, professional hunter, smuggler, bush pilot, crocodile hunter, public-relations rep, travel-agency manager, salesman, gold prospector, anti-poaching expert, English teacher, spare-parts manager, entrepreneur and spy. His hastily cobbled résumé reflected only a small portion of this vast experience, modified to approximate normalcy. Nevertheless, the caseworker, a pleasant young woman who seemed anxious to help, frowned at the freshly typed piece of paper. "Well," she said finally, "I've never seen anything like this before."

She paused, considering. "You are fifty," she said at last. "That makes things a bit tougher." He wished she had simply said, "What in God's name am I supposed to do with an out-of-work bush guide in Paris?" Maybe then he would have felt he had a chance.

There was only one place for him to go, and that was back to Africa. When he told the nice young woman at the unemployment office that he had found a job as the general manager of a safari company and would be moving to Tanzania, she practically leaped over her desk to congratulate him.

The house provided by Ranger Safaris was far from town; the contract had said it would be furnished. The furniture consisted of a second-hand bed, a nightstand, and a wooden chair. When Patrick asked Abbas Moledina—the older of the two brothers who owned Rangers—for more, they had their first kelele. Finally, grudgingly, Abbas sent a truck with four more chairs and a table.

The house, your basic cinderblock box, had one redeeming feature—a stunning view of Kilimanjaro, twenty-five miles to the east. The view, however, was completely blocked by the brick wall that encircled the house, its top studded with broken bottles to discourage thieves.

Patrick spent his first Christmas at the office. "Being in the travel business means working holidays," Abbas told him. Patrick didn't mind; he had nobody to spend Christmas with anyway. Thomas was still in France, where he would remain until the beginning of the next school year, some ten months away. Patrick spent most of his free time alone. Evenings, he sat on a wooden chair in the empty house, smoking Marlboros and rereading worn paperback suspense novels until it was late enough to go to bed.

In the night, he often lay awake for hours, turning the same thoughts over and over in his mind: what to do about Abbas, what to do about Thomas, how to get his life back on track. The daylight banished these troublesome thoughts; the darkness brought them back.

When Thomas came to Arusha, Patrick took over Sento's job. He woke Thomas in the morning, fed him breakfast, got him dressed, brought him to the school bus, picked him up in the afternoon, fed him dinner, and put him to bed. When Patrick did the shopping, Thomas went with him. When Patrick fixed dinner, he picked Thomas up and sat him on the kitchen counter next to the two-burner kerosene stove so that Thomas could stir the soup. They set the table, ate dinner, and cleared the dishes together, stacking them in the kitchen for Jenni to wash the next day. After dinner, they kept each other company—talking, reading, playing cards—until Thomas's bedtime. Then Patrick arranged Thomas's mosquito net, turned off his light and said, *"Bon nuit, mon grand."*

After they moved to town and Patrick had a bit of money, they often went to a pub in the evening. Thomas would sip Fanta Oranges and listen to the grownups talk until he fell asleep on a bench; when Patrick was ready to go home, he'd scoop Thomas up and carry him to the car. There were not many single fathers in Arusha, and several families adopted them, inviting them for Sunday dinner and making sure they had somewhere to go for Christmas.

As a single parent, Patrick discovered there were a thousand small details to remember; naturally he forgot a few. The headmistress at St. George's sent notes home in Thomas's schoolbag to remind Mr. Texier about such important matters as Thomas's uniform (the necessity of wearing a tie every day), lunch money (missing), homework (missing), and school fees (late). There were the many times when the tooth fairy (which in France is a small mouse) forgot to come. Then, after the baby teeth had been replaced by a mouthful of crooked ones, there was the retainer that spent very little time in Thomas's mouth before taking up permanent residence in a dark corner of Thomas's room. There was the time Patrick dropped Thomas at school as usual, not realizing it was a public holiday, and came back in the evening to discover that Thomas had been alone in the schoolyard all day. It was during this era that he spent a few of his precious shillings on one of his favorite T-shirts, now worn and frayed: the one that states in big letters across the back, "Nobody's Perfect."

The life Patrick described to me during those long evenings in Njiro, candlelight flickering, rain coming down, was full of setbacks and chaotic in the extreme, its highs as stunning as its lows. "No regrets," he said, and for the most part, I believed him. Somehow he had managed to escape the bitterness and cynicism that infected so many of the weary souls around us.

And yet something was motivating him to be a different kind of father from the one he had known, and to succeed with Thomas where he had fallen short with Valerie and Lionel. He and his older children had grown apart after the divorce, and he had let it happen. He was, after all, Maurice's child, and yes, he had regrets. Thomas was his last chance to get it right.

A settlement in northern Togo.

Chapter Thirteen

Guests began to trickle in, giving the staff something to do besides fixing the Texier family's meals and making our beds and doing our laundry. Gaspard hastened from bungalow to bungalow, noisily clanking his long-handled dustpan and whistling tunelessly, calling attention to the fact that he was working and not, as we might have supposed, taking a little nap in one of the unoccupied rooms. The guests were mostly muzungus from Lomé or from neighboring countries where Patrick had lived. Sometimes, in fact, they were people he knew, disconcertingly aged since the last time he'd seen them. One of them, a Frenchman from Abidjan, had brought a butterfly net and other bug-collecting paraphernalia with him. He was a big fan not only of bugs but also of snakes. He and Thomas became fast friends, discussing creepy crawly things at length. Thomas went about the hotel grounds, collecting butterflies with the net that Alan had fashioned for him and putting them to death by gently pinching their abdomens the way Alan had taught him, then enclosing them in carefully folded bits of newspaper and storing them in our kitchen fridge.

Every day, more guests arrived. Many had driven for days to get to this rather dowdy resort with so-so food, expensive drinks, and few attractions, but complaints were rare. The rangers took them on excursions into the forest in the big truck, a few couples swatted some balls around the solitary tennis court, and our dwindling supply of Ping-Pong balls dwindled further, but mostly people seemed content to congregate around the pool, which I had come to think of as my pool. From my chaise, I eyed them resentfully.

With the rooms filling up, Patrick had no time even to think about *les braconniers*. There were menus to plan, provisions to buy, reservations to keep track of. Each night he fell into bed exhausted. The staff rushed about, unaccustomed to having so many things to do all at once. Gaspard dashed from bungalow to bungalow in silent concentration, toting laundry, carrying bags, attacking long-neglected corners with his broom and his rag. Only Martine seemed unperturbed, clopping steadily back and forth between the bar and the patio with her drink tray, pausing now and then to flirt with the gendarmes, who were suddenly more numerous now that bonus time was here.

On Christmas Eve, the dining room was nearly full. Earlier in the week, Patrick, too busy to make the trip himself, had dispatched the cook to Lomé to shop for groceries; the cook had returned with lobsters, which he had unwisely decided to serve in the shell. They were Togolese lobsters, their shells rock-hard, and while a Togolese would probably have made short work of them, our dining room full of ex-pats was flummoxed. The cavernous room became a battleground, echoing with the clash of metal and the crack of skeletal tissue as the guests wrestled the lobsters around on their plates, armed only with a standard-

issue knife and fork. Not only that, but having tri-
umphed over their lobster, they had no time to sit
back and savor their victory, for the task was not yet
finished, because there was a second lobster. They
were small, you see, so everybody got two. The good
part was that dismembering and consuming the lobsters took enough concentration to slow the pace of
dinner, giving the servers and the kitchen staff time to
catch up. Hussein had managed to recruit some extra
hands from the village, but it was still mayhem.

Despite the now prolific mosquitoes, the three of
us and Paganelli were stubbornly eating, as usual, on
the patio, which put us somewhat outside the fray.
Halfway through our meal, however, Patrick turned
to Thomas: "Help Hussein serve the people, *mon
grand*."

Thomas schlepped toward the kitchen, and pretty
soon we saw him on the other side of the glass, walking toward one of the bigger tables, a plate in each
hand. Hussein was right behind him with several
more plates; Hussein's young cousin, Dominique,
brought up the rear. Hussein and Dominique set
down their plates and zipped back to the kitchen;
Thomas lingered, drawn into conversation by the
guests, who must have wondered who he was,
because he looked in our direction and pointed. The
guests looked our way, smiled and nodded. Patrick
returned the nod sheepishly, then set down his knife
and fork. "Excuse me, darling," he said. "I think I better help Thomas." He rose from the table, drew back
the sliding glass doors and stepped into the dining
room. My inability to communicate with either the
guests or the staff except on very specific topics, most
of which, like roller-skating sheep, were unlikely to

come up for discussion, gave me an excuse to sit and enjoy my dinner in peace.

So far, I reflected, our second Christmas together hadn't produced the germ of anything promising in the way of time-honored family traditions. We could only hope that, years from now, Hussein would not be the one to decorate our tree and we would not be sitting down to eat with a lot of paying guests. Staring into the illuminated pool and listening to the gurgle of the water filter, I recalled how, a year ago, Patrick and Thomas and I had taken Jenni's blue laundry bucket, filled it with rocks, and jammed the trunk of a spindly tree down in it. The tree, which was really the branch of a tree, had leaned a bit to stage right, so we rearranged the rocks, which made it lean a bit to stage left. We decorated the tree with ornaments made from art supplies found in the kitchen cupboards: Plastic grocery bags became elegant bows; baking flour became papier-mache angels and gingerbread men. On Christmas Day, we sat down to a dinner of good roast beef and real figgy pudding in the home of actual friends. Everyone had a good time except Pat, our hostess, who had a migraine from the pressure of preparing all that food, and Thomas, who had a small chunk of his left hand bitten off by Pat's rottweiler. This exacerbated Pat's migraine, particularly since it was not the first time the rottweiler had bitten a houseguest. Several people had already suggested that the dog be put down, but Pat argued that the dog was not to blame because he was, after all, a dog, and didn't understand why it wasn't okay to bite little boys who came to dinner, especially if they stuck a finger through a hole in the fence and waggled it.

The year before, we had celebrated Christmas in the German tradition, with our friends Udo and Renata. It was handy having friends who ran a luxury lodge, especially since they ran it so well. Christmas Eve dinner at Plantation Lodge was served at a long table with everybody gathered round — family, friends, and paying guests. Udo sat at the head of the table, dressed as Father Christmas. A child was chosen to sit next to him, usually the youngest. Thomas, when he was ten, was the chosen one. At one end of the room was a fifteen-foot-tall tree, with presents underneath, placed there by the parents for their children. The year Thomas was the chosen one he received a soccer ball and a .22-caliber rifle.

That same year, we managed to stretch our stay with Udo and Renata into New Year's, the excuse being, if I remember correctly, that our car had to be repaired before we could leave. The car was suffering from the automotive equivalent of osteoporosis, especially affecting the leaf springs, and the road to Plantation Lodge was long and full of bumps. More than once we arrived at Udo and Renata's with a busted leaf spring that had to be welded back together before we could return home.

While a team of local mechanics worked on our suspension, New Year's Eve came, with a big feast and dancing in the gazebo. Just before midnight, the men disappeared into the main house and came out with a collection of fire arms, which, at the stroke of midnight, they began blasting into the darkness. Considering the amount of alcohol everyone had consumed by that hour, it's a miracle there were no fatalities. The most serious accident of the evening occurred when Bernt, a stocky German septuagenarian, swung me a bit too vigorously during a polka, lost his balance, and tumbled to the floor, pulling me down on top of him. He lay on his back for a moment, staring in astonishment at the ceiling, then leaped to his feet and started whirling around the gazebo again.

The next year was much quieter, despite its being the end of 1999 and lots of people were welcoming the new millennium as loudly and boisterously as possible. On New Year's Day, the streets of Arusha were covered with broken glass from all the bottles that were exploded the night before. We, however, were far away in the bush with Patrick's nephew and six friends from France. Mesuli's little son Nelson was with us, and after dinner he sang, sweetly, some of the songs that he had learned at his school. "You sing very well, Nelson," I said. Nelson explained that he had better sing well, because anybody who didn't got rapped on the head with a ruler by the music teacher.

This second Christmas, unless it improved markedly and soon, would be less fondly remembered. "I know you have it," Thomas had said, over and over, in the days leading up to our departure for Togo, bursting with an eleven-year-old's eagerness to receive his one and only Christmas gift. "When are you going to give it to me?" Somehow he had figured out about the Game Boy, which I had bought in town for an astronomical sum with the intention of keeping it firmly away from him until we were in Togo, or at least en route. He finally stopped asking when, in one of the many stepmotherly moments that I would erase if I could, I walked into his room with the Game Boy and chucked it, unwrapped, on his bed with a cross "Here!"

Among the hotel guests was a rugged-looking Frenchman who recognized Patrick from Sierra Leone. He and his wife used to vacation at Tokey Village when they were living in neighboring Guinea-Bissao. Their group—middle-aged French ex-pats who'd been around Africa for some twenty years or more and were now living in Lomé—spent several afternoons sunning themselves by the pool. The women were tan and chic, with expensive-looking hair and pedicures. Gingerly, they descended the steps at the shallow end of the pool, then launched themselves into the sparkling turquoise water, heads held high. With languid strokes, they executed a couple of slow laps before emerging, coiffures intact, to dry their oil-scented skin in the sun.

While the women swam and sunned themselves, the men talked politics and I tried half-heartedly to follow what they were saying, occasionally helped by Patrick, who leaned toward me at one point in a particularly opaque discussion of Togo's current political misfortunes and explained that the rugged Frenchman was now an advisor to Eyadema. They were talking, he explained, about the next election, to be held three years hence. Would there be more accusations of fraud, more violence, more tightening of the screws by the EU? Bets were heavily on the affirmative. The constitution prevented Eyadema from standing for reelection, but a little thing like that had never stopped the president before—it was not for nothing that his official biography described him as "a force of nature." He could simply rewrite the constitution. There was also the possibility that his son, Faure Gnassingbè, would take over the office. Either way, sparks would fly. I ventured a difficult question about the last uprising—difficult since it required the past tense: *Le violence, c'etait quoi, exactement? Qu'est-ce-que se passait?* Well, I was told, during the last election, which the president won by a landslide, hundreds of protesters were killed, gunned down by government security forces.

A friendly-faced Dutchman whose two children attended Thomas's new school as day students turned to me. "Don't worry," he said. "If there is another coup and riots break out in Lomé, I will personally see to it that your son is safe."

The man patted my arm. He did not say whether he was willing to brave artillery fire, tear gas, and Molotov cocktails to achieve Thomas's rescue. We, of course, would be many miles and armed checkpoints away.

瑞

On a mudflat in the northeast quadrant of Fazao National Park, we found the tracks of the missing elephants, a sun-baked mass of milling footprints left by the herd during the rainy season. "There are babies," said Patrick, examining the prints. "And a couple of young calves. That's a good sign." But though we looked everywhere, driving to distant corners of the park and striking out on foot, the herd continued to elude us.

If the elephants were mercurial, the big boss was more so. Email after email failed to rouse his attention. Most of the emails were reports of our recces, which were yielding alarming discoveries. There were the smoking caves in one corner of the park, where poachers cured bush meat for sale to restaurants in Lomé. There were the plots of land cleared by subsistence farmers along the park boundary, which was being steadily whittled away. And there was the extensive road system built and maintained by a well-financed team of timber poachers. The timber was sold in Sokodé to make furniture.

"What sort of furniture?" I asked Patrick. We had been following the road all morning. It kept branching, fanning out across a wide area. Each branch led to two or three trees, mostly mahoganies, each tree worth at least twenty thousand dollars on the open market. In one clearing, three big mahoganies a good four feet in diameter were lying on the ground.

"Flashy stuff," said Patrick, "for the local market. Flashy but cheap." He stared ruefully at a stump. "Junk."

Some of the stumps were freshly cut, and a few felled trees hadn't yet been removed. Surveying the damage, Patrick grew quieter and quieter. "It's a big operation," he said at last. "Much bigger than I thought."

"Do you suppose Monsieur Gaumieau knows about this?" I asked, wondering what the minister in charge of national parks and forestry would think of somebody stealing his trees.

Patrick was silent a long moment before he answered. "Oh, yes," he said finally. "He knows."

The ranger station nearest the logging site was tucked back in the woods far from the main road. Patrick spent a long time there, talking with the men. It was a place without comfort — hot, lonely, without electricity or running water, no mosquito nets, little furniture, and nothing to do. Around the periphery, fastened to tree trunks and branches, were several small bundles of feathers and bird claws and bones and such — talismen to ward off evil spirits.

Most of the rangers, one suspected, would happily have chucked their jobs if they could. They were away from home for weeks at a time, living in forest camps, with no women to cook and clean for them. Their work was difficult and dangerous, the pay lousy, their equipment poor. The best of their weapons had come from the poachers, seized during arrests. What's more, they were unpopular: Many of their countrymen saw them as the goons of that Kabye bandit Eyadema, the latest in a long line of thieves.

No wonder they sat around playing cards most of the day. Who could blame them for not wanting to risk their lives to protect a few trees?

Samideau, however, was different. Though small, he kept himself in superb condition, like a good soldier. He kept his thoughts mostly to himself, and his eyes were shrewd. It was Samideau who had told us about the timber operation, having studied it carefully for many months. He had made it his business to know everything that went on in Fazao, and Patrick had learned more about the park from him than from any other single person. "I trust him," said Patrick. "He wouldn't hesitate to shoot a poacher. He is deezgussed by what is happening to this park."

Being disgusted by the poachers and not hesitating to shoot were important: Antipoaching is a kind of war. The rule was, shoot first or be shot. A ranger who hesitated was worse than ineffective; he was a threat to himself and his teammates. It took training, however, to turn men into good soldiers, and training, as Patrick had pointed out, took money.

As the silence emanating from Switzerland grew more prolonged, Patrick, normally so patient, began to seem itchy. Before a contract could be drawn up and signed, he and the big boss had several important matters to discuss, such as whether it made sense to have your chief warden prowling through the guest rooms with a clipboard, making sure the lampshades were dusted and the soap bars replaced, while well-organized gangs of thieves made off with precious chunks of the country's heritage.

"Don't worry," Patrick said, whenever I raised the subject of the contract. "It's all gonna work out." I tried not to mention it too often. He didn't need reminding that this job, which he had spent the better part of a lifetime preparing for, could slip through his fingers.

From the office in Sokodé he fired off another email to Switzerland. Surely a multi-million-dollar tree heist would capture the attention of the big boss. The few emails we had received from him were filled with news of his other projects, about which we cared only in a negative sense, selfishly wishing they would go away. From one such email we had learned, for instance, that the boss was establishing a world court to uphold animal rights—alarming news, since it threatened to divert his attention from our own animals and their problems in a big way. We needed jeeps and radios and radio collars to keep track of them, and a big fence to keep them from wandering off when people like the big boss had their backs turned.

As our supply of diesel waned, Patrick cut back his use of the park's two off-road trucks, announcing one morning that he was going to do a solo recce on the dirt bike. "If I'm not back by noon, you have lunch without me, okay?" he said, lifting his canvas vest from the back of a chair.

It was not even midmorning—the remnants of breakfast had yet to be cleared away by the gentle Hussein—and I realized with dismay that I was to spend another day doing nothing. Instantly, I was both resentful—how come he gets to go off on the dirt bike and have all the fun?—and ashamed: Who is this jealous creature, and what has happened to the me I know?

"Where are you going?" I asked, sounding horribly peevish, as he slipped the vest over his T-shirt and collected his Zippo and a packet of smokes from the breakfast table.

"Not far."

"Which direction?"

"That way." He pointed toward a corner of the living room.

"Past the village?"

"You know where the road forks just after the small stream?"

"No."

"Well, that's where I'm going."

"And after that?"

"I want to follow a road to see if I find any tracks."

"What road? What sort of tracks?"

"Tracks of these hunters who are going for bush meat."

So he was going off alone to chase poachers on a dirt bike. Surely if there existed an antipoaching manual that even mentioned such a strategy, it fell under the "Don't do" category.

"Why don't you just go with the truck?"

"The truck can't get through. The road hasn't been maintained for a long time."

"Hm. And what should I tell people if you don't come back? Where do I tell them to look for you?"

"Don't worry. Nothing gon' heppen to me." And with that, he was gone.

Alan had left, and without a bug-collecting partner Thomas's interest in his new hobby had waned. We spent most of the morning in the pool, playing water soccer. At noon, there was no sign of Patrick. At one o'clock, Hussein came to the edge of the pool and politely inquired if we would be having lunch.

We ate on the patio. Paganelli was asleep. He rarely came out any more, often skipping meals. When he did turn up at dinner, he looked droopy and wan, picked at his food, and said he was tired and didn't feel well. Even Patrick, who tended to rely on modern medicine only as a last resort, said he should see a doctor.

At two o'clock, Patrick was still not back. I tried to concentrate on the Lewis and Clark book, which Patrick had abandoned without finishing, but by now I was really worried. What would I do if something happened to him?

Thomas threw the ball into the air and caught it, inviting me to play as if I was a ball-loving retriever. "Sara!"

Where would we go?

After a while, I went inside and tried to study French, but it was hard to concentrate because I kept thinking things like "If Patrick falls in a hole or gets ambushed by poachers and dies there will be no point in learning French."

It was three-thirty when I finally heard the sound of the dirt bike growing steadily louder as it came up the drive. The engine stopped. I waited, refusing to run out to meet him. Thirty seconds later he opened the front door. I pretended to be reading. He stood in the doorway, saying nothing.

"Hello, darling," I said, absent-mindedly, allowing myself to look up only after marking the page and closing the book.

Patrick was covered with dust from head to toe, the dust streaked and smeared with sweat. Straw and bits of leaves clung to his hair and his clothes.

"What happened to you?"

"I got stuck on the bike."

He entered the room. Sprigs of dry grass were stuck in his hair, his boots, his belt buckle. Reaching into his pockets one by one, he extracted bits of chaff, which he deposited in a little mound on the breakfast table. Silently, I watched this pantomime, refusing to be amused. When he was satisfied with his little pile, Patrick gave me an abbreviated account of the incident it denoted.

Rounding the side of a hill next to an open field, he had come to a place where the road banked steeply, and the bike had skidded down into one of the ruts. The rut was so deep that when he straddled it and grabbed the handlebars of the bike to lift it out, his feet were level with the saddle.

"It took me over an hour to get it out of that damn hole."

I could fake it no longer. "I was worried about you."

"I'm sorry. This bike." He shook his head. "I just couldn't lift it. Jeez, what a pain in the ass. I am filthy. Look at this." He plucked bits of straw from his belt buckle and added them to the small pile on the table. Then he looked at me and heaved a sigh.

"You should not have gone off alone on the bike like that."

"I'm sorry." He hung his head to advertise how contrite he was.

"It was not smart at all, and if you ever do it again I hope you have to walk back."

"You are absolutely right. Please forgive me."

He took off his vest and hung it over the back of a chair. When he turned around to face me, his face was bright with excitement.

"You'll never guess what happened."

"There's more?"

"While I was there, messing around with the bike trying to get it out of the hole, I heard something, a kind of rustle. I looked up, and there was a big male hartebeest. He was as close to me as that wall. This hartebeest—ah, he was so nice! He was standing there, right in the middle of the field, looking at me. And then, he started doing this"—his hand hopped across the table—"bloop-bloop-bloop! I never saw anything like that before. I never saw a hartebeest dance like that."

He was breathless with the description of the dancing hartebeest.

"You know what I gonna do now?"

"No idea."

"I gonna go for a swim."

Stripping off the rest of his clothes, he disappeared into the bedroom, reemerging in a pair of old bathing trunks from his boating days in Sierra Leone.

Outside, Thomas was lying, bored, on a lounge chair. He watched as Patrick walked toward the water's edge.

"Daddy! Are you going swimming?"

Patrick kept going. Thomas sat up.

"Daddy? Sara, look!" Thomas was now out of his seat. "Daddy's going swimming!"

The two of us watched as, without a word, Patrick walked to the deep end, turned, and fell in backward with a loud splash.

"Daddy's in the pool!"

Patrick did a brisk breaststroke with a splashing kick to the shallow end of the pool and emerged, dripping, his swim finished. Years from now, I thought, as Thomas ran to fetch a towel, Patrick will remember this as the day he saw the dancing hartebeest, Thomas will remember it as the day Daddy went in the pool, and I will remember it as the day I almost became a widow. Somehow, I need to get a grip.

෬

At the eleventh hour, just days before our return to Arusha, the big boss flew in from Switzerland, bearing gifts. Not the longed-for radio equipment but a set of walkie-talkies, which he presented to Patrick with a ceremonial flourish as we were sitting down to dinner on the patio overlooking the pool. We arranged ourselves on either side of a long banquet table: Patrick and me on the boss's right, Paganelli and Thomas on his left, the staff of the Sokodé office and somebody from the Togolese press opposite us. Silently we raised and lowered our forks and chewed, all eyes on the big boss, who spoke in sonorous soliloquies; before becoming a conservationist, he had had some success as a poet. Tall and beaky with big hair that fell almost to his shoulders in long, thick silver waves—I couldn't help but think of a woman's wig—he talked and talked, skillfully modulating his well-trained voice and glancing up and down the table to make sure everyone could hear him. I had been worried that my job as hostess would be compromised by the fact that I still spoke very little French, but there were times when not knowing what people were saying could be useful, and this was one. I alone remained impervious to the boss's speech, a fact that seemed to nag at him, for he kept glancing in my direction and making remarks in his minimal English such as "It's a pity you don't understand."

The boss's hairdo reminded me of my old hair salon in Washington Heights, where a procession of elderly husbands used to drop off their wives' wigs on Saturday mornings for Juanita and her coworkers to groom. A row of Styrofoam heads on one of the counters held the various wigs until the husbands returned in the afternoon. I was thinking about the wigs, in fact, and Juanita, and my ex-husband, and my old life, not necessarily with regret but with an intense nostalgia, when the boss turned to Patrick and said, "You should translate for her." It sounded like a reprimand.

Patrick sighed. "I know," he said. "But it's a big job."

The boss was here for one night only, so Patrick had little time to corner him before he got away. He did so after dinner, the two of them sitting down at a table in the bar, alone. I retired to a lounge chair on the patio, and waited. From Paganelli's bungalow came the softly mournful strum of his guitar: The answer, my friend, is blowin' in the wind, the answer is blowin' in the wind...

Already, I missed Arusha. Grubby Arusha, with its inflatable monuments, open-air butcheries, noisy neighbors, and overpriced shops. I missed Jenni—forgetting for a moment that she didn't work for us anymore. Remembering brought a little shock of sadness, until I reminded myself that Jenni was far too capable to be our housegirl for the rest of her life. I thought about our lonely askari, who, like Jenni, was more careful with our things than we were, covering the car's stuck-open windows with a tarp when it rained and bringing us the keys when we left them in the ignition. I even felt a surge of affection for Loto, who was steady and reliable in his own way, with his endless supply of ailing relatives and his rasta hits pouring from the garden shed promptly at naptime.

I missed the Mambo Café and Emilio's ciao-bellas; the griping around the big table at Masai Camp; the Discovery Club, where we'd celebrated our nuptials after Mr. Happy God Matoi finally married us, and Max's Patisserie and Cyber Café, where we vied for Max's computers with truckloads of overcaffeinated college kids. I missed Old Moshi Road's blue canopy of jacaranda blossoms, the exact color of my wedding dress, and Meru's peak, so distinctive with its missing chunk. I missed Patrick's habit of keeping his eye on Meru as it slumbered, a habit that was enabled by our house's superb vantage point; nobody else we knew, except Mesuli, could do a volcano check from his front porch.

Moonlight rippled on the surface of the pool; Paganelli sang his lonely refrain. I was still brooding when the two men emerged, shook hands, and said good night to each other. Then Patrick came to join me on the patio.

"Okay," he said, "it's all arranged. We have our contract."

The next morning, before the sun was up—while the night watchmen dozed and the generator that powered every light in the compound slumbered on— I dressed in the dark, and, unlatching the glass double doors of our suite, let myself into the courtyard. As the stars faded, I walked down the little hill to the road. When I reached the bottom, I started to run.

In semi-darkness, I passed the guard who spent his nights slumped in a chair beside the access road to the airfield where Paganelli parked his plane. A few paces beyond was a checkpoint maintained by the gendarmerie and a shack set back from the road that served as its headquarters; a shadowy figure in the doorway acknowledged my passage with a wave. A couple of farmers trudged toward me, walking sleepily to their fields, rakes and hoes resting on their shoulders, big rubber boots on their feet. We exchanged bonjours and backward glances.

As I ran, the sun came up, burning through the dust of the Harmattan. The countryside was brilliant in the early morning light, like a superrealist painting, each blade of grass illuminated and distinct. My pounding feet flushed birds from their nests beside the road; they exploded out of the grass and rushed up into the air with a loud whirring of wings. The air smelled of dust; the sun was a neon disc in the pale sky. My skin glowed a bluish white in the strange light. The road stretched out ahead, running straight and even for twenty miles until it joined the highway to Lomé. I could run all the way to the junction if I wanted, and keep right on going. Back to Lomé, back to America, back to my old life. I could walk in the door, throw my arms around my ex-husband, and say, "I've come back."

At a certain river crossing, I stopped running. The river was dark and slow, its banks shaded by eucalyptus. I stood on the little bridge and stared down at its glassy surface. My silhouette peered up at me.

On the road near my shoe was a small white pebble; I picked it up and polished it against my shirt, noticing again as I did so the skin of my arms and legs, still glowing like something radioactive in the dust-filtered light. Somehow I had to make this work. I would learn French—I could hire a teacher from the village school to tutor me. I would make friends, despite being an outsider, despite being shy and tongue-tied. If the village children couldn't come to Fazao then I would go to them. And to help fill up my time, I would write, with or without electricity—who needs a computer? I would write by hand. Instead of putting myself to sleep with bedtime stories, I'd write a book about Fazao's miraculous turnaround. I would will things to work out, the way Thomas had willed away hives.

I dropped the white pebble into the dark water flowing under the bridge; my silhouette rippled. I waited until the ripples died, then I turned and retraced my steps.

Thomas in the garden with Nelson Mesuli, at left, and a neighborhood friend.

Chapter Fourteen

The morning we left Fazao, the staff clustered in the hotel parking lot to wish us bon voyage: Hussein, Martine, Gaspard, Antoine, even Hussein's mother, which both surprised and touched me until somebody explained that she merely wanted a lift to the nearest bus stop. We were forty minutes down the road when I realized I had left my wallet behind. Fortunately, there was nothing essential in it—our passports were still in Lomé, and Patrick had the airline tickets and our travel money in his safari vest.

In Lomé, we went straight to Monsieur Gaumieau's office to collect the passports, which had, we hoped, been stamped with the visas necessary for us to remain in the country for a couple of years on our return from Tanzania. The ministry for national parks was housed in a quiet, leafy neighborhood, its streets lined with well-preserved colonial mansions. We pulled into a semicircular gravel drive that swung past a white portico, parked under the arched fronds of a convenient tree, and Patrick ran up the front steps of an elegant white stucco building with wooden shutters and through an ornate wooden door. Thomas and I waited in the car.

The minister's gardener was delicately removing leaves from the gravel drive with his broom. We watched the man with the broom, and waited for Patrick's return. It was hot, and we were hungry—we had not eaten since breakfast, and that was hours earlier. I was just about to leave the car and investigate the cause of our delay when the ornate wooden door opened and Patrick emerged, scowling, an unlit cigarette clamped between his teeth. He passed in front of the car and, standing by my open window, lit the cigarette, closed his Zippo with a familiar clank, and exhaled a long puff of smoke.

"Well," he said briskly, smoke pouring from his nostrils, "our passports are not here."

I squinted up at him, raising a hand to shield my eyes against the bright sun. "What do you mean they're not here? Where are they?"

He blew another puff of smoke out of the corner of his mouth and stuck his Zippo back in his breast pocket. "I'm not sure."

It took us three days to locate our passports and get them back. Monsieur Gaumieau had given them to somebody, who had given them to somebody else, who had given them to yet another somebody. And so on. The delay was maddening: Every hour we remained in Togo was one less hour we'd have in Arusha to wrap things up and complete the round trip before the start of school.

At long last, the passports turned up at the Office of Immigration; they were returned, with smiles and handshakes and laughter from the Togolese, and sullen gratitude from us, and we made it to the airport just in time to catch our thrice-rebooked flight.

In between all the running around, we had stopped by the boarding school so Thomas could take his one-hour entrance exam—which lasted not one hour but two. The stress of our departure must have addled Patrick, for he suddenly came up with the idea of leaving Thomas behind. We could drop him at the boarding school in Lomé, he pointed out, while we returned to Arusha to pack up. "No, darling," I said, gently, "he needs to say good-bye to his friends." Patrick's mind was simply too busy with its own thoughts to imagine what somebody else's mind might be thinking right now, and for a moment I felt like the mother Thomas deserved. "You're right," Patrick said, and there was no more talk of Thomas remaining behind.

Arusha was cool and breezy, and so refreshing after Togo's stifling heat that I began to wonder why on earth Patrick wanted to renew his acquaintance with West Africa, but such a question at such a time would not have been helpful—we were going, heat or no heat. Still, the old town looked particularly fetching, lush from the erstwhile rains, the jacarandas and flame trees in full flower. Old Moshi Road was a corridor of blue and yellow and red, and Mount Meru's snow-dusted peak rose above the treetops into a clear blue sky.

In our absence, Esther had kept the house immaculate, despite the dust that was on a renewed campaign to engulf the town now that the rains were over. She had even cleaned Thomas's model Citroën rally truck, a gesture that reminded me of Jenni, scrubbing down the Land Rover on the day of our wedding. But there was no time to waste on sentimental daydreams—we had too much to do. Our main task was to sell as much of our stuff as possible as swiftly as possible: the Land Rover pickup, the Toyota Tercel, the furniture, the camping equipment, and other household odds and ends. We had a scant two weeks.

All over town there were signs up for people who were bailing out and selling furniture, cars, refrigerators, stoves, you name it. They were posted on the wall at Max's Patisserie, at Mambo Café, at Meat

King, at the Outpost, at almost any place you could think of where muzungus gathered. Itinerant teachers from the UK who, after two years in Arusha, were off to teach English next in Abu Dhabi or Bangkok; U.N. officials who had been reposted; people whose businesses had failed and were starting over elsewhere. People came, people went, especially in Arusha.

We didn't bother to put up notices that we were selling—there was no time for that either. We told a few friends who passed the word on, and within a couple of days, everybody knew that we were out of there. An accountant friend made an offer on Patrick's laptop; the special ed teacher at St. George's expressed interest in the Land Rover. Jenni's aunt bought most of the furniture. Moses came with a van and loaded it all up; the aunt paid cash, carefully counting out a thick wad of ten-thousand-shilling notes. Jenni bought some of the dishes, and Patrick gave her the rest. I gave the gardener and the askari most of our clothes, including Patrick's father's much-worn sweater and my blue wedding dress and matching shoes, worn once. Nelson acquired the outgrown toys, including a once-cherished set of Legos.

The mornings were crisp and dewy; the schoolchildren who stuck their small hands through the hole in the front gate and waved as they passed the house were dressed in warm navy blue sweaters. Loto came to work each day wearing Maurice's old yellow cardigan.

We planned a hasty good-bye party, and advertised it through word of mouth, as we'd done with our wedding just over a year earlier: Saturday evening, Mambo Café. Now that we were really leaving, I had nothing but affection for Arusha.

Meanwhile, we waited for Patrick's contract to arrive.

"How is he sending it?" I asked. Time was growing short.

Patrick seemed unsure.

"By email?" I suggested. We were also awaiting plane tickets.

"Mebby."

"You don't know? He didn't say?"

The school in Lomé had sent several emails. They were holding a place for Thomas, and the emails were starting to sound impatient: Was he coming or not?

"He just said I'd receive it within a week."

"But it's been longer than that. Does he know that Thomas has to start school? Does he realize that we are moving, all of us, from one country to another? That we have to pack and, and all that?"

"I gonna call him."

The deal fell through the day after we sold the last of our furniture. Patrick received the news by email, in Emilio's office at the Mambo Café—we were among a handful of regulars who had free use of Emilio's personal Internet connection. While Patrick went in to check his email, I sat in the bar and waited.

It was midafternoon; the lunch crowd had dispersed, and the late-afternoon bar crowd had not yet arrived. The clientele had changed since Emilio took over the place, becoming somewhat more respectable. Gone were the out-of-work regulars who had sat around all day running up tabs and getting under Martina's skin, and in their place were lawyers from the Rwanda Tribunal, teachers from the local private schools, and carloads of wageni on tour with up-scale companies. Emilio had lured them with a steady series of improvements that included a canopied terrace and a real bar managed by a professional bartender named Buddy, who had springy blond curls, electric-blue eyes, and looked about twelve years old. Buddy approached the job of bartending with the enthusiasm of a twelve-year-old, too, along with the discipline and purposefulness of a general, and the bar was very popular. It was usually mobbed in the evening, starting with the four-o'clock stampede of teachers from the school parking lot. But for now, all was quiet; not even Buddy was around, having gone away for a while to attend the funeral of his grandfather, a retired Lutheran missionary who, in his nineties, had been killed by rebels at his home in the Congo.

After not five minutes, I heard footsteps and Patrick appeared in the barroom doorway. The set look on his face told me there was trouble. He took two steps into the room and I could see he was not just upset—he was furious. He could barely speak he was so mad. "We're fucked," he said. He cast a glance around the barroom as if he was looking for something to punch. Finding nothing suitable, he sat down on the banquette, breathing heavily, and stared at nothing in particular for a moment before he spoke again. Then he said, in the controlled tone of somebody who might erupt at any moment, "There is no contract."

Instead of the contract that he had been promising for weeks now, the big boss had sent an email saying that his board of directors—a group of decision makers we'd never met and had clearly underestimated—had calculated the organization could not afford a full-time warden's salary. They wanted Patrick to work six months out of the year. The rest of the year, during the rains, the hotel would shut down, and the entire staff would go on hiatus.

"Even the rangers?" I asked, dumbfounded.

"Even the rangers."

We spent the next day or two going around town buying back our furniture. Fortunately, nobody had resold it yet, and there was no quibbling—only nods of sympathy and understanding, and then everybody just accepted back the money they had given us days before, and we loaded everything into the pickup and drove it back home. We did not ask for the return of the wedding shoes, the Legos, or Maurice's sweater.

It was too late to cancel our good-bye party. When our friends arrived at the Mambo to bid us farewell, we simply told the ones who hadn't heard it already that we were staying.

るき

We went back to doing safaris, but something was different. Having been so close to bolting, we couldn't get comfortable again. We were like a house that's been picked up by a tornado, spun around a few times, and set back down. We were rattled, and certain thoughts nagged more than ever, such as how long it would be before our legs gave out and we were forced into retirement, and what would happen to us when we were in our eighties, God willing we should live so long—the age of Rick and Putschi's mother, Helinka, who could barely see anymore and was cared for by her ex-daughter-in-law because Martina, despite her cantankerousness, was really a kind person. We would be lucky indeed to be cared for in our old age by somebody like her.

The lost opportunity hung over us. Part of me was greatly relieved to be able to set aside the book about the roller-skating sheep and the question of who would run the hotel, not to mention who would rescue Thomas when the next riots broke out. But I could see that Patrick had been dealt a great blow, though, in typical fashion, he tried to play it down. Ever since he had left Sierra Leone, he had missed West Africa. He literally dreamed of it. West Africa was where half his life had been spent, the setting of a thousand cherished memories. West Africa, for him, was home, something that could not be said of a former British protectorate where "they have no clue what is a decent baguette."

After the deal fell through, he spent another six weeks in Togo, up to the rainy season. Thomas and I stayed behind in Arusha. We needed the six weeks' pay, and Patrick wanted to be there to take two nephews from Paris on safari, a trip that had been arranged weeks earlier. And he needed to settle a few things.

In the short time he was there, he spent several days going around Sokodé, talking with furniture makers, who confirmed his suspicion that the park's valuable mahoganies were being chopped down and sold by high-level civil servants. It wasn't the only illegal activity at Fazao that had the government's fingerprints all over it.

While on a recce in the forest, he heard a chopper overhead and, above the whir of the blades, a series of shots from a high-powered rifle. In Lomé a few days later, he described the incident to the French advisor to Eyadema. There were only two helicopters in the entire country of Togo; one belonged to Eyadema, the other to his son. The president's advisor called the president's official pilot, another Frenchman, with Patrick standing at his side.

"You were in Fazao last weekend?" he asked casually. "You were doing some hunting?"

"How did you know?" said the pilot.

That's how Patrick traced some of the animal poaching at Fazao to Eyadema's inner circle.

The nephews came, and he spent the last week or so of his brief career as a national park director traveling around the country, enjoying himself. One of the nephews went up in the plane with Paganelli but barely made it off the runway before the right wing caught a branch and went down; at the hospital where they had their abrasions treated it was discovered that Paganelli's fatigue and loss of appetite were due to advanced typhus.

Patrick, however, wondered aloud whether Paganelli and the former hotel manager had been poisoned by people who saw them as interlopers. An image of the gentle Hussein, nervously hovering as his young cousin helped carry plates to and from the table, flashed through my mind, and I remembered the day soon after Christmas when all three of us came down with something that we decided, in the end, was malaria.

"They might have tried with me," he mused, "but I'm immune."

"Immune to poison?" There was a time when the poison theory would have made me laugh.

"To whatever kind of poison they were using." He scratched his chin absent-mindedly, reflecting. "They were complaining a lot about me."

"Who was complaining?"

"The villagers, to the tourism authorities, because I wouldn't let them farm inside the park." His pensive look gave way to something more purposeful. "There is only one way to protect a park: It's to be tough. Catch a guy poaching, it should be five years in jail; not a warning."

In his absence, Samideau had been transferred to a highway checkpoint, where he was basically useless. "But why?" I asked, stupidly. "He was too good at his job," said Patrick. "Too efficient. It made him a pain in the ass."

And he was particularly mad at the big boss, who had turned a deaf ear when presented with evidence of government poaching. "He denied the things," he sputtered. "He just denied everything."

Beneath the anger, though, there was something else. Both of us knew that such an opportunity would not present itself again, and that his time in the bush was coming to an end.

ಎಲ

As the school year drew to a close, we took a bunch of students and a few teachers on a camping safari to Lake Eyasi, where a handful of hunter-gatherers known as the Hadzabe had set up a small tourist business, to the chagrin of missionaries and anthropologists who wanted them to remain hunter-gatherers. The schoolkids were at that awkward age when the girls are considerably taller than the boys, and certain body parts are growing faster than others, so that noses look too big on some, legs too long on others. They were city kids; most had no clue what to do in the bush. We hiked along the lakeshore to a Hadzabe encampment; the men showed them how to make fire and helped them shoot a few arrows, but the kids were not into walking, an exercise for which they could see no point when we had a perfectly good overland truck to take them places in comfort. They shuffled along, complaining, their column getting longer and looser with every step. "What are you going to do this summer?" I asked one, a girl. "Watch TV," she said.

The teachers were ready for the school year to be over, and for them, the safari was an opportunity to relax; they looked forward, in particular, to the evenings, when they could pack the kids off to their tents, break out the whiskey, and have the campfire to themselves.

The kids struck me as more demanding than usual. Maybe they were as tired of the teachers as the other way round, or maybe they were too used to having household servants wait on them. Or maybe I was tired of being a hostess. Whatever the reason, it didn't take me long to get my back up.

"May I have some tea?" said one of the smaller boys when he reached the head of the chow line, where the adults were serving. I was in charge of drinks.

"May I have some tea . . . what?" I prompted.

The boy thought for a moment. "May I have some tea . . . bags?"

"What's the magic word?"

The boy looked completely confused, as if he wanted to run away. I turned to Patrick, who was serving noodles. "Do you know the magic word, Mr. Texier?"

"Oh, yes, I know the magic word."

I turned back to the kid. "Okay. Try again. And don't forget the magic word."

The boy, now panicky, said in a small voice, "May I have some tea . . . with brandy?"

The teachers cracked up. Meekly, the kid held his cup while I poured the tea, then he slunk away as the guffaws died down.

After dinner, the teachers tried to get the kids back into a group to sing a song. The kids, who had been so listless all day long, had become charged with energy as soon as the sun went down, and they ran about hooting and hollering in the dusk, ignoring the teachers. Mrs. Valentine, the teacher with the loudest voice, started to bellow. The two Hadzabe men who kept watch over the campsite at night regarded the chaos with amused expressions.

Coming back from Lake Eyasi, after dropping off the kids and the teachers at the early-years center in town, we overtook Nelson, who was walking up the hill toward home. Patrick stopped the truck and Nelson climbed in the back with Thomas. At our gate, he hopped out and shot over to his house without a word. We were just climbing out of the truck ourselves when Nelson reappeared with Mesuli.

"Habari za leo," we said—how is your day?

"Not good," Mesuli answered, gazing at the ground in front of him, as if unable to look at us. "Very bad," he added, shaking his head. He walked in silence along the gravel drive, head down, then stopped in front of the truck and just stood there, pointing toward a dark spot on the gravel driveway where something had spilled.

"What is it?" said Patrick, staring at the spot. He looked at Mesuli and lowered his voice almost to a whisper. "The askari?"

We stared at the bloodstained gravel. The spot was more than a foot in diameter. Leading us around to the back entrance of the house, Mesuli muttered something I couldn't hear, so I asked Patrick, who was between us: "What happened to the askari?"

"He's dead!" Patrick said loudly, almost angrily.

Mesuli turned. "No," he said. "Not dead. He is in the hospital."

The askari, he said, had received a blow on the head with a sharp object; he had a bad gash, but was expected to recover. He was lucky: As he was lying on the gravel drive, motionless and bleeding, he heard the thieves, standing over him. "I'm going to slit his throat," said one. "Don't bother," said the other. "He's already dead."

The back door was bashed in and there was stuff strewn about. Mesuli led us from room to room, pointing things out—he had already made a careful inspection with the police. The house had been ransacked in a very disorganized way. The boom box was gone, and some other odds and ends, but amazingly, an envelope containing about six hundred dollars in cash, which had been tucked in a pile of shirts in the bedroom, was lying in plain view. It had been discovered and then inexplicably left behind. The three bicycles were still in the storeroom. So was all of the camping equipment. The only thing that seemed to be missing from the storeroom, in fact, was a well-worn pair of men's hiking boots. Also untouched were two pairs of binoculars, the printer, the scanner, and my laptop.

"The guns are missing," said Mesuli. "You had them with you?"

"Don't worry," Patrick assured him. "They are at a friend's house."

Another laptop, said Mesuli, was found in the garden, where the thieves had dropped it as they fled. The police took it with them "as evidence."

"You will have to go to the police station to sign for it," Mesuli explained. "I have a friend who will go with you—he is a retired police officer. He will see that you get it back."

We heard footsteps at the back door and a woman's voice calling "Hodi!" and Irene, Mesuli's wife, appeared with little Emily. Mesuli instructed Nelson to help unload the truck, which was packed with camping gear, and the three children trotted outside; a moment later I caught sight of Emily waddling toward the house carrying a campstool almost as big as she.

"Pole sana," said Irene: So sorry. She and Mesuli were way more upset for us than we were for ourselves. Knowing them, I suspected they felt somewhat responsible: As our nearest neighbors, they had failed to respond quickly enough in our absence to prevent the break-in.

"There were fifteen who came," said Irene. Fifteen robbers, against our one poor little askari. "They went to two other houses," she continued. "Both in Sekei, the same night. It was around one or two o'clock." In one of the homes, people were watching TV; the thieves took the TV and the VCR and loaded them into their pickup truck. The second was the home of a priest who was well prepared for a break-in: Either he or his askari blew a whistle, which was promptly answered by a chorus of whistle blasts from the surrounding neighbors. The thieves took off.

"Don't feel bad about the missing things," I said to Irene. "They're not important."

Mesuli called a fundi to repair the door, and we cleaned up a little. Perusing the shelves in the living room where he kept his most precious mementoes, Patrick discovered that among the missing was the owl-shaped silver flask that had been a gift from Huguette—one of the last tokens of that fifteen-year marriage—and the pair of papier-maché birds that were a first-year anniversary gift from me. Also stolen were his meershaum pipe and his Mont Blanc pen, which the thieves would probably sell as cheap tschotchkes. The fake Zippos were gone, but the real one was still there. Picking things up off the floor by the shelves, Patrick studied a small object, turning it over in his hand. "Ah," he said finally, "I know what it is." He picked up Thomas's rally car. "It's the wiper," he said. He placed the car back on the shelves where it belonged and put the wiper inside. "I put it under the seat," he said. "Like in my old Nissan."

That night, in the wee hours, I awoke and couldn't go back to sleep. Finally, I got up and went down the hall to the living room, where Patrick was reading a book in his favorite position: leaning forward, hands clasped, elbows on knees, feet flat on the floor, book open in front of him on the coffee table. It was three-thirty in the morning; he had been awake for two hours and had done a further inventory. "They took the electric cattle prod," he said.

In fact, they had taken only half of it. The other half was still in a drawer in the kitchen, useless now. They had also taken the electric teakettle but left the cord, and Patrick's blood pressure kit but not the armband.

"I'm making coffee," I said, and went into the kitchen to heat water on the gas burner, since our electric teakettle was no more. Patrick made himself a snack of some bread and jam. Coming back from the pantry, he said, "At least they haven't stolen the organic couscous. Thank God for that."

At the police station, we parked the car and followed Mr. Havalite Lima, Mesuli's friend the retired police officer, past a row of smashed cars to the building entrance. Inside, the corridors were lined with unclaimed stolen goods, sorted into piles—radios, TVs, a stack of bicycles. One large pile consisted entirely of bags of cement. Mr. Havalite Lima spoke to one of the officers and then escorted us upstairs and down an unlit hallway lined with moldering stacks of unfiled documents. In an office so small that whenever somebody moved everybody else had to move too, two clerks wrote out separate police reports, one for Patrick and one for me. The clerks wore overcoats to protect themselves from the cold air that came in through the windows, which had no glass in them, but they had nothing to keep their hands warm; with stiff fingers they moved their pencils slowly across the lined paper. Around the edges of the room were more towering stacks of mildewed documents, ideal for harboring mice and beetles. I imagined a clerk placing our reports on one of the stacks.

Downstairs, we waited while Mr. Havalite Lima took charge of getting our laptop back. Outside a row of padlocked doors that appeared to be jail cells, two handcuffed and shoeless young men sat on the floor, backs against the wall. At the front desk, Patrick signed for the laptop, and the clerk set an ink pad in front of him. "Your thumbprint, sir, please, right here." Patrick put his thumbprint next to his name in the ledger, and we walked back out past the smashed cars. "They need some new ink for their pad," he said, examining his thumb.

At the hospital, the patients were two to a bed. Mr. Havalite Lima showed us to the men's ward and then excused himself, saying he had other business to attend to. We thanked him and tried to give him some money, but he refused.

"Please, no," he said, waving his hand. "That is not necessary. When somebody has misfortune, it is good to help. It is the right thing to do."

We walked slowly past the rows of beds, searching, unsure whether we would even recognize the askari, whose face we had seen so seldom. But there he was, at the far end of the long room, curled on his side in a narrow bed with someone else's feet next to his bandaged head. He looked even smaller and more fragile than ever, and I noticed that he was wearing a pair of warm socks that used to be mine. Over him was a thin sheet, useless against the cold that came through the open windows; even the hospital, it seemed, was too poor to buy glass for its windows. I took his hand and, mustering a few words of Swahili, thanked him and said I was very sorry and asked him how much to pay for the hospital. It was about ten dollars. Did he need food? No, his wife was bringing food. We told him we'd come back with a warm blanket.

"He was wearing your socks," said Patrick as we drove away.

For the next few days, we went about in a daze. Patrick was uncharacteristically glum. He'd been robbed before, plenty of times, but it had just made him mad. He tended to grab whatever weapon was handy and fight back, once charging naked and barefoot through the garden in the darkness armed with his crossbow. Now, he seemed shaken, almost depressed. And it's not even like we lost much.

In the sunny garden of the Mambo Café, he liberally dosed his toasted ham-and-cheese with black pepper and then just stared at it. "Well," he said finally, "I'm down."

We were driving through town on one errand or another when I said to him, "Maybe we should move to America. I can get a job in New York—all I have to do is call a friend or two—and you can set up your own tour company."

"Maybe you're right," he said, surprising me. I was expecting something vague and noncommittal.

"Let's think about it for a couple of days," I suggested.

Within a week, we had made up our minds.

ॐ

We left Africa in the summer of 2001, in our second year of marriage. When I asked Patrick if he was sure, he said yes. I sent a few emails to friends in New York, telling them I was coming back and bringing Patrick and Thomas with me. Within two weeks, I was working for a hip new business magazine headquartered in a sleek Soho loft. While I scoured the Jersey suburbs for a two-bedroom apartment, Thomas went to France to spend the summer with his grandmother.

Patrick stayed behind to make some money—the summer tourist season would soon be in full swing—and to sell the cars and collect on a couple of debts.

Why didn't we hesitate? Suddenly the future was a bright blue sky. Optimism moved in where uncer-

tainty had been. We would have no more worries
about work permits and rainy-season dry spells, when
business slowed and the matador stood guard over an
empty cupboard. Nor about gangs of armed thieves
coming in the night, or Al-Qaeda setting off bombs in
our backyard. In Westfield, a suburban town in
northern New Jersey, we would be safe. Our duplex
apartment was a short commute from the office in
Lower Manhattan where I'd be working; you could
almost see the World Trade Center from our doorstep.
The view, which encompassed an auto body shop and
a dumpster, wasn't as picturesque as Meru, but Patrick, for one, would sleep more soundly knowing he
was not within range of an active volcano. He looked
forward to the vast international selection of cheeses
that awaited him in America's grocery stores, and
drifted off at night dreaming of blue-dimpled wedges
of Roquefort and creamy white mounds of chevre. I
looked forward to Sunday dinners chez Texier with
my New York friends. Thomas looked forward to
watching TV in his very own living room instead of at
Mesuli's house, and to seeing snow fall out of the sky;
this year, he informed us, he would ask Santa for skis.
He even said a few positive words about going to a
"real" school, one with lockers and bells.

One of Patrick's last acts before leaving Africa was
to sell his most valuable possession, the Land Rover
pickup. The special ed teacher bought it, mostly to
drive around town, which was a little bit like retiring an
old workhorse from the bulk of its labors—even
though in this case, Patrick claimed the old horse had
many kilometers of off-road driving left in it. Mesuli
got most of the furniture. The matador painting where
we'd hidden our cash went to a Spanish friend.

If not for Thomas and me, Patrick might have
stayed with the job in Fazao and tried to make it

work. He might even have succeeded. But probably not; rescuing a wilderness the size of Fazao is slow work, and in a country like Togo it's very slow work. He no longer had the years to see it through.

To this day, however, he has never said a word about what might have been. No regrets, he told me, way back when I barely knew him; it wasn't a fact so much as a philosophical habit. Regrets will snatch happiness right out from under your nose. To banish them takes discipline.

When he boarded the plane for America, he had a few dollars and two suitcases, little more than he'd come with. His souvenirs from the past four decades were a handmade bow and nine arrows, a worn safari vest, a disorganized box of photographs. Thomas's Citroën rally car made the crossing, too, along with his Goliath beetle, sent to him from Abidjan by his bug-collecting friend Alan. So did Patrick's teeth, and my Swahili pocket dictionary, now just another useless memento. The cork from our bottle of wedding champagne was tucked among our socks and T-shirts, its good-luck shilling held in place with cellotape.

When it was time to leave, Patrick didn't make a drama out of it. He just went on to the next thing. "I can't wait to see you . . . and more!" he wrote in his emails during the month or so we were apart. "I got $4K for the pickup . . . I miss you big deal . . . only twenty-one more days," et cetera. Then he said good-bye to the place he loved most in the world.

"What took you to Africa?" people ask. "A plane," he always says. It really isn't a joke. He wanted to go, so he went. It was that simple. He left the same way.

ॐ

Thomas in the sky above southern New Jersey.

Epilogue

Our six years in the Jersey suburbs were a rigorous test of the contract we signed in front of Mr. Happy God Matoi, and there were moments when I wondered if the wedding boss hadn't inadvertently hexed us. "Don't come back here if you change your mind" wasn't much of a blessing.

Our new home had certain advantages over Arusha, it's true. In Westfield, we were nobodies. For the first time in years, I could go for a walk without drawing stares. In Westfield, Thomas could leave his brand-new bicycle lying on the front lawn in plain view of the street and nobody would touch it, even if he left it there all night. In Westfield, a prosperous town studded with million-dollar homes, we hardly ever bothered to lock our front door because one glance at our driveway was enough to discourage a potential burglar. Our car, Buttercup, was a little yellow Honda with pop-up headlights and a bashed-in door, which we had bought for $174 from a mechanic who wanted to get it off his lot. "I hate this car," said Thomas every time he squeezed himself into the back seat.

"You should love this car," I told him. "It is because of Buttercup that we are able to afford Coco Puffs." But I had to admit that, parked beside our neighbors' giant SUV, Buttercup looked pretty meager.

Our home was the top floor of a duplex that over-looked a busy street. New Jersey Transit buses rum-bled past our living room window, and feral cats prowled around the dumpster in the parking lot. Pat-rick used to sit on the stoop blowing smoke rings and dreaming of far-off places.

The Jolly Trolley, a noisy pub where weary rail commuters revived themselves after a hard day on Wall Street, provoked a flood of nostalgia for the crabby congeniality of the Mambo Café, and every time I did a load of laundry or picked up Thomas's messy room, I missed Jenni. But at least in Westfield we felt safe.

The morning Al Qaeda bombed Lower Manhat-tan, I stood on a street corner in SoHo, two miles north, looking and looking at the empty place where the Twin Towers should be. Patrick stood on the front stoop facing east, studying the same smudged patch of blue. In the afternoon I called him to say I wouldn't be home that day; the wait at Penn Station to get on a train was still several hours long.

After September 11, we abandoned our plan to start a tour company. Patrick spent more and more time playing solitaire on his computer and sanding a chair that he had found beside the road on trash col-lection day, until he finally gave up on the chair and concentrated on the solitaire. That's what he was do-ing one afternoon when he began to tremble and real-ized he must be having a heart attack. The trembling went on and on, and he waited for the end. This was not where and how he had expected death to come, in the living room of a duplex apartment in an American suburb, snatching him away from a game of solitaire. To his surprise, it was remarkably painless, this heart attack. As it continued, he started to relax. Then he noticed a steady thumping coming from the utility room: the washing machine was violently spinning, shaking the walls and floorboards of the flimsy duplex, the cause of his palpitations.

We all missed Africa, Patrick most of all. Once his green card came through, he got a job behind the counter at a car rental company and tried to be philosophical about it. "I had my adventures when I was young," he said. "Most people wait till they retire. I'm not sorry I did it the other way round." He started out as a car prep, working alongside someone named Stinky. "And what will you be doing in your new job?" asked my mother. "Hosing down the outside and vacuuming the inside," Patrick replied. It was August when he landed the job, and he went to work in shorts and sandals, washing the cars in the shade of a tree. By the time the weather turned cold, he'd been promoted to an indoor spot. "I've never owned so many white shirts," he said.

On a wintry night in January, at the beginning of our second year in Westfield, Patrick and I awoke to find Thomas standing beside the bed, bright light coming from the hallway. "Papa," he said, "there's a lady on the phone. I think it's my grandmother."

A midnight call from France could only mean trouble. Patrick sat on the living room couch, listening to the caller, saying a few words now and then, while Thomas and I hovered. "Who was that?" Thomas asked when Patrick hung up the phone. "Just a lady" was all the answer he got.

The lady was Thomas's mother, Anne. She had been looking for him for some time. "I knew it!" Thomas exclaimed, when we finally told him, two weeks after the phone call. "I knew it was her!" He had said nothing in the interval that followed the phone call, but Anne had said plenty, begging Patrick to let her speak to Thomas. He told her to wait until midyear exams ended. The day after the last exam, we called Thomas into the living room. "I've heard from your mother," said Patrick. "It was she who called the other night."

Their first conversation was long. "We talked for more than an hour," Thomas told us. "That's the longest I've ever talked on the phone." He wanted to meet her, and we said he could go to France during the summer holidays.

Meanwhile, Patrick had done some investigation. Anne was living in the small village that had been her childhood home. She had made a courageous effort to pull herself together, and her life had been restored. Thomas wanted to spend the entire summer with her and her family, a construction worker named Ian and a blond ten-year-old named Luc. Patrick said an entire summer was too long for a first visit; Thomas could go for three weeks.

As summer approached, I made a gift for Anne, an album of pictures, glimpses of all the years of Thomas's childhood that she had missed. I dreaded meeting her. Thomas and I were heading into a long and difficult phase; her sudden reappearance rocked me. I was jealous and insecure; my role was being usurped, by Thomas's real mother, what a twist. I tried not to mind, or at least not to show that I minded, but several times I threw myself, weeping, into Patrick's arms, feeling terribly sorry for myself and ashamed that I wasn't happier for Thomas. One part of me was glad—every child should have an opportunity to know his mother—but another part was deeply forlorn.

The little gang of Westfield boys Thomas hung out with was excited about his adventure, a doubleheader: trip to France and reunion with mystery parent. Everybody seemed to know about it—Thomas's teachers, the neighbors, his friends' parents. I'd never known him to be so chatty. I braced myself for the reunion, not at all sure I wanted to witness it. It bothered me, too, that here would be another situation where I didn't speak the language. As a stepmother I would be out of place; as a foreigner, deaf and speechless.

The drive to Anne's village from Paris was interminable. Patrick took the scenic route, speeding through mountain passes while I watched the time and Thomas grew more and more silent in the back seat. We were expected for dinner at the home of Anne's friend Claudie, a retired country doctor. By the time we arrived, the dinner hour was long past, and the sun was setting. We parked the car and a slender woman with Thomas's eyes emerged from Claudie's house.

Since our move to Westfield, Thomas had become a fan of that great American pastime known in our household as couch-potating. Patrick and I refused to chauffeur him around town, so he walked a lot, but the end result was still a little pudgy. Patrick had insisted that Thomas prepare for this reunion by paying a visit to Supercuts, and Thomas had emerged with bangs. He looked much younger than fifteen, except for his height. He had shot up fast, and he bumped into the furniture a lot. Anne was tall, but Thomas was taller. She gave him a quick hug and a little kiss, and the moment I'd braced myself for passed before I had time to react. Everybody exchanged greetings, and we went into Claudie's house.

It was nearly ten o'clock at night when we sat down to dinner; Claudie had prepared a large feast. We had almost finished desert when the tension of the day caught up with me and I excused myself from the table. When I came back, some ten minutes later, my eyes were red. "What's the matter, Sara?" Thomas asked. "Nothing," I said. "I'm going to miss you, that's all." And I burst into tears.

275

Everybody except Claudie was terribly dismayed. "It's normal," she kept saying. Thomas, who was sitting opposite me at the table, with Anne on his right, looked very worried. "I'm just tired," I told him. "And I can't understand what anybody's saying."

Thomas was to spend the night at Anne's house; Patrick and I were staying with Claudie. We would drive back to Paris in the morning after saying our good-byes. Thomas took his bag and left with Anne and Ian and Luc. I gave Anne Thomas's toothbrush. "Make sure he uses it," I said. Then Thomas was gone.

Within five minutes he was back. "We ran into your car," he said to Patrick. Everybody went out to survey the damage; Thomas and I stayed behind. "I don't want to go," he whispered. "Don't worry," I said. "It's easy to make a mistake like that, backing up in the dark. You'll be fine."

"That's not what I mean. It has nothing to do with the accident. I just don't want to go."

Everyone came back inside the house. "He doesn't want to go," I said to Patrick.

Thomas spent the night with us. He and I lay side by side on the bed in one of the guestrooms, taking turns reading the last book in the Harry Potter series; Harry was ahead of Thomas in school, graduating from Hogwart's when Thomas had two long years ahead of him at Westfield High. Meanwhile, Anne and Patrick were quietly arguing on the patio where we'd had wine and hors d'ouevres. She wanted Patrick to insist that Thomas follow the program, and she was appalled that I was reading to him. "He's too old for that," she said. "She is treating him like a baby." I found this out much later.

We did what we could to encourage Thomas to stay, delaying our own departure by a full day in the hope that Thomas would change his mind. He spent the second night at Anne's house, but he didn't sleep much, and when we came in the morning to hear his decision he said right away, "I'm coming with you." Anne was devastated.

She tried to keep in touch with Thomas by email. It didn't work. "Call him," I advised her. "Thomas doesn't write letters; we have to go through hell to get him to send a thank-you to his grandmother." Anne called a few times, then she stopped. I couldn't understand why she gave up so easily.

For the rest of that summer, Thomas mostly slept and played video games. The next summer, Patrick crashed his Harley and was laid up for three months, and I was determined that Thomas wouldn't hang around the house all day. Thomas said he wanted to get a summer job. Every morning, I woke him up at eight o'clock and sent him out to look for employment, instructing him not to come home before noon. I suspected he was going to a friend's house, but he told us later he went to Starbucks and read books. If he had said in the beginning that he wanted to spend the summer reading books, we would have been delighted. But of course that wasn't what he wanted to do at all. He felt terribly persecuted. I remember looking out the living room window and seeing him on the front stoop with his backpack—I now realize his pillow was stuffed inside, along with his book, in case he wanted to take a little nap at Starbucks. I had made Patrick's breakfast and his midmorning snack and his lunch, and I was waiting for Thomas to disappear so I could go across the street and catch the bus into the city. I didn't want Patrick to know that Thomas was sitting on the stoop, downcast. He had enough on his mind. I remember suggesting to Thomas that perhaps he would like to escape this torture and spend the summer with

Anne. "She'll make sure you have a good time," I promised. His response was a resolute no.

In our darkest hour, we turned to somebody named Dennis, who advertised himself as a family therapist. His office was on the top floor of one of Westfield's grand old mansions, right around the corner from the little duplex apartment we rented from a Mr. Angelo Appezzato.

"We're stuck" was the way I explained our collective presence in Dennis's office. "We are unable to talk about the future. Nobody even wants to think about the future, except me. Thomas is the only student in his class who hasn't taken the SAT. We just can't get it together. The form doesn't get filled out, or it doesn't get handed over to his guidance counselor. And that's just one example of the kind of thing that happens all the time. Thomas says he wants to go to college, but he doesn't act like he wants to go to college, and whenever I try to talk about it, everybody gets all silent and sullen. So we've given up. We've become a family of people who don't talk to each other."

To prove my point, I stopped talking. The four of us sat in silence. Thomas was on my left, slumped in the corner of a shabby love seat, legs akimbo, jacket on, its collar hiding as much of his face as possible; Patrick was on my right, perched on the edge of a chair, looking about as relaxed as a grasshopper. "I see what you mean," said Dennis. "There's a heavy feeling in this room."

As Dennis studied us in all our misery and confusion, he himself looked very relaxed, casually dressed in a plaid flannel shirt and brown corduroys, tipped back, feet raised, in a Lay-Z-Boy recliner—on account of his bad back, he explained. Couch-potating, in other words, one of the many activities that Patrick and I had been parentally trying to discourage.

"Do you want to go to college?" he asked, smiling at Thomas in a friendly way, one couch potato to another.

"Sure."

"So what's stopping you from filling out this application?"

"I dunno. I've been kinda busy."

Thomas agreed to fill out an application before the next session; Patrick handed Dennis a check, carefully writing it out in front of Dennis as we said our good-byes—a gesture that was clearly meant to give Dennis a stab of discomfort. It seemed to work. "You don't have to do that now," said Dennis, to which Patrick responded, "I'm sorry but it's just my way. You know I lived in Africa for many years; I prefer to pay as I go." His words had a certain Old Country ring, as if we were simple, honest peasant folk who could ill afford such expensive nonsense, and anybody with half a scruple would be ashamed to charge so much to listen to a few small gripes when there were plenty of decent folk who would do the same for no more than the cost of a pint.

On the way home, Patrick let off steam: If anybody should be reclining in that office, shouldn't it be the three of us? What kind of logic said that the therapist got to stretch out while his customers, with all their costly burdens, occupied the cheap seats?

Thomas never did fill out the application, and after three unproductive sessions, Dennis admitted he had run out of ideas. Perversely, we all felt slightly better for having stumped our therapist: He was no smarter than we were! Driving home after the third session, we reached our first unanimous decision in months, and the next day I called Dennis and politely told him he was fired.

Dennis, to be fair, was only the last in a long line of experts—teachers, guidance counselors, archery coaches, orthodontists—whom we'd consulted in our efforts to get Thomas to do things we thought would be good for him, like homework and flossing. When it looked like our child might distinguish himself as the only student in the class of '06 not to graduate, we revved up our efforts on his behalf. But as an army of agitated adults bore down on him, Thomas defended himself by withdrawing until he was spending every waking moment in his room with the door shut and the curtains pulled, deeply immersed in the fantasy world of his favorite video game.

"From now on, I'm going to eat only healthy food," he announced over dinner one evening, causing me to choke on a lettuce leaf.

"What for?" I asked.

"For my senior project. We're supposed to set a challenge for ourselves."

"What kind of challenge?"

"Any kind. But it's gotta be something really, really hard."

"Hard doesn't have to mean torture. Think of something else."

"Like what?"

"Something hard but . . . exciting."

"Like parachuting out of a plane?"

Two weeks later, Thomas and Patrick drove to western New Jersey. Thomas was at the wheel, having finally gotten his learner's permit, the last one in his wide circle of friends to do so and the only one sensible enough to view the prospect of becoming a New Jersey motorist with deep skepticism. He had barely slept the night before, so anxious was he about his ability to safely navigate that stretch of highway, with its rumbling trucks and rushing traffic.

At a small airfield, the two of them spoke with a bunch of French paratroopers, one of whom took Thomas up in a small plane. Then, as Patrick stood on the ground, chain-smoking, Thomas tumbled through the sky and floated gently to earth.

"There's only one problem," he said to me on the phone a few minutes later. "It was too easy. I can't wait to do it again."

The hard part turned out to be the paper he was supposed to write, describing the challenge and how it was met. The task of putting all those words down on paper proved insurmountable.

"Do you want to graduate?" I asked him. We were sitting in the hospital cafeteria, having dinner. In a room of the hospital, Patrick was recuperating from the business of having a pacemaker installed.

"It's too late," he said, picking at his fries.

"It isn't too late. I talked with Miss Glasser." The guidance counselor and I were on very friendly terms. It irked me that Thomas had so little regard for her: How could he be so disinterested in such a flagrant oddball? Miss Glasser, who was on the verge of retirement, looked like any other Westfield matron and yet she was not, for did she not have her pilot's license, and was she not riding the lead camel in the photo of a desert caravan that hung on her office wall? And was there not, above her office door, a sign that read "Karibuni," the Swahili word for "Welcome"? "Where did you get that?," I had asked her, seeing it for the first time. "In Tanzania," she replied. "I went there on a safari."

I watched Thomas pick at his food, his face a mask of defeat.

"Miss Glasser says you need to write three overdue papers for English and hand them in, in order to graduate. That's all."

"That's a lot."

"I'll help you."

The three papers got done, but not on Thomas's computer. They were composed on my ancient laptop, the one that had been stolen in Tanzania and retrieved from the police station with the help of Mr. Havalite Lima. That's because I had confiscated Thomas's keyboard, in a fit of pique, so he couldn't play World of Warcraft until after the essays were done. He composed them at the kitchen table, with a good deal of coaching from me.

"Now can I have my keyboard back?" he asked when the last of the papers had been turned in. I was on my way out the door, headed for the grocery store. "Not yet," I said.

"Why not?"

"Because I'm still mad." I closed the door and headed down the stairs. The door opened.

"Then when can I?"

"When I stop being mad."

The door shut. As I reached the bottom of the stairs, I heard a muffled *blam* from within. I kept going.

When I came back a half hour later, Thomas greeted me at the door, looking contrite. "I pulled a Tyler," he said, naming a friend who was famous for his temper tantrums. "I hurt my hand." He rubbed his knuckles.

"How'd that happen?"

"I hit the wall."

"What wall?"

He lifted a throw pillow off the back of the living room couch, where he had propped it against the flimsy wall to cover a fist-size hole.

"That was pretty stupid."

"Sorry."

I didn't know what else to say—nothing like this had ever happened before. I left the house and started walking, intending to think things over. Patrick was home from the hospital, but it had been a hard week for everybody, and I didn't want to make things worse.

I hadn't reached the corner when I realized I didn't give a damn about the hole in the wall. I went back. Thomas was in his room, lying on his bed with a book. I stood in the doorway.

"I've decided it's a good thing you hit that wall."

Thomas regarded me with suspicion.

"I mean it. You probably needed to hit something. Sometimes it's good to get things out. How's your hand?"

"It hurts."

"Let's see." The hand was slightly pink.

"It'll be okay. I do have one piece of advice. You wanna hear it?"

"I'm not sure."

"Next time, put the pillow there *before* you hit the wall."

As Thomas's senior year at Westfield High drew to a close, I remembered something he had said to Patrick and me when graduation was still far in the future: "I just can't imagine not living with you guys," he had told us, during one of the long dinners we had at the end of each day, a tradition we had kept since Arusha. It had seemed like a compliment at the time. When we were his age, we couldn't wait to grow up and leave home. So when it became obvious that he would not be going off to college with his friends—the college applications, buried in the debris of his room, were no longer mentioned—I softened a little. He was eleven before he had what he considered to be a real family; he needed more time, that's all.

The morning after graduation, Thomas handed me his diploma. "Congratulations, Sara," he said. "Where shall we put it?" We gave it a prominent spot on the same set of shelves that housed the cork from our wedding champagne.

Thomas hung around the house for another year and then, when he was ready to leave, he went clear to Prague, where a friendly little college had accepted him on the basis of a two-page application form that had taken him ten minutes to fill out.

"I don't want to talk about it," Patrick said, a few days after he and Thomas said their good-byes at Kennedy Airport. I had long suspected that Thomas wasn't the only one unready for college. "It's like turning the knife in the wound. For a long time, it was just Thomas and me; we're like an old married couple. You know what I mean?"

Once Thomas was safely launched, I wrote to Anne for the first time in several years. She wrote back immediately. In her letter, she wondered whether Thomas had graduated from high school. "He has traveled a lot for someone his age," she observed, "like his father. How nice for him; you have done well; he is lucky to have had you for a mother." Her gratitude was humbling; I don't know whether Thomas was lucky on that score or not. Then she added, "I had to work hard to come to terms with Thomas's absence, but in the end I managed. A child should be comfortable in his skin, and it's enough for me to know that he is happy."

After a couple of emails, we ran out of things to say. But in that brief exchange, I learned something important about her. I was wrong to think she let her child go a second time without a fight. How foolish of me. Our hardest battles are with ourselves. Thomas's wishes were clear, and Anne chose to respect them. But she didn't give up easily.

After Thomas left home, Patrick and I moved to Vermont, to the house I grew up in. Our household now includes my mother, who will turn eighty-seven the day before Thomas turns twenty. Our first Christmas in Vermont was a proper one, with rare roast beef and real Champagne and presents underneath the tree. Thomas flew in from Prague on Christmas Eve, landing in Boston between snowstorms.

Patrick quit his job with the rental-car company and went to work for an airline, the job that had taken him to Africa. As he drives to the airport in the predawn darkness, snowflakes in the headlights, he thinks about all the places he and I can fly to free of charge: To Hanoi with a gift for his little granddaughter and a box of maple candy for her parents. To Paris to spend time with his daughter, and his sister, and his mother. To Prague, to see how Thomas is doing.

We have not been back to Africa, and we talk about our time there less and less. The cork from our wedding champagne is now tucked in a box of handkerchiefs; the stories Patrick courted me with are seldom told. Our family mementoes are scattered about the upstairs rooms of my mother's house. Among them is the little sign that hung above our front door in Sekei: Texier Household, Est. 1999.

One of the last messages we received from Arusha was an email from Moses, soon after September 11, announcing the birth of a son, whom he and Jenni christened "Innocent." After that, we lost touch. When you move a lot, over great stretches of land, it is sometimes easier to let the past go. If we could transport ourselves to Masai Camp on a Friday night, we would see only strangers. I can tell you which of

285

our old friends remain; they are the ones with deep roots. Mesuli is there, working hard to get the youngest children through school; Putschi and Penny are living quietly back in the shambas. Innocent is a schoolboy in shorts and kneesocks. And I wouldn't be at all surprised to find Loto listening to "Buffalo Soldier" in our old garden shed, and the nameless askari guarding the house.

"My home is with you," Patrick often tells me. He has no other. And yet he misses Africa every day. He never expected to live so long in a place where the trees are naked half the year. Now he has an iPod, a closet full of white shirts, and an American passport. After studying him for quite some time now, I've concluded that his best qualities are incomprehensible. What is the secret, for example, of his enduring optimism? In the face of much evidence to the contrary, he actually considers himself lucky. "Do you know how much money they've spent on me?" he asked the other day. He was talking about our medical insurance; the receipts in his hand represented an astonishing sum. "If I were still in Africa," he said, "I'd be dead by now." It was a cheerful observation, as if he was pleasantly surprised by his own net worth. I've taken to calling him the half-million-dollar man. He loves nothing better than a good joke, even and perhaps especially when it's on him. "I remember when I was working for Air France," he said; we were having lunch at the kitchen table, and the snow was coming down. He was about to begin the long drive to his job at Burlington Airport in a blizzard. "I used to look out at the tarmac, and I'd see those guys in their jumpsuits, shivering in the cold, and I'd think, 'I'm glad that's not my job'—and now it is!" Then he laughed.

This morning, he came upstairs as I was writing these final pages. He'd been having his breakfast in the kitchen with my mother; the Sunday comics were in his hand. "I found something so good," he said, and he showed me a cartoon. Later I found it, neatly clipped from the page, in a pile of mail he is saving for Thomas: Two novice parachutists, portly with middle age, plunge through the clouds in freefall; one of them is leaving a trail of school backpack items: notebooks, pencils, a ruler, a sandwich. "Imagine how your son feels," says the other, "walking around school with your parachute." Patrick laughed until his sides hurt, remembering Thomas's small figure drifting down through the New Jersey sky. Then he pulled off his glasses and collapsed beside me on the couch, wiping tears. We sat like that for a few minutes, thinking about the wisdom of jumping out of planes, and about how scary life is, and how brave one has to be. Then Patrick wiped his eyes again, and with the comics page in one hand and his glasses in the other, he went off to find the scissors.

Patrick and Thomas on the veranda
of our house in Arusha.

Glossary

Asante sana — Thank you
Askari — Watchman
Dala-dala — Bus
Dik-dik — A small antelope
Duka — A small shop
Fundi — Mechanic
Hamna shida — No problem
Karibu — You are welcome
Korongo — Ditch
Mzungu — White person
Pole sana — I'm sorry
Shamba — A small farm or vegetable plot
Shida — Problem
Taka-taka — Trash
Wageni — Tourists, visitors
Watu — People

Printed in Great Britain
by Amazon